The First Fifty
Lessons Learned in a Half Century of Living

Cory Ellsworth

© 2014 Cory P. Ellsworth

All rights reserved. No part of this book may be reproduced in any form or by any means without permission in writing from the publisher, Bacecace, LLC, 1655 N. 26th Street Mesa, Arizona 85213.

ISBN: 978-0-9960011-1-3

Printed in the United States of America

For Amy, Ethan, Ben, Atley & Camden, Emily & Brigham and their Little Ben, Cade and Colby, and all future grandchildren.

Acknowledgments

Thank you to everyone whose name appears in this book. You have helped shape my life and create so many great memories.

Thank you to everyone who helped read, edit and correct including Rowan, Atley, and Amy.

Thank you to Emily for driving the process of getting the book published.

Contents

Forewords

Preface

The First Fifty Introduction

Chapters:
    The First Fifty 2

    Dairy Lessons 7

    Mission and Church Lessons 50

    World Lessons 87

    Marriage and Family Lessons 120

    Business Lessons 140

    Life Lessons 161

    Handcart Lessons 230

    Wheelchair Lessons 286

    The Next Fifty 366

Foreword I
By Tom Larsen

"Every life is worth examination." That is a quote from my good friend Cory Ellsworth. That sentiment is true. However, more can be gleaned and the benefit greater by examining some people's lives over others. Cory's life falls in that category. Life's lessons learned and shared in this book are well worth the read.

I have known Cory for a long time and know him well. We are close – as close as friends are in Cory's life. We have experienced much together, i.e. personally, spiritually, medically, service, musically (including musicals), and professionally. His life experiences are unusually diverse. The man is complicated, yet very simple. Cory is well educated and wise, yet he possesses much common sense. He is so personable and loves to cultivate relationships with all he knows. Humor is a trait you will discover woven throughout this book.

Cory is an extremely gifted communicator, i.e. from the pulpit, with the pen including written scripts and poetry, composer of some of the finest music I have ever heard (that is saying a lot coming from one who is a real music snob), and is a master communicator in his relationships with people. Most importantly, Cory is an excellent communicator with Heaven dealing with spiritual things. Cory's life is full of God-given opportunity, tragedy, sadness, courage, faith and hope.

So, why read the autobiographical thoughts of someone's life? You will find this book interesting, amusing and inspirational. Since there are a wide variety of topics discussed, surely you will find several of personal interest, even if you have never known Cory. More deeply, reading these pages will give you unique insights that have beneficial application for all. I am convinced God uses good people like Cory to be an answer to people's prayers and challenges faced in this place we call mortality. Cory offers inspiration and courage to help deal with life's trials that are an inevitable part of life. Why read this book? You will be better for your time spent.

I began with a Cory quote. Allow me to end with another.

"Yes, I am still standing tall, despite the rough terrain, . . .

My wings are torn and tattered, but I know I can still fly, . . .

Record it in the book of life and bind it with a seal, . . .

That I, unbowed and unbroken, I am standing still!"

By his own experience, Cory can help teach you how to stand through it all. Thank you for sharing, Cory!! I love you.

Tom Larsen
(Friend, neighbor, and 'Man with no name' in *1856, The Musical*)

Foreword II
By Carlos Dominguez

Humble, Faithful, Optimistic, Funny, Multi – Talented, Smart, Observer, Friend, Global Citizen. There are many adjectives that can describe Cory and these are what quickly came to mind when I recalled his smiling face and the eternal twinkle in his eye. Cory, by any measure, is a unique human being. I've often wondered how someone with so much going on intellectually and spiritually is able to radiate such simplicity and calmness. It's contagious and when I get my Cory fix I always leave with the inspiration to be a better person. Amazing!

Cory and I met for the first time in 2000 when he had the daunting task of supporting me as my Controller in the Service Provider (SP) business of Cisco Systems. The SP business was the hottest growth area at Cisco at the time and had grown from $500M to $1.8B. The expectations were high for the next 12 months as we were assigned a $3.8B billion goal. Things were exciting, things were happening fast. We were on a magic carpet ride that seemed too good to be true... and it was. In a matter of weeks, the Dotcom bubble burst and so did our business.

The next few months were full of change, stress and anxiety as our customers disappeared and so did our business. Our new reality forced us to reduce our team from 1,423 people down to 742. As you can imagine, this played heavy in our hearts as we had to lay off some amazing people. The emotions at that time were high and extremely volatile. I discovered quickly that Cory not only served as a great advisor, providing me input on people, business ideas, and priorities, but became a trusted friend that I relied on to keep my sanity. I remember him telling me, "lead with your heart, it will get us to the right place." His faith in my leadership, his sense of humor, his teamwork with Anand and Ruthann (other members of our team), and his undeniable faith were foundational in my survival. Crises all have a finite lifespan and this too passed with time. Hooray!

I've gotten to know Cory well over the years and one of the things I enjoy the most is his dry, witty sense of humor. When you least expect it, he will whisper something calmly and quietly that makes everyone bust out laughing. Cory took the team to one of his favorite restaurants in Hong Kong to eat Garlic Prawns and our discussion that evening was one of the funniest nights of my life.

Cory is also full of surprises and is exceptionally multi- talented. The more time you spend with him the more in awe you become of his talents. One day out, of the blue, he started speaking fluent German with our Sales team. I said to him, "I didn't know you spoke German," to which he quickly responded, "you never asked."

Another time he gave me a CD and told me that he had just written a musical called "1856". I must have appeared totally shocked by his comment because he quickly put his arm around me and said, "Are you ok?" Gosh, how does one casually write and compose a musical? How the heck does he do it!?

I should have known about his musical capabilities since we spent an evening on a Karaoke machine in my basement until one of my daughters pulled the plug. In fairness, the plug was pulled due to my singing in the wrong key. I can always make dogs howl for miles. Cory, on the other hand, made it look easy.

We've been together for many happy moments and through some painfully sad situations on both sides. I've always admired his family values, ethics and, most of all, his faith. Cory is a great man that was put on this earth to teach us how to be the best we can be. He always looks for the best in people even when they have significant flaws. He makes us laugh and smile. He's the first in line to dish out a hug when needed. He's a great listener and charismatic communicator. I am blessed to know Cory and even more blessed to call him my friend.

Open up your heart and minds and enjoy his story. I sure did.

I'll conclude with a simple sentence.

I love you, Cory!

Carlos

Preface

I wrote this book to create a record for my family of many of my experiences and the lessons I have learned and to perhaps offer an insight or a laugh to my family or anyone else who happens upon it.

Every life is worth examination. In some ways mine has been diverse enough to allow for some insights that might not be found elsewhere. I have been a dairy boy, a missionary, an avid sports participant and fan, an international resident (twelve years in four countries), a businessman in the corporate world, a lifelong volunteer in the LDS church, a creator of musicals, and the father of sick and deceased children, among other things.

So, here, for what it's worth, is a glimpse into my life. I have minimized my defeats and disappointments but have also tried not to dive too deeply into accomplishments. My focus here is on formative experiences and the lessons I have learned as a result. In most cases I have not called out the lesson learned, as it may be very obvious or, in some cases, different for each person.

[Note: Other than the references in the text, I have not compiled sources or a bibliography. All of the "1856 The Musical" pictures were taken by my friend, Steve Porter. If you have questions about attributions or veracity of the several references to statistics, please contact me.]

The First Fifty Introduction

I passed 50 years of living a few years ago. For me, turning 50 was a reflective time. It was the first time that it hit me with certainty that my life was at least half over. That caused me to pause and take stock. Who am I exactly? What have I accomplished? What should I have done differently or better? Have I helped my loved ones? Have I added to society? Am I on the right path? What should I focus on now?

It wasn't a mid-life crisis but rather a time to take inventory and to make course corrections and renewed commitments. Amy, my sweet wife, and I have joked that a classic male mid-life crisis usually involves a used convertible sports car, a dyed mustache, or chasing women. None of those appeal to me. But I did recently buy two Jersey heifer calves that we intend to raise, breed, and milk. Amy says that is my mid-life crisis – getting in touch with my dairy roots.

I didn't adequately answer all the questions I posed but taking stock was a still a very meaningful process. It drove me to document parts of my life and create this book.

I do think that I know who I am.

I was raised on a dairy.
I had great, loving parents and great, loving siblings.
I have survived a heart attack.
I can clean my tonsils with my tongue (I have yet to find anyone else who can do that but, then again, it doesn't come up that often in conversations).

I love all sports but especially basketball. I am pretty good at all of them except golf. I am the worst golfer I have ever known.
I do not wish to live my life over – I am happy with where I am – but if I had another live to live I would want to be a teacher and a coach.
I was a spelling champ in grade school but also misspelled 'of' in the second grade.
I am a hugger.
I am too often sharp-tongued but am making progress.
I am an active member of the LDS (Mormon) church.
I speak fluent German.
I am married to a saint. I love my wife very much.
In sports, I follow fascinating individuals more than I follow teams.
I am the father of six wonderful children. I love them very much.
I/We have buried our oldest two children and will almost certainly bury our two youngest children. I hope and pray that's it.
I have hiked the Grand Canyon rim to rim to rim (48 miles) alone in less than 24 hours.
I lost 50 pounds and gained half of it back.
I am the creator, writer, producer, executive producer, recipient, guardian, and babysitter of two stage musicals.
I am an introvert but few people suspect that.
I have been to about 40 countries.
I don't like crowds.
I love old wood furniture, home made quilts and home made bread.
I have many deep friendships but have no 'buddies' that I revert to or do things with on a regular basis. I take no 'boy' trips.

I have always been a B+ or an A- student. One semester of Zoology was enough to make me drop my pre-med major.

I graduated from Brigham Young University.

I have become a cleaner but was not always so. As a freshman at BYU, my mother changed my bedding in October. When she visited next in April, she noticed that my sheets looked dirty. She asked when I changed them last. I asked her, "When were you here last?"

I graduated from the University of South Carolina with a Master's degree in international business.

People tell me I make them feel good and loved.

People tell me I am a good speaker and teacher.

From a distance I find reasons why I won't enjoy this or that person but I always end up loving them when I engage. I do love people.

I love history and, particularly, LDS history.

I collected Lincoln pennies.

I have lived in five countries.

I keep letters, cards or emails that I have received that make me feel especially good or valued.

I served a two-year mission in Germany for the LDS church.

I live to eat rather than eating to live. Maintaining a proper weight is difficult.

I am a child of God.

Those points are not chronological or in order of importance but do sum me up pretty well.

Additionally, to know anything meaningful about me, you need to know a little about the people who matter most to me.

Good parents raised me. Joseph Franklin Ellsworth - great father, dairyman, native of Mesa. Carrie Allen Ellsworth – great mother, born and raised in the Gila Valley in Arizona. She loves learning.

I was loved and influenced by good siblings – Rowan (12 years older than I), Keller (9), Marta (8), Dorne (5), Matt (4) and Beryl (2 years younger).

I married Amy Lynn Bowden on December 29, 1981. Best decision I ever made. Amy was raised by good parents, Bob and Jeri Bowden. In addition to Amy, they raised three sons – Rob, Jim, and Brent – all of whom are very dear to me.

Amy and I have had six children together. Ethan, born in 1983. Fiery redhead. Passed away from the effects of Muscular Dystrophy at age 25.

Benjamin, born in 1986. Happy, driven. Passed away in a train accident in Argentina in 2005 while serving an LDS mission.

Atley, born in 1988. Beautiful, vivacious, owns the room. Atley married Camden in 2007. Camden is solid, good to the core, great addition to the family.

Emily, born in 1990. Beautiful, sweet. Emily married Brigham in 2009. Brigham is solid, good to the core, great addition to the family. As of this writing they have one little guy, Benjamin, named for his uncle Ben.

Cade, born in 2000. Smart, talented. Affected by Muscular Dystrophy.

Colby, born one minute after Cade. Sweet, smart. Also affected by Muscular Dystrophy. [Note: I remember the twins' birth, which happened by C-section. The doctor was dressed in scrubs and goggles. I remember thinking that the goggles were a little much. I stood by Amy. Amy wanted all of my attention but I was also interested in the happenings on the southern half of her body. I had never seen a C-section. So I stood about even with her large tummy, able to focus on her face when necessary but also able to watch what was happening below. Doctors are interested in keeping the horizontal, lower abdominal incision as small as possible (for healing and bikini reasons, I assume). The doctor made the small incision with a scalpel then began the process of squeezing the first baby through the inches-long incision. It was a tight fit. The pressure of the head coming through the cut caused Amy's water to break in a fountain-like kind of way. The amniotic fluid streamed into the air and covered at least half of the doctor's smock and goggles. Ah, now I know why they wear goggles.]

For this book I have separated many of my experiences and lessons learned into categories. Since my formative years were spent on a dairy, I'll start with 'Dairy Lessons'.

Dairy lessons

The Recker Road Ellsworth dairy, circa 1965. Dad never liked this picture because he couldn't find anyone working in it.

Introduction

My parents, Joe and Carrie Ellsworth, moved their small dairy operations to a larger place on north Recker Road in Mesa, Arizona in 1954. I was born in 1960, the sixth child and fifth son. Dairy life was all I knew until the age of 10 when Dad moved the dairy away from our Mesa home to Chandler. My formative years were spent working and playing on a 600-cow dairy in the desert.

Growing up on a dairy had many benefits. With twenty acres, all of the tools necessary for farming and plenty of toys that Dad slowly accumulated, there was always an adventure waiting on the dairy. We had animals – at one time or another we had cows, horses, dogs, cats, chickens, pheasants, peacocks, sheep, pigs, goats, goldfish, homing pigeons, and rabbits. We had tractors and trailers. I was driving tractors at age five or six. We had haystacks and forts and chicken coops and milk barns. My Dad could squeeze a cow's teat and squirt milk in my mouth from 15 feet away. Of course most of it went all over my face but the game was fun. The rhythmic sound of the milking machines and its effect on the ever-present AM radio is a sound that I can still recall. A huge milk truck came to take our milk every morning.

We had sand piles for playing, a huge pit for silage (chopped corn stalks and cobs), guns for hunting doves and sparrows and anything else. We had a junkyard with no end of pleasures like dead washing machines and metal rods. Under everything in the junkyard was a scorpion, snake, or centipede. In the workshop we had gas tanks and oilcans and table saws (which one brother used to saw off one of his fingers), and a loft with bales of fleece and other treasures. We had a desert next door. We had a full court basketball court, a swimming pool, a swing set, motorcycles and quads and bicycles. We even had a thing with a center peg and a hoop larger than a person with straps for each hand and foot. The idea was to spin around doing continuous cartwheels in the metal contraption. I haven't seen any of those for 30 years - OSHA, the ACLU and other acronyms probably had them banned. We had a Jeep, two boats, and a Model A Ford.

We had pets - a dairy dog named Maverick who seemed much smarter than most people and a dumb, fluffy, magnificent Saint Bernard named Hannibal. I had an ugly red cat named Tony. Once, we had somehow climbed to having 17 cats around the dairy, mostly stray and untamed. A wave of Distemper raged through and killed (as we supposed) all 17. Some we found dead, others we found only once they began to rot behind a wall or object, some including Tony, we never found. A full six months later Tony returned to me on the dairy and remained our only cat for a while. I supposed he sensed death in the air and took a walk-about until the air cleared.

We had plenty of citrus and fruit trees, grapes, figs, pomegranates, bamboo, palo verde trees, manzanita, chapparal, saguaro cactus, and several more types of trees and shrubs.

Almost every extended family gathering was at our place. My cousins loved to be with Uncle Joe and

Aunt Carrie on the dairy. I still love hearing cousins and friends talk about the happiness and adventure they experienced on the dairy.

Dad washing down the "holding" corral.

Of course a dairy is a business and a tough one at that. My Dad, who could stretch the truth a little, said that there was a 12-year period when he milked at least a 12-hour shift every single day. If that is even near the truth, and I believe it is, it speaks to the dedication required on a dairy. Cows must be fed and milked regardless of weather, emotion or illness. Feeding the calves was my main responsibility from age 6 to 10. They had to be fed morning and afternoon, period. Every morning, every afternoon and most of my Saturdays were full of dairy work. And, as the last boy and with the dairy moving when I was 10, I got off with the least amount of total work. My brothers all have many more accumulated dairy work hours than I do.

A happy birth! Triplets! Our breeder and Dad show them off.

With that many animals there is birth and death and sickness and injury every day. There were difficult calf births, the sad demise of cute little calves or any other kind of animal. We steeled ourselves most of the time but some deaths were especially hard. Birth brought happiness. Dad had a habit of bringing babies – it could be rabbits, chicks, lambs, whatever – into the house for Mom to play with for an hour. Many mornings I watched Mom snuggle with little babies, sometimes putting them in the oven on 'low'.

Medically, I enjoyed administering shots or forcing pills down calves' throats.

The dairy had just about everything. I wouldn't have traded those years and experiences for anything.

Me, center right, with Hannibal. Keller is looking at me.

Standing Too Close to the Fire May Result in Injury

Growing up on the dairy, I became an employee on my sixth birthday. I had one key duty and several smaller tasks. I assisted my brothers, Dorne and Matt, with feeding the newborn calves before and after school. Up at 6 a.m., feed the calves, wash up, get home to change and eat breakfast and then go to school. After school we repeated the calf-feeding process. That process included loading two 10-gallon metal cans into a red wagon in a room next to the milking barn, filling the cans with hot water, mixing milk replacer powder (Land O' Lakes brand, usually) into the water, and pulling the heavy wagon along with multiple 4-pint bottles and rubber nipples the 100 yards to the calf pens. Then we would sink a bottle into the can and let it fill, stretch a nipple onto the bottle and then feed a calf through the fence of their individual, small pens. Occupational hazards included the calves ripping the nipple off and spilling the milk, or most annoying, the calves knocking me over by their inborn rooting behavior (every 30 seconds or so, with no warning, a calf will surge suddenly forward, acting as though they want more milk faster). The key was to keep your arm flexed a little to be ready to absorb the shock of the surge. If I lost focus and was unprepared I found myself on my butt.

The other hazard was wintertime. We always got very wet with the milk mixture. Arizona winters can get cold, especially for the morning feeding. On perhaps 10 days a year when it was really cold (high 30's or low 40's at 6 in the morning), one of the brothers would build a fire a few yards away from where we parked the wagon. It was still dark. In between individual feedings we would stand by the fire to warm our hands for a while then feed another calf. On one particularly cold day, I was standing in the dark by the fire which had apparently burned down a bit so that there was a ring on the outside of the fire which was not actively burning but was still very hot. I could not see that and inched forward to get warm.

In the midst of my shivering and extending my hands over the fire, I heard my brother, Keller, who is nine years older than I am, yelling at me as he sprinted towards me from another part of the dairy. We are a fun-loving family so I figured he was having some sort of active fun to warm himself up and amuse me. I couldn't understand his shouting and watched as he neared me. To my surprise he ran right up to me, picked me up, threw me on the ground, and rolled me over and over again in the dirt. Somewhere in that process I realized what was happening. I had caught fire and he was putting me out. He had looked across to the calf area and had seen a flame on my Levi's pant leg (Levi's and a flannel shirt was our daily uniform). I was hurt and was crying. After ensuring there was no serious damage, Keller walked away, finishing with something like, "You are such an idiot." I stood further away from the fire after that.

Aluminum Might Be a Metal

Flies are a constant nuisance on a dairy. In the middle of the calf pens we kept a large fly zapper. It was electric; perhaps three feet square, with multiple narrow wires stretching across every surface, except on the bottom. It looked like a box that had been framed in with wire but not completed. In the middle we placed rotten food scraps. Flies, attracted to the smell, would fly in through the wires and receive a jolt of electricity sufficient to fry their little minds. That jolt would give a person a significant shocking experience but not enough to do any lasting damage. The zap was a combination of a white/yellow and a blue light that was almost entrancing to look at in the dark. I regularly spent minutes just watching the flies die in their blaze of glory.

There was always a pile of dead flies in the middle with the food scraps. One trait of the zapper – I still don't understand it – is that you could rest your hand on the surface of the wires without getting zapped. But put even one finger through the wires and ouch – ZAP! Occasionally something larger than a fly – a bird was the usual suspect - would get stuck in the wires and create a constant blue zap stream while sucking large amounts of electricity. In such cases the foreign object needed to be removed. I learned how to do that. Take a stick or other piece of wood and jab around until the object falls through into the middle. I was taught that it was urgent to get the object out of the zapper and not to use anything metal as that would result in an electric shock to the user.

So one morning a bird got stuck. I was the only one around. I couldn't find any wood of any kind so I grabbed the only thing I could find. It was an aluminum pole. It was much lighter and a lighter color than any metal I had ever dealt with so I was pretty sure it couldn't be metal. So I shoved it into the zapper and promptly received a very large electrical jolt that sent me flying. There were a few seconds of pain, some numbness, and much sheepishness as I glanced around to ensure no one was watching. But the science experiment was complete – aluminum is a metal.

Never Look a Gift Horse in the ……Hmmm

I usually liked to help with doctoring the animals – shots, pills, trimming hooves, whatever. On the new dairy in Chandler, when I was 11 or so, one of my older brothers took advantage of my zeal for his own purposes one day. He asked, "Want to help doctor a horse?" Of course, I replied eagerly. He grabbed a bag, some tubes and off we went. We found the horse standing but clearly uncomfortable. My brother explained that she hadn't pooped for days and needed our help. Cool. He filled the bag with water, stuck the tube into the bag and moved to the rear of the horse. He shoved the tube into the horse's backside (Very Cool!) and got on a stepladder and held the bag above the horse so that the water drained into the mare's bum in a minute or two. All along I had asked every few seconds how I could help. After the bag emptied, he said, "This is where you come in." He said we needed to repeat the process 3 or 4 more times to get enough water in the horse. He needed to go fill up the bag a few more times. But, while he was getting more water each time, we didn't want the existing water to escape from the horse's rear. My job was to stick my finger in the horse's butt every time my brother pulled the tube out so that the existing water could not get out.

I was up for that without even a moment's hesitation. Standing behind a horse is seldom a good idea but I knew she was too sick to kick me across the corral. As I stood behind the mare, I realized it worked fairly well as I was about eye level with her bum. I could keep my finger in the proverbial dike with little effort and could monitor the situation. I

17

made it a little game. If I eased my finger out a little, water would begin to spurt out. I moved to the left or the right to avoid getting too wet. Each time my brother came back he lauded my efforts. After the last bag went in I held it all in with my finger for several more minutes. Then I let go. We proudly watched as the horse, over a period of several minutes, dumped what seemed to be her entire bodyweight. She was cured. I was the doctor or at least the doctor's assistant.

In subsequent years I have wished I could see a picture of the 11-year-old boy standing there quietly, but with a huge smile, with his finger in a horse's backside.

Getting Big

Saturdays on the dairy were often reserved for larger projects that couldn't be done during the grind of the normal schedule of milking and feeding the cattle. On Saturday all of the boys were available to help. Typical projects might include branding, ironing, a deep cleaning in the barn, or 'cutting' cattle into various pens. Cutting meant separating out specific cattle from one corral to be moved to a different corral or off the dairy. For example, we would have a bull in only one or two of our nine major corrals so any cow in heat (i.e. needing to be impregnated) would need to be moved to where a bull could service her. Along the south edge of the corrals was a lane, maybe 15 foot wide. Each corral had a gate that opened into the lane. At one end of the lane was the entry to the milking barn. So the lane was our means of moving cows from their corral to the milk barn and for moving cows in and out of corrals.

The process of cutting cows started with a few of us, usually led by my Dad, entering a corral, identifying the cow to be moved, slowly isolating that cow as we moved around the corral, then driving that cow toward the gate, where one of us was stationed with the assignment to let that cow out but not any others. Sometimes another one of us was positioned down the lane somewhere with the assignment to stop the cow near a certain corral. A grown Holstein cow (black and white milk cow - 90% of our cows were Holstein) weighs about 1,200 pounds. As an eight year old I must have weighed 60 pounds. Almost all of the cutting activities, at some point, involved a smaller human convincing a half ton cow that it needed to bend its will and direction to the little person. Cows are not evil by nature but they have fears, are high-spirited, and can create tremendous momentum.

Stopping a scared cow that is running at 10-20 mph is not an easy task. It always involved 'getting big', which meant loud yelling, jumping up and down, and arm waving. My Dad regularly tasked us with it. Failing at it often resulted in physical pain (getting pushed over, run over or, if lucky, brushed by) but also psychological damage. None of us wanted to disappoint Dad or create more work for everyone so most Saturdays were an opportunity to 'man up' in the lane. My reputation was good. Dad and my brothers knew I was not afraid to get big and stand my ground. If a cow wanted by me it could win but not without a good effort. I found that confidence mattered. A cow, it seemed, could sense my fear. Success was usually proportionate to my confidence.

Up, Up and Away

Each of the nine corrals had 50-100 adult milking cows, which were milked twice a day. Dad had about 600 milk cows when I was a boy on the Mesa dairy. Six cows could be milked at one time. On the south side of the corrals was the lane, which was used to get cows to and from the milking barn. On the north side of the corral was a manger where feed was deposited. The cows would eat the feed by putting their head through designed ports in the metal-based fencing.

When a cow calved she usually did so in her corral. My Dad looked around every few hours to see if a cow was calving and to see if any needed assistance. After a calf was born we would allow the calf to bond with Mama Cow and get some much-needed colostrum from Mama Cow's udder for a few hours. Then we would remove the calf from the corral and put it into a small pen where we could monitor, protect and feed it. Cows (female cows are called cows), as opposed to bulls, are not malicious. The only time they can be intentionally dangerous is when their newborns are threatened. So removing the calf from its mother could be dicey. When it was my job, I always needed to act confidently, steer the calf out while keeping my head on a swivel for what the Mama Cow was doing. Often I needed to step toward her and make plenty of noise to stop her building aggression. A few times I had to abort the mission, flee for my life from a menacing cow and fetch an older brother or Dad for help.

The calf pens were only 50 yards from the row of corrals. Occasionally calves would escape their pen or run away while they were being encouraged along the way to their new little pen (steering a calf was best done by pushing from behind). Once, a calf that I had not removed from its mother but was assigned to get into a calf pen, got away from me and ran surprisingly quickly to the manger and climbed through a port and into corral #2. I tried to stop the calf but was too late. As the calf got into the corral I did notice that she did not immediately bond with any specific Mama Cow. That led me to believe that the calf's mother was not in corral #2. That mattered because an agitated calf with its Mom was a dangerous combination. So, assuming the calf was not with its mother, and because I did not want to bother Dad, I climbed into the corral to start over again with our little 'runner' calf.

As I steered the calf along, I heard a guttural mooing behind me. It sounded offended and unhappy. I turned in time so see a cow so agitated that I knew it was the calf's mother. Her look informed that I would not be removing her calf today. Even as a little boy I knew the temperaments of cows. I started to use my usual tactics of 'getting big' by yelling and waving my arms. At the same time I was planning an escape route. Despite my efforts the Mama Cow pawed at the ground, snorted, and moved closer. I kept the calf between her and me. Just as the cow was a few feet away and I knew she would not back away, I darted for the corral fence between corral #2 and corral #1. I had to cover about 30 feet, scale the fence and catapult into the safety of the next corral. As I sprinted I heard the Mama Cow on my heels. She was not satisfied with me just leaving. She wanted to kill me (my interpretation at that point).

I recall getting to the fence, putting one foot onto the lowest of the 3 or 4 rebar rods that formed the fence, and lunging upwards with the intent of using the other foot on the second or third rebar rod to then hurl myself over. Just as the first foot was doing its job and I was focusing on where the second foot would plant I felt Mama Cow's head square in the middle my backside. She lifted me up and over the fence with great force. I have always imagined the sight as something like a pole-vaulter clearing the bar. I must have soared a foot or two over the top rung and then came crashing down in the manure of corral #1. Had I been a little slower the mother would have punished me against the rebar in the fence. It hurt. The adrenaline was flowing. I quickly looked around to see if Mama Cow had any accomplices in corral #1. I headed for the manger and crawled through to complete safety. After checking myself for wounds and finding none, I ran to find Dad in the milk barn, whereupon I cried alligator tears at length while telling the story.

I could have avoided the pain and drama with a quick check with Dad or a brother about the residence of the calf's Mom.

Hard Work

Becoming a de facto employee of the dairy at age six created the opportunity and necessity to work hard. Chores came before play. Chores had to be done even if we were sick or tired or sick and tired. Looking back I am deeply grateful for being put in that position. At the time it was not always pleasant. The same was true for my four older brothers. One was especially infamous for not wanting to be awoken in the morning and for doing harm to those who did wake him. One of the worst tasks I could be assigned was waking my brother, Keller. The best results were achieved by ascending the staircase to his bedroom, yelling loudly, then darting back down the stairs before he threw a shoe or a chair at me. Usually the first foray did not achieve success as Keller would yell and try to go back to sleep. It took two or three attempts before he was sufficiently awake. Then I was sure to keep my distance from him for the next hour or so.

I built a reputation as a very good worker. Looking back I realize that I liked the reputation, liked the praise and was mindful of building that reputation. I worked best when I was being watched and complimented.

When I was ten years old, Mom and Dad moved the dairy from my house to Chandler, about 20 miles away. The next several summers were full of very hard work on the Chandler dairy but school years were not full of daily chores. I became quite lazy. I know I disappointed both my Mom and my Dad several times on that front. I was into basketball and other sports and playing with friends.

My work ethic returned when I was went on my two-year mission to Germany for the LDS Church and has not waned since. My motivation is now less focused on other people's view of me, (although it is still a motivator) and more on getting things done, getting ahead, and doing a job well.

I attribute whatever positive work habits I have to those formative years from age 6 to 10 on the home Dairy.

Quite a Charmer

Dad liquidated the Mesa dairy when I was ten and moved it to a more rural setting in Chandler. He owned the dairy there for four more years. Whereas we had about 600 cows in Mesa, now we had 2,000 on a beautiful, new dairy complex. Instead of milking six at a time, we milked 16 and milked for 20 hours a day. Friendly Spaniards of Basque descent did our milking.

Dad drove the 20 miles each morning and afternoon. Managing a dairy involved a lot of 'Management By Walking Around' and 'Management by Driving Around'. Both activities allowed Dad to take note of cows in heat (and therefore needing to be bred), distress (needing doctoring), delivering calves, and so on. It was not uncommon to spot Dad either wandering around in a corral or driving slowly around the corrals, stopping every 50 feet or so in his Chevy pickup.

Breeding is a constant concern on a dairy. To make economic sense, dairy cows need to be bred at about 15 months, have their first calf at two years old, then to be bred again a few months after they calve. That cycle is repeated over and over until they are too old to milk productively. A dairy cow will milk for about 10 months after calving, then rest for two months before having the next calf. It is important to note when a cow is in heat and ready to breed. Once that occurs the cow needs to be put into a corral with a bull or be artificially inseminated. We usually kept two or three live bulls on the dairy to service all of those cows. Noticing heat cows and getting them into a corral with a bull was always a priority.

One day Dad was in a corral of first-calf heifers (15 month olds being bred for the first time). A young bull, Charmer, was also in the corral. Bulls are mean as hell, period. Charmer had been de-horned, which made him less lethal but his 2,000 pounds of testosterone could grind a man to pieces with his head (his brother, Stylemaster - is that a cool name or what? - had broken a man's leg simply by ramming a fence against which the man leaned 15 feet further down the fence line). Dad had been around bulls and cows all of his life and knew, as well as anyone, how to control cattle. I was not allowed into a corral with a bull, but he never hesitated himself. He knew how to deflect their anger, how to call their bluff. As he wandered through the corral looking at the heifers and taking mental notes, two heifers moved out of the way. Perhaps 40 feet away stood Charmer, bent on proving that this was his corral. This was nothing new to Dad. This is where noise, slow movement, and arm waving if necessary always calmed the situation. Not this time. Charmer would have none of it. The dance – Charmer pawing, snorting and moving closer and Dad motioning, moving, yelling – continued until Dad realized this was different. He knew it was time to run. He almost made it to the manger but Charmer caught him, knocked him down and pummeled him over and over again against the cement foundation of the manger, breaking ribs and tearing them from the sternum and inflicting internal damage. Dad, in a dazed state, would play dead. Charmer wandered away. As soon as Dad realized there was some distance and tried to move his broken body through the manger, Charmer would attack again. That was repeated a few times. Then

Dad tried the aggressive approach and stuck his entire thumb into Charmer's eye socket. That just enraged Charmer more.

After several encounters Charmer decided he had won and wandered off. With great difficulty Dad climbed through the manger onto the dirt road used by tractors to distribute food to the cattle. Dad did what he could to move toward help. That consisted of a slow, agonized army crawl.

That's where I came in. It was summertime on the dairy. I was eleven. After hours of morning chores that started before 5 a.m., we usually rested around midday and did odd jobs or entertained ourselves in the afternoon. I was on my way, alone, to the calf barn. As I reached the center of the dairy, where in each direction a dirt road led past corrals, I heard something like a moan. As I looked to the sound, I saw something on the ground perhaps a hundred yards away. I moved toward it slowly. It made a sound again. As I moved closer I thought perhaps it was Dad. Now Dad was a great practical joker but I had never known him to go so far as to fake an injury on the ground. He groaned again and called my name. I ran to him. A mixture of blood, manure and cow feed covered him. His eyes rolled back in his head again and again. He asked me to get help.

I sprinted to the barn area, finally found my oldest brother, Rowan, and told him Dad was in trouble. A few of us went to him, did some basic first aid, cleaned him up a little and prepared to get him to a hospital. Being a man's man (with its pros and cons) and barely conscious he insisted that we drive him home to Mom. So Dad was placed by the far door of the pickup with Beryl, Matt and me sandwiched in the middle and Dorne, with his driver's permit, driving. Dad told Dorne that, if Dad passed out and could not be woken up, he should get him to a hospital. That was a hard 30-minute drive home full of anxiety and fear. At home, Mom got him settled into bed where he stayed for weeks. As far as I know, he never went to a doctor.

Dad was never the same. He never again played catch in the backyard with me. Any attempts to shoot baskets were intermittent and short. He grew odd calcium deposits on his sternum. I have always assumed it was re-growth to attach the bones to the sternum.

We put Charmer down a few months later.

My Dad

When I was four or five, Dad and I went into the chicken coop to gather eggs and have a look around. As I typically had no reason to be afraid and was quite independent, we separated to speed up the process. Soon I realized that a certain rooster, which I had never pestered, wanted to attack and possibly kill me. And I wasn't that much bigger than he was. His spurs were gleaming and his eyes were fixed on me as he ruffled his feathers and started to charge. I remember thinking that if I could get to Dad everything would be OK. But Dad was all the way on the other side of the coop, perhaps 40 feet away. I started to run, screaming, "HELP, DAD, HELP!!" I thought I wouldn't make it and that Dad would have to pick my remains out of the rooster's beak. As I rounded the center set of roosts I saw Dad and felt the rooster behind me. I sprinted past Dad, planning to circle behind and hide between his legs. Just as I passed I heard a terrible screech-moan and turned in time to see feathers fly and the rooster flying through the air.

Dad had dropkicked him into the next life with one swift kick of his boot. I should have run over to spit on the bird and confirm that he was dead but there were other chickens and they had eyes and beaks and spurs. I stayed between Dad's legs for the next ten minutes, even walking back to the house. At that point the only safe place was with Dad.

My Dad was a very giving man. He and Mom bought 12 burial plots in a new cemetery in east Mesa. A young man from the local LDS Ward occupies one of the 12 spots. He was a war veteran, had his own demons and took his own life shortly after moving into the ward. No one knew him well. His family was either not found or was not contactable or helpful. Instead of seeing the boy buried in a pauper's grave (no headstone, no name) Dad offered up one of our spots. Three more friends, who were short on funds, occupy three more of the 12 spots. My father lies there, awaiting my mother. Two of my sons are lying there as well. My wife and I and our two younger sons will eventually be there. Every time I go to visit the graves of my sons and my father I see the grave of that young suicidal man and am reminded of the goodness of my father.

In 2005 we bought a getaway home two hours away from Mesa in Strawberry, Arizona. It is a beautiful property at 5900 feet of elevation where the temperature is always about 20 degrees cooler than in the Phoenix area. Our two-acre property backs to a creek bed. On the other side of the creek is a larger property. Sometime in the first few months of owning the property, Amy and I spotted a couple near the creek and correctly supposed they were the owners. We walked across and introduced ourselves. Upon hearing our surname, the lady asked if I was related to the Joe Ellsworth who owned a dairy in east Mesa. When I said I was his son, she started to cry and then told us a story. She said that her first husband had been a struggling farm equipment salesman who regularly called upon Dad. As the husband was not a great salesman the couple was usually struggling financially. She spoke emotionally about how my Dad had slipped her husband a $50 bill more than once and that, each time, it made the difference between having food on the table and not.

With only slight plot twists, I heard many more similar stories about my Dad. He was an extraordinarily giving man.

I have always liked this picture of my dad with my pregnant sister-in-law, Nancy. My mom's note on the back of the picture says, "Joe's still the biggest- and will be- the longest. May 1980

It's a Dog's Life - Maverick and Hannibal

From my first memories Maverick was there. He was mostly black but had light brown around his eyes. He was a large dog but not quite as big as a German Shepherd. I don't know what kind of dog he was. I could lean on Maverick, both physically and figuratively.

Maverick in front of our home on Recker.

Maverick was the wisest dog I ever expect to meet. He was an employee of the dairy, doing as much work as any of us. He would 'cut' cattle, meaning he would help us separate specific cattle in a corral and get them out of the corral. He was a master at cutting cattle. If we were especially tired or just wanted to test Maverick's abilities, we would go into a corral, point out the cow we wanted cut, tell Maverick to take care of it (sic 'em, Maverick!) and stand back and watch. Nine times in ten he would deliver. It involved a lot of nipping at heels, biting at tails, cutting off escape routes, and re-directing. There were a lot of pieces of tails in the corrals, all thanks to Maverick.

He was gentle with me. He had kind, knowing eyes. He only bit a child once. The stupid neighbor child was repeatedly jabbing Maverick with a fork in the back and even in the face. The stupid parents of the stupid child insisted we quarantine him to determine if he had rabies. He went away and came back a different dog. He was confused and tired. Soon thereafter signs of age crept in and he slowly went blind. I watched him run into things and would go re-direct him.

Dad finally put him down. I miss him still.

Hannibal was a Christmas gift for my brother, Keller, but he felt like the family's dog. He was everything Maverick was not. He must have been the biggest, dumbest, sweetest, clumsiest Saint Bernard that ever lived. As a pup he was irresistible - cute and fluffy and playful. I would wrestle with him and take naps on him. He would share his ticks with me (Mom found several juicy ticks in my hair over the next few years). He would bite my Levi's near the ankle and drag me around the yard. He brought great joy and immediate smiles to all of us.

At full weight he was a little less than 200 pounds. He was useless on the dairy, barking at the wrong things. He was not smart enough to understand cutting cattle. He was not an employee of the dairy. He was not ever trained. He did what he did. If we younger kids walked outside with food he would take it from us. My brother, Matt, liked to finish his breakfast while walking to the barn to begin the process of feeding the calves. He would pay me to walk out the back door and attract Hannibal's attention while Matt would sprint-walk out the front door and down the main road to the barn. That way he could avoid a painful tackle and could eat his own breakfast.

We also called him Piddles for what he would do as a pup on the carpet. Dad called him Tuck, because he would tuck in his tail in a major way when scolded.

When he was older, we moved him to our farm in Idaho. I spent a few summers there. It was hard to watch him age. When Dad realized it was time to put him down (read: take him out and shoot him), he loaded the gun, loaded Hannibal in the pickup and headed down the road. He came back several minutes later with tears streaming down his face and Hannibal very much alive. He handed the gun and the keys to my brother-in-law, Jim, who had not grown up with Hannibal and did not have the same attachment.

I miss Hannibal still.

My little sister, Beryl, with Hannibal as a puppy.

The Weekly Invasion

LDS missionaries have a preparation day (P-Day) once a week where they are 'off' from sun-up to dinnertime. They use the time to do wash, write letters and shop. Any time left over after that is used for fun and relaxation.

Nothing allowed for more fun than our dairy. With the full array of things to do and ride, our dairy was the place to be on P-Day. Usually we had two or four missionaries but it was not uncommon to have eight or more. Our record was 20 or 22, achieved more than once. They would play basketball, football (we had amazing, often bloody touch/tackle games in the desert right behind our basketball court), roam the dairy, assist with chores, ride horses, or ride motorcycles.

The missionaries all saddled up and ready for a ride.

Elders (the fully dressed ones) in the pool.

Swimming was not allowed for missionaries. Despite that rule, they did end up in the pool a few times. Once an entire zone of 20 missionaries ended up in the pool in their suits. One fell in or so they said. Then one was pushed in, and then another. After a while all missionaries were in. They also ensured that every Ellsworth was thrown in, including my mother. We have pictures. Everyone is smiling from ear to ear.

We think that the worldwide ban on missionaries riding motorcycles came about because of an accident on one of our motorcycles. Two Elders were riding, took a spill and Mom ended picking gravel out of their arms and legs. The new rule was our family contribution to the global safety of our missionary force.

Missionaries were full of life and often full of mischief. I recall a game that a few of them made up. One climbed to the top of a haystack. Another would drive our golf cart along side of the haystack at a predictable speed. The haystack missionary would time his leap and try to land right in the short bed of the golf cart. It required precise timing. As soon as the jumping missionary got adept at the process, the other Elder made an adjustment. As soon as the jumper leaped, the driving Elder hit the brakes. The jumper landed on the dirt and fell down. The driver ran over him with the golf cart. Ah, good, clean fun.

That's how it went with those guys. Mom loved having them there and would feed them non-stop. I loved having them there. They liked me and played with me. Looking back they were great examples to me.

Everyone Has Crosses to Bear

David (not his real name) was a year younger than I. His father, mother and little brothers lived in a home at the far end of my Dad's dairy. His father worked on the dairy for a few years. I never knew much about the family. Later I learned that they came from Michigan looking for a new life. The father was strict and mean. David quickly built a rap sheet at the dairy. We caught him stealing from our house. He and I had a fistfight over some small thing. As he stormed away he screamed at me, "Just wait until I'm older than you". He shot my finger with a BB gun. [Note: That was partly my fault. We played a game where one of us would hold out a small piece of paper in our fingers about thirty feet away. The other would try to shoot the paper out. I shot the paper. He shot me.] From our trampoline he urinated on me once. He was a mess of a kid.

Looking back and adding puzzle pieces makes me wish I could have a do-over and try to be a more positive influence on him. I am sure that I tolerated him but did little to help. His father was abusive. He owned a very long black bullwhip and used it on the little boys. He drank and cursed and threatened. While he was working on the dairy the FBI came and arrested him for his history of passing bad checks in Michigan. I don't know how that was described to David but it cannot have been good.

This story and others like it have driven a lesson deeply into me. Everyone has significant crosses to bear. Many are visible but most are unseen. It helps me be kinder, more polite, more inclusive, and more tolerant.

Bad Dog

When I was six or seven and Beryl, my little sister, was four or five, she and I wandered unusually far from home. We were in uncharted territory for us and were walking on the edge of a golf course. Some distance away we heard the barks of an angry dog. Turning our attention that way, we saw a large dog headed our way at full speed. Beryl and I had been around animals, including dogs, all our life. We were not bad at judging the intentions of animals. We were immediately convinced this dog was nasty and was going to attack us rather than just get blustery and fake an attack. Its growls and barks were serious. We could not have outrun the dog and had almost no time to react.

In retrospect I reacted very well. I pushed Beryl behind me a little and devised a plan on the spot. As the dog lunged forward, teeth bared, I kicked it in the mouth as hard as I could. It made a screeching sound and headed back from whence it came. We were saved and walked home quickly. [Note: I have corroborated the story with Beryl. She remembers it the same way. I needed that confirmation, of course, as I could have really stretched the truth, being so small. And I was so unreasonably unkind to Beryl so many times in my youth that she could not be faulted for remembering things to my detriment.]

Switching gears, I was in a company-sponsored class once where the teacher claimed that we have no control over our 'fight or flight' reaction (also 'fight, flight, freeze, or fawn'). He argued that it is instinct built into the most primitive part of our brain. In an emergency we will always do what that instinct tells us to do.

Through the years, stories like my dog story with my little sister have caused me to consider and finally disbelieve what the teacher was saying that day. I believe that our reaction can be informed and manipulated based on conditions and inputs. I do not consider myself heroic but I was brave that day with Beryl. Had I been alone, I believe I would have run, cowered, and probably been chewed to bits. But I was influenced that day by my role as protector. I was not acting for me but for her and for us. Therefore, believing myself to generally be a wimp if I was alone and I thought no cameras were on me, I have chosen to adopt a mindset that, in troubling times, I am being watched and that my response will matter to others. I think that gives me the best chance of being strong.

Just Memories

[Note: At the end of some sections I will add memories that are less tied to lessons learned.]

Many of my best times were playing basketball in the back yard with family and friends. I spent countless hours on that court. I think I hit 86 free throws in a row once. I first dunked there (I think the hoop was an inch short of 10'). I would play with friends in the summers until they begged to quit or jump in the pool. I seldom wanted to stop. Dad, as he aged, had to play dirtier and dirtier to get his way. The bigger brothers and visiting family and friends often found themselves getting tugged and shoved. They sometimes had to pick themselves out of the oleander bushes that ringed the court after a hip check from Dad.

My mother was never sick. She always said she couldn't afford to be so she wasn't. I cherish the memories of being sick and having Mom attend to me. It always included gentle words, stroking of my hair, and Vicks Vaporub on my chest.

Our kitchen was always full of pies or cakes. Mom baked often and well.

Dad would pay us, as he lay on the floor, to sit on his back and pull gray hairs from his head. I was always surprised he could lie flat on the floor as he had a huge milk belly (people nicknamed him "The Mountain").

The backyard basketball court. Left to right: Dorne, Matt, Jim (my brother-in-law), me, Rowan, and Keller. Good times.

At night the dairy was mysterious. The overriding sound was the clanking of the cows' neck chains. Other sounds included some mooing and coyote yelps. It was always scary and enchanted to me.

My Dad was never one to let form get in the way of function. It made for interesting times. I know a very reputable man (distant cousin) who reminded me that Dad once bailed him out of jail. I asked for the story since this man seemed incapable of doing anything that would put him in jail. As a teenager he drove a silage or hay truck for Dad. He was pulled over and arrested as the plates on the truck were for a boat – and the boat tags were expired. Double whammy. Tags, tags – who needs tags? At age 13 or 14 I drove a very large truck for Dad on the Chandler dairy for a few days that had NO brakes. The only method of braking was the emergency brake and gear downshifting, which would slow me – amidst terrible smoke and screaming of the brakes – but not fully stop me. Dad reasoned that all of the stops I needed to make on the four-mile drive to the cotton gin were 4-way stop signs. So I could slow, make plenty of noise and count on the other guy to stop.

It seems like most of the male members of the family got hurt more often on the dairy than did I. Rowan broke an arm, had a rod driven though his upper thigh (long, nasty story) and several other similar issues. Dorne mangled some fingers under a running lawnmower and crashed a go-cart into the back axle of a truck. Matt sawed off one of his fingers. Dad, as described earlier, was crushed by a bull, and had a myriad of other accidents. My favorite was when a cow moved quickly, causing Dad to inject a planned anti-mastitis shot into his eye socket bone. Within a few minutes he looked like a prizefighter with a massive black eye. The good news was that he never developed mastitis.

When a cow had trouble delivering its baby calf naturally, the normal intervention was to 'pull' the calf out. That involved getting the cow into a stall where its head could be locked into place. Then a ratchet-like crank was fit firmly onto a wall or fence behind the cow. A chain was attached to the crank on one end and around the front legs of the unborn calf (The front legs were sometimes protruding, sometimes not. If not, we had to reach into the back end of the cow, find the forelegs, and attach the chain). Then the ratcheting started. As the crank took up the slack, the cow would feel the pressure and be pulled backwards. The headlock stopped her. Subsequent slow cranking pulled the calf out amidst pitiful moaning by the cow. Looking back it all seems a bit cruel but it got the job done and I don't think methods have changed much since the '60's. Most cows deliver while standing up so the first activity of a newborn calf is a three-foot freefall to mother earth.

The Carnation company's milk truck in the background.

Dad sold his milk to the United Dairymen of Arizona, as I recall. A driver in a large truck would come each morning to suck our large tanks dry. The driver had a secret compartment, which served as a refrigerator. He often had small cartons of the coldest rich chocolate milk in the world. I was

46

always very kind to the truck driver in the hopes of getting some chocolate milk.

In the later years our dairy was surrounded by a retirement trailer park, a golf course and homes. Before those popped up it was desert all around. There was endless opportunity for a child to have adventures in the desert. There were washes (called arroyos these days) and hills, jackrabbits and snakes. There was a dump where treasures could be found among other people's castoffs. Near the dump was a hill that we used for shooting practice. I must have pumped thousands of BB, then pellet, then .22 rounds into that hill. I remember that we didn't follow many rules and it's a wonder we all made it through alive.

Further to the point of encroaching neighbors, one of the reasons Dad eventually moved the dairy was because of all the complaining the neighbors did about the smells of the dairy. We were there first but somehow their olfactory sensitivities trumped that. I am amazed at the pockets of stupidity I find in the world.

There was always plenty of alfalfa hay on the dairy. Bales of hay are perfect building blocks for forts and other buildings – sort of like massive, scratchy Lego blocks. We made a few elaborate forts. It was mysterious back in the dark lanes of the forts. When tearing one such fort down we found two very large scorpions. I didn't enter any dark hay forts for a while after that.

Twenty miles from the dairy was a lake. When I was young we boated often as a family. Many of our old no-audio home movies are of our family boating and skiing at Saguaro Lake. The Salt River exited from the lake and provided a great summer activity – floating the river. All that was needed were large inner tubes. A two or three-hour float on a 110 degree day was refreshing. There were a few places with outcroppings that allowed for jumps off the cliffs into the river. With the additional traffic that metropolitan sprawl has brought to the Phoenix area the authorities have blown up or otherwise removed any opportunity to jump.

Horses are only OK on their good days. I trust and understand cows. Horses are not to be trusted. Small horses - ponies - are borderline evil. I was given a Shetland Pony as a boy. He was beautiful, full of life, and small enough that I could imagine us being a real team. Then I learned that he was a mean son-of-a-gun. Cinnamon - a cute, misleading name - refused to let anyone ride him successfully. When I mounted him, he would go only where he wanted to go. He always bee-lined to the nearest pole or wall and scraped against it. His intent was to remove my leg from my body so that I would fall off. I knew just enough about horses that I must impose my will with urging, steering, and, if necessary, kicking. I had some success with large horses in the past. None of those things worked on Cinnamon. He cemented my lifelong belief that horses are tools of the dark side.

A man in our local LDS ward asked Dad about raising chickens. Dad kindly gave him a rooster and a hen and wished the inexperienced would-be farmer luck. At this point in the story, I have to inform that chickens mating can look like a violent event. A rooster, while mounting a hen, can peck the back of the hen's head consistently, leaving a bald spot and even drawing blood. A few weeks later Dad asked the man how the chickens were doing. The man was anguished as he told Dad that he had been forced to kill the rooster with a baseball bat. "He was pecking that poor hen and just wouldn't leave her alone, Joe." ☺

Mission and Church Lessons

Elder John Hill and I with one of my favorite people, Uli Hoppe (now Beer), whom I was privileged to baptize in March, 1981.

Introduction

Over the years, as I was a hiring manager or assisting other hiring managers with the interview process I must admit to being biased. If I interviewed a returned Mormon missionary (RM) and found that he had completed his entire two-year mission I mentally gave him credit for about 10 years of job experience. Nothing matures a young man (or young woman) quicker than an LDS mission. A missionary is thrown into a foreign culture (even if it's Alabama or Boston), often foreign-speaking, and is asked to be a master salesman within months. A missionary usually works harder than at any other point in his life. He is asked to protect and be protected by a missionary companion and to, therefore, stay with his companion 24 hours a day, even when the companions have little in common other than membership in the LDS church and the desire to share what makes them happy. He is separated from home and hearth and asked to communicate only sparingly with family (so that he can focus on the task of sharing the gospel of Jesus Christ). In the end, a missionary usually comes home describing his mission as the best two years of his life.

I could write at length about the spiritual lessons learned on my mission and I will do that someday. As many of them are precious to me and should be shared in a slightly different context, I will forebear writing about many of the experiences in this book.

After my mission, while pursuing a degree at BYU, I taught at the Missionary Training Center from 1981 to 1984. That experience was also formative and I include a few thoughts from that period.

German

The word 'circumlocution' means being able to describe something without knowing or saying the actual word. Swimming could be described, for example, as 'staying afloat in the water by paddling'. About nine months into my mission I reached fluency in German. I remember thinking, "I can say anything in German". I might not know the exact word but I could circumlocute. That thought and realization was empowering. I was seldom tentative or apologetic about my German after that.

I love the German language. It is not a pretty spoken or sung language and it takes more words and letters to describe something in German than in English. It is not the world's business or science language. It is getting less important all the time. But it feels like it's my language, the language of my mission, the language in which so many important things happened to me.

German can be tricky. I was told early on about one particular consonant switch that could be embarrassing. "Be" and "ge" are prefixes. 'Schneiden' means to cut. So in the past tense 'geschnitten' means cut. If you swap the "ge" out for "be", the word 'beschnitten' means circumcised. So, telling someone in German incorrectly that you just cut yourself a little could turn into a longer discussion about why you were performing a personal circumcision.

I have remained fluent through the years, partly because I am a nut who will talk to myself to retain fluency if possible. But I have been lucky and blessed to have German speakers placed in my life at regular intervals. After my mission I taught in the MTC for three years. In my master's program, we lived in Germany for eight months. In Canada my secretary spoke German. In Hong Kong I had an Austrian assistant for a while. In London my boss and key colleagues were all Germans in Germany.

German will always be an important part of me.

Rejection of All Kinds

LDS missionaries in Germany know all about rejection. Tracting, or knocking on doors, was the most common form of contacting during my mission. I must have averaged eight hours of knocking doors and ringing doorbells every day of my mission except for the weekly preparation day and Sundays. Let's see – 5 days, 8 hours a day, say 100 weeks in Germany – that's 4,000 hours of tracting. Only about 1 in 100 would stop to talk or let us in. Another 10 or 20 would politely decline. That leaves about 80 or 90 out of 100 who would emphatically decline. That could include slamming the door, opening then immediately closing the door when they saw us, or verbally abusing us. It was humbling and frustrating. Especially since we deemed our message to be of critical importance for all humanity.

One of the keys for survival on the doors was to not take your frustration from the last door to the next door. Compounded rejection and frustration could lead to insanity. We tried to mix things up, changing our door approaches and trying to inject a little humor. It didn't improve our odds but it helped pass the time.

It can get a little wilder than door slamming and verbal rejection. In Goettingen we had a man chase my companion and me down three flights of stairs with an axe in his arms, yelling loudly about how he was going to cut us into pieces.

We had vehicles purposely brush by us at fairly high speeds - literally touch us - while we were riding bicycles. We had people call the police on us. The worst instance of that happened on Karl Marx Street. Nothing good comes from Karl Marx.

I am sure that those constant levels of rejection made the occasional positive interaction sweeter. When people invited us in we were thrilled.

I have made it a point to converse politely with anyone who comes to my door and offer him or her a drink of water. I have been in their shoes.

Germany's Dying Faith

WWII knocked whatever faith Germany had left right out of them. When tracting, I heard at least a thousand times, "I don't believe in God. If there was a God, he never would have allowed this to happen." "This" meant World War II. Every adult I talked to who was over 50 years of age lost at least a parent or sibling or child in the war. As far as I remember, it was every single person! The suffering is incalculable. Add the shame of losing the war and the atrocities carried out by its government and soldiers and you had deep national shame, depression and a profound loss of faith.

I arrived there 35 years after the war. Much of the older generation, which had suffered so much loss, wandered around like zombies. One lady expressed it to me this way, "I will only be happy when I can finally close my eyes for good". She said that to me as she opened, then slowly closed her door after we had knocked. Her little face haunts me from time to time.

I met clergymen who were not shy or apologetic as they explained that they did not believe in God. They viewed their roles as social workers. I attended Lutheran and Catholic meetings in Germany. Excluding widows over 70 years old and kids from 12-14 (they came because, at the end of their catechism, when they turned 14, they would receive substantial, traditional gifts), there was almost no one in the building. Regular attendance at church in Germany stands around 2-3% and that includes the widows and the kids. Take them out and it's likely below 1%.

Communication Could Save Your Eyebrow

A missionary spends more time during the week with his companion than he will ever spend with his wife. Learning to communicate is a critical skill for a missionary.

In one city my companion and I worked as hard as anyone in the mission. He was 27 and an Army veteran. I loved and respected him. One night we needed to go to the rooms that masqueraded as our Sunday church meeting space. It was up a dark staircase. The light was burned out. We fumbled our way up the stairs and stood on the landing in the pitch black. Elder Apgood had the keys and was fumbling around unsuccessfully with them. I stood patiently. We each got an idea at the same time. His idea was to kneel down and get oriented by looking through the keyhole (large German keys). My idea was to pull out and use the cigarette lighter that I used occasionally (when going door to door we liked to note down the responses from each address like "they slammed the door and told us to never come back". It was often dark so the lighter was helpful). We each implemented our ideas at the same time, he kneeling down next to me in the total darkness and me burning off his entire eyebrow. It was another reminder that communication is important and that burned human hair smells really bad.

On a more serious note, I had one companion who really annoyed me with his eating habits. He ate like a pig, with his food often falling out of his mouth around the corners. I am picky with things like that anyway but this was extreme. I tried to avoid sitting directly across from him during meals. Other companionships gave me best wishes for my suffering. After several weeks of mounting frustration (read: I wanted to kill him) I finally confronted him, semi-politely even, with his eating habits. He apologized profusely and explained that a deviated septum made it necessary for him to always breathe through his mouth, making mealtime messy. Boy, did I feel horrible. My companion had a handicap. As the context of the situation set in over the next days and weeks, I came to the conclusion that it was as if I had a one-legged companion and complained that he couldn't run faster. After that I became his defender when others complained about his eating style. I had come full circle in the way I viewed him. And it was as simple as knowing that he had a physical handicap. Communication solves so many problems or at least puts people on the same page. I could have avoided massive amounts of frustration and anger if I had just raised the issue politely weeks earlier. I vowed to do better.

My Little Flock of Sorts

Luise Niedorf
Beate Glaesener
Annette Hartmann
Annette's daughter
Norbert Pohl
Uta Paulus-Pohl
Florian Paulus-Pohl
Schwester Gebauer
Stefan Gebauer
Iris Grell
Ulrike Hoppe
Michael Tetteh
Petra Kaczmarcyk

These are the thirteen people who were baptized into the LDS Church partially or mostly because of my efforts during my mission. In my mission the average missionary had two convert baptisms. I felt exceptionally blessed to have been involved with so much success, comparatively. I love each of these people. I can see their faces. I can recall meaningful experiences with each of them. Just more than half of them have not remained active in the church. But several have. The LDS scriptures tell of unspeakable joy for those who bring even one soul to Jesus Christ. I have felt and still feel that joy. It is one of the choicest blessings in my life.

Companions

As mentioned earlier, a missionary is with his companion more than he is with his spouse later on. You are never to be apart, basically. I loved each of my companions although there were times where I would have traded each of them. I am sure I drove them crazy, at least occasionally. I learned from each of them. During a mission we call our companion brother or Elder so it's not uncommon to have no clue what a companion's first name is. Even now it feels odd to refer to them by their first names.

Ken Berbert – two months in the MTC.
Michael Prescott- two months in Luebeck. He was my trainer and I depended on him for everything but air, it seemed. He never let me down.
David Hales – two months in Luebeck.
David Apgood – two months in Goettingen.
Bob Atkinson – two months in Goettingen. Elder Atkinson was my first of two 'Goldens' i.e. I trained him.
Michael Puhlmann – one or two months in Bremerhaven.
Curtis Bond – two or three months in Bremerhaven. I trained Elder Bond.
Julius Graf – five glorious weeks in Hamburg Langenhorn. The best missionary I have ever known.
Chris Call – two months in Hamburg Langenhorn. I heard he has passed on. I loved being his companion.
Russell Weinheimer – two months in Hamburg Langenhorn.
Marcus Hausleitner – an Austrian – one month in Hamburg Langenhorn.

John Hill – my last three months, in Bielefeld.

My MTC district was so close that each of them felt like companions. In addition to Elder Berbert, there was Laura Shaw, Tracie Lamb, Mark Hirschi, Taylor Newman, Jerry Gerhardt, and Steve Tew.

Companions come in all shapes and sizes. I had 11 companions in 24 months in the Germany Hamburg Mission. In those days there was a transfer every month. The shortest companionship I had was one month and the longest was three months. Companionship choices are made by the Mission President, after much prayer and thought. I teamed mostly with Americans – from Missouri, Utah, Idaho, and Arizona – but also from Germany and Austria. After only about four months there I started using the phrase, "I could room with Godzilla" as I had learned the basics of getting along. Those basics were hard earned and learned at the expense of my first few companions. I am sure they wanted to knock me silly me a few times as I wanted to do the same to them.

The basic principles of getting along were difficult yet simple: pay less attention to what you want, help your companion, and don't get too wound up about anything. Much easier said than done, of course.

The combined effect of my 11 companions was tremendously positive on me. They had such varied personalities, work ethic, senses of humor, etc. that I benefitted from each of them.

A Farewell to Germany

My mission had a few phases. The first four to six months were all about just hanging on. The language was hard. The culture was foreign. Getting along with companions was hard. The germs were different. Homesickness set in from time to time.

Then things settled in with the language, companions, etc. I became stronger in my teaching abilities and even my conviction and testimony of the work. For the middle year of my mission I was a good, functioning missionary who loved the Lord and loved the people. The last eight months I was on fire. I was a good or great teacher. I led a group of 20 missionaries. I solved problems. I loved the Lord even more and loved the work. Most of all, I loved the people with all of my heart.

Somewhere in the last six months another change slipped in, almost imperceptibly at first, then stronger. It was that I was where I was supposed to be, that I was loving it and that there was no place else that I wanted to be and no other work I could ever imagine doing. The corollaries of that feeling were that I felt little desire to go home, had zero homesickness, and would have sincerely been pleased to have my mission extended indefinitely. It was a strange and wonderful feeling.

Recently I spent time with a couple who had just returned from three years as mission presidents in South America. They spoke of how hollow they felt in some ways upon re-entering non-missionary life such as secular employment. Everything, they said, paled in importance to the work they had just been privileged to direct in a small part of the vineyard for three years.

I was in that zone. At the end of the 24 months, I was given flight details and invited to conclude my mission. I did not want to leave MY people, MY country. I felt so empty during the flights. I was not unhappy to be in my mother and father's embraces - just the opposite. But I had left behind a large part of me.

Peace Lovers

The post-WWII generation recoiled from anything that represented German might or military. Germany was also 'green' before any other country. They were anti-nuclear power and anti-war to an extreme. There is a saying there, "Nie wieder Krieg" or "Never again war". Hitler books and references were banned. Anything aggressive was wrong.

We taught a sweet family in Goettingen. LDS missionaries encourage people investigating the church to read the Book of Mormon as we believe it is scripture and that it is the best way to test the validity and claims of the church and of Joseph Smith. In the first 20 pages of the Book of Mormon, a good man named Nephi is commanded, in desperate circumstances, by an angel to cut off the head of a very bad man with the direction, "It is better that one man perish than a nation dwindle in unbelief." The father of this family read to that point, closed the book and refused to read any more. Nothing could justify murdering another person. Period. I tried to reason with him. I asked what he would do if he was threatened. He would give them anything they wanted and would die before fighting back. Getting desperate now, I asked what he would do if robbers held his little boy at gunpoint and threatened to shoot him dead. Would he fight back? He responded that he would not but would rather watch his son die than inflict any violence on anyone else. His view might have been extreme but, if so, not by much.

The Best Missionary In My Mission

If a missionary works hard and follows the rules he is usually rewarded with leadership opportunities as his mission progresses. Starting out as a junior companion, an Elder can become a senior companion, a trainer (which is a real compliment since a trainer is the senior companion to a new missionary, thereby imprinting on him his first and lasting mission lessons), a district leader (over 4 to 12 missionaries), a zone leader (over ~20 missionaries), and an assistant to the president (there are usually two of those at any one time).

Halfway through my mission I was 'promoted' from district leader to zone leader (ZL). As I had had success in my previous city and had some sweet experiences, I felt like I was ready to be a ZL. I was made a junior ZL in Hamburg to a German missionary who, by all rights, should have already gone home. The mission president extended his mission for a 25th month for some reason that I still don't understand.

Within hours of being paired with him, I felt like a brand new missionary. Everything about him screamed great and wonderful. He had a great smile, a loving way, and he was an amazingly powerful teacher. I had never felt so inadequate. I vowed to listen and learn from this best missionary in the mission.

Over our five weeks together, I learned about this remarkable man. He came from the very southern tip of Germany. He came on a mission despite hardships at home. His younger brother was a sometimes-violent alcoholic. Several times, including once while we were together, he received letters from his mother after being beaten or abused by her younger son. She would wonder if she could stand it any longer. Each time my companion said that he would plead with the Lord in prayer for his mother's safety and his brother's rehabilitation. He would ask if he should end his mission and go home. Each time he felt strongly that he needed to stay and be the best missionary he could be.

He gave me a summary of his mission. In the first 17 months he had been blessed to participate in four baptisms. While that was well above the mission average, all four of the previously baptized people had stopped coming to church. He felt like a failure. At the time he was a ZL. He felt unprepared to be a leader of missionaries when he had so little success. He presented all of these feelings to the mission president in an interview. As he spoke he said that our mission president got a far-away look in his eyes and seemed to be distant. Noticing that, my companion went quiet. After a minute or two, he said, a feeling filled the room. It overpowered him with love and clarity of thought. The mission president added to the moment by pounding his desk a moment later (he was a pulpit-pounding Prussian, after all) and saying, "Jetzt geht's los!" which means "Let's get going!" or "Now we will get going!"

They shared their thoughts with each other. My companion walked out a changed person. He was somehow more dedicated, more resolute, more determined to be a great missionary.

Over the first 17 months he helped 4 people find their way to Christ through baptism. Over the final 8 months, he baptized 21 people. He baptized every month. On the day I met him he told me that he would go home in five weeks and that he wanted to have his luggage in one hand and a bag of wet baptismal clothes in the other. The night before he got on the train for home, he and I baptized a family of four.

I felt so humbled and blessed to have been with him for his last five weeks. I knew I had a huge responsibility to apply the things I had learned from him. I tried very hard to live up to that responsibility. I still do.

The Best Job I Will Ever Have

After my mission I returned to BYU. I needed to have a part-time job. The dream job, at least for me, was to teach German at the Missionary Training Center (MTC). Through some nice coincidences, I got an interview, did well and was hired to teach a district of ten missionaries four hours a day, five days a week.

I fell in love with the Elders and Sisters on the first day of their two-month stay there. I loved the aggressive teaching style we used and I loved the faith-based learning that the MTC provided. One non-LDS language expert deemed the MTC the finest language learning institution in the world. Missionaries learned 11 hours a day, 5 days a week.

After a school year in which I taught four groups of missionaries, I was promoted to the role of Zone Coordinator, the boss of all the German teachers. In our zone we also had a few other languages so my role was to hire, train, and monitor all of the teachers in the German, Polish, Greek, and Russian languages. I had the Zone Coordinator role for two years. It will forever be the best job I will ever have. Missionaries who wanted to serve their Lord and mankind surrounded me. I hired and worked with teachers with amazing capabilities. [Note: the application process for prospective teachers required letters from an applicant's mission president and bishop. There were so few positions that I could afford to be very selective. I joked – but it was not far from the truth – that I didn't even interview an applicant unless their bishop said he/she was the best missionary he ever sent and the mission president said he/she walked on water.]

I saw miracles happen there.

The Bee

While working at the MTC, I was exposed to an object lesson in a training session that has remained with me. I sat in a dried out weed patch on one of the hottest days of a Utah summer and was told to learn a lesson and come back to class to report on it. I sat for a long while feeling hot and mildly annoyed but also determined to complete the task. Then I had a nice little epiphany. A bee buzzed by me. I followed his path for a full minute. The bee made me realize that, even in this very brown, dry place there were a few small flowers here and there, not even enough to provide color. I hadn't noticed them. The bee had noticed them. It buzzed around until it found a flower, landed on it, enjoyed the nectar, then moved on until it found another little flower in the sea of brown. 90% of the bee's environment was a brown, arid space but 90% of its time was spent in the 10% of color and happiness. The moral: find the good things wherever you are and dwell on those. Flee the yucky stuff as quickly as you can. It's simple but particularly useful.

Hands In The Circle

In the Mormon Church we believe that we can hold and exercise the priesthood, the power to act in God's name. That power was restored to Joseph Smith and has been passed down uninterrupted to the current day. I hold that priesthood. It has blessed my life and the lives of others around me. For example, during my mission, my companion and I rode our bikes to visit a newly baptized member. This sweet young lady lived with an LDS family and was the nanny for their three little kids. We rang the doorbell. Seconds later the door burst open. The mother of the house was crying and holding their baby, who was obviously very ill, as she was dark red, almost purple. Her eyes were rolling back in her head. The mother blurted out, "My baby's sick. Please bless her now!" After a few seconds of gathering myself I laid my hands on her hot little head (107 degrees at the time), invoked my priesthood and asked the Lord to give her relief. I closed the blessing. Within a minute or two, the baby's temperature dropped to around 100 degrees, she fell asleep in her mother's arms, and the Mom was able to get her to a hospital for treatment. The blessing did not heal her. That sweet baby had ongoing health issues, before and after that. But the faith of the mother and my priesthood allowed for relief. Every LDS person could tell stories of faith rewarded and priesthood power.

A ritual in the LDS Church is for an infant to receive a blessing in a Sunday meeting. I remember, one Sunday in Ohio, participating in a baby blessing. The father holds the baby and all other invited priesthood holders form a circle and put a hand or two under the father's arms so that everyone is connected. The father and several of the participants were dear friends of mine. During the blessing I did something I have never done in that setting – I opened my eyes slightly and worked my way around the circle of faces. As I gazed briefly at each face I felt deep love and admiration for each person there. I remember thinking, "where else in the world am I going to find a group of men like this?"

I am so grateful for the LDS Church. There are many reasons. But one is the caliber of fine men and women that assemble every Sunday in chapels across the world.

Prayer Works in Texas… and Other Places Too

After graduating from BYU in 1984, I applied for and was accepted in to the Master in International Business program at the University of South Carolina (it's THE USC, we like to say, not the copycats in L.A.). I worked at the MTC as long as I could, said a very sad goodbye to Provo, the MTC and friends as dear as family, then headed to Arizona to spend time with both families for a few weeks.

To make it easier on Amy and Ethan, who was 18 months old, I loaded our meager belongings into the smallest trailer that U-Haul made, hooked it up to my 1976 pick-up, and made the 2,100-mile drive alone from Mesa to Columbia, South Carolina.

On the outskirts of Fort Worth, on I-20, the pickup experienced serious problems. The Hot/Cold gauge fixed itself on Hot. Steam was coming from the engine. I pulled over onto an exit ramp and tried to survey the damage. I am not a mechanic but, after a minute or two, I determined the problem. The main rubber hose that carried water from the radiator to the engine had split – exploded, really – so that I lost all water from the system in a matter of seconds. I clearly needed a replacement hose. The problems were that I didn't have a replacement hose, wouldn't know how to fix it or have the right tools, and it was Saturday night after closing time for most businesses (and they would remain closed through Sunday), and the off ramp was still a mostly rural place. These were pre-cell-phone days.

I surveyed the damage several times and walked around the pickup and trailer checking for other damage. I was really just pacing and determining if I had any options. I was committed to be in a 'welcome to the program' class in South Carolina the following Monday morning and, therefore, trying to avoid laying over for the weekend. I thought of a friend of a brother who was living in Dallas but I didn't know his number and didn't have access to a phone. I spotted one house about a half mile away. I was mulling over whether to walk there and see if anyone could help.

After perhaps 20 minutes of pondering I happened on an idea. I had been taught all my life to pray, including in times of need. I felt ashamed that I had taken so long to think of it. I stepped in between the pickup and trailer by the hitch, knelt down and offered a prayer, beginning with an apology for taking so long. I am sure I thanked God for many things, then got to the subject. I told Him I didn't have a plan and that I needed help. I finished.

I stood and took a step or two. Within ten seconds of saying Amen, a car pulled up. The driver, leaning over nearer the passenger side door, asked if I needed help. I explained. He pulled over, turned his car off, and assessed the damage with me. He confirmed that I needed a new hose. He told me he was on his way home from his work. He operated a garage in Fort Worth and specialized in freeway breakdown assistance. He said that if he had the right hose, I was in luck and he could help me. If not, I was probably out of luck until Monday morning. We got into his car and headed east to his garage.

Often, in a car repair facility, they keep hoses on a large pegboard. The outlines for the hoses are traced in black, like the white lines around dead bodies on TV. The purpose for the black outline is so that a garage mechanic knows where to put the replacement hose when one is used and a new one ordered. On this man's shop wall was a huge display of black traced lines with the possibility for hundreds of hoses. Filling only about 10% of the outlines were hoses of all shapes. My heart sunk, thinking I was out of luck. We searched the board, narrowed it down to a smaller area, and FOUND the right hose.

We loaded the hose and some water bottles into the kind man's car and returned to the pickup. He replaced the hose, and then I filled the radiator with water. The hose worked fine and the engine seemed to show no ill effects. I was on my way. I made it to my Monday morning class, full of gratitude. I am less slow to remember to pray.

If I recall correctly, the man's name was Herschel Crump. Bless him.

Princes Among Us

When we lived in Hong Kong we attended the Victoria Ward, which was the LDS congregation serving the island of Hong Kong (H.K. is made up of the island, and two areas on the mainland called Kowloon and the New Territories). The ward was full of families like mine – Dad working for a multinational company and Mom and young kids along for the adventure. Additionally, since the Church's Asia area was headquartered in H.K. we enjoyed having some senior missionary couples and even some General Authorities of the church in the ward.

We developed some nice friendships with a few of them. I jumped at the chance to spend any time with any of them since they were so wise and experienced. One of the sweet couples was the Grobergs - John and Jean. They are as good and kind and sweet as people can possibly be (Note: For the last year or so I served in the ward Bishopric. With the difficult travel schedule of the Bishop and other counselor, I conducted meetings often and sometimes as the only Bishopric member on the stand. Usually I had one or two General Authorities sitting behind me. While they were not the kind of men to criticize, I always felt watched and pressured to do everything perfectly. Only once did one of them speak to me about my conducting skills. It was Elder Groberg, who put his arm around me and, with a loving look and smile, asked, "Do you think we can start on time next Sunday?" We started on time the next Sunday and every one thereafter that I had anything to do with.)

Jean was motherly or grandmotherly to each of the ladies in the ward. Amy adored and idolized Jean. So did I and I loved Elder Groberg – his way, his unassuming smile, his books, everything. They invited us all over for a Family Home Evening on our last Monday in H.K. They fed us well, we enjoyed a spiritual message and then we played a game. All the time I was hopeful that our spirited children would mind their manners, not set the place on fire, or do any other heinous thing. All was going well as we started the card game.

None of us had ever seen or played this particular card game. The Grobergs explained it and we jumped in with a few practice rounds. I could see as each of us Ellsworths grasped the rules and got a feel for the game. The game involved knowing the cards in your hand and playing them onto piles on the table at breakneck speed. I was sitting close to Atley, then almost eight years old. I could see that she was frustrated by the game. I watched her closely (she was the child most likely to set the house on fire, after all) as I played my own hand and was pleased to see some progress. I saw her face move from anger and frustration to some level of understanding. Then a little smile as she finally got it. Then a bigger smile as she pondered an opportunity to play a card. It took a while to connect the thought to grabbing the card to putting it on the appropriate pile. But she grabbed the right card and leaned in to make a play. Just as she gloriously laid the card on the pile, Elder Groberg saw the same opportunity (he was cruising through the game, playing cards here and there, and was oblivious to this little sub-plot) and beat her to the pile with his card by a millisecond. Atley realized immediately what had happened and that she had been beaten to the punch. She looked again at what had happened, then peered up to meet his eyes with her own fiery eyes. "Watch it, sucker!", she snapped at him.

Time froze. I froze. Couldn't she just have set the place on fire? That would have been nicer than an eye to eye personal insult to the man of the house, who happens to be a hero of mine.

Elder Groberg laughed. Hard. We all laughed and then laughed some more. I could tell he thought it was genuinely funny and nothing more. We played on. I jokingly passed my LDS Temple Recommend to Elder Groberg, offering to forfeit it. He passed it back. We laughed again. Kids will say what they will say. Elder Groberg - and every other senior leader in the church that I have ever personally encountered – was a prince in every way.

[Note 1: Another General Authority moved into the ward and assumed his seat on the stand on the first Sunday. We usually sat on the second or third row from the front. The new Authority was a dear man and was obviously suffering from something like Parkinson's Disease. His head bobbed consistently. It drew attention at first. Once I had watched for a moment, I moved my gaze to other things. After another minute or so, Amy poked me with that 'do something!' poke and directed my gaze downward urgently. Sitting next to me was Atley, mesmerized by the new man on the stand and, staring intently at him, perfectly mimicking his tic. I quickly took her face in my hands and we had a whisper fest about how to proceed from there.]

[Note 2: Elder Groberg's first book, originally titled *In The Eye of the Storm* but changed to *The Other Side of Heaven* when it was adapted as a major motion picture, has had a profound impact on me. I recommend it highly. Take your time. Read it slowly.]

A Faded Light

In my nearly three years working in the Missionary Training Center, I had about 600 missionaries whom I felt like were 'my' missionaries. That means that I taught them personally or I was the Zone Coordinator when they came through the MTC.

Of the 600, I could probably put together a list of 20-50 that seemed like A+, 'can't miss in life' Elders and Sisters. One of them was a charming, smart, witty young man. I'll call him Elder Jones. He had great eyes that connected immediately with others. He was a natural leader.

In the MTC we didn't have a process to keep updated on the missionaries who came through and then went into the mission field. Occasionally we would receive ad hoc information. I heard a year later through a returning missionary that Elder Jones was on fire on his mission. He was the lead assistant to the mission president after a year.

I learned later that he stayed in that role for the rest of his mission. I was not surprised. This was an exceptional young man. His mission president became quite ill and Elder Jones really ran this mission for several months.

Years later I got the rest of the story of this remarkable young man's life. Apparently a few days before he was to conclude his mission, he went out and did something that was so far outside the church's mission rules that, after confessing it, he was sent home immediately and was subsequently disciplined by the church.

Anyone who knows the church and the discipline process also knows that it is done with love and with the best interest of the person in mind. I do not know the details but I believe Elder Jones would have been loved and encouraged through this process. He and everyone involved would have wished for and expected his return to full fellowship in the church a few years down the road.

But it did not go in that direction. Elder Jones, ever the star, ever the overachiever, was now in totally unfamiliar territory. Only a few people knew that he had been disciplined but somehow Elder Jones, over time, felt like everyone was watching him and judging him. He felt uncomfortable attending LDS meetings. He felt unloved and unwelcome in the place that had been most important in his life.

He slowly withdrew. He stopped coming to meetings, stopped hanging around the people who were trying to support him. It is a long tale and had many turns. But the sad ending was that he bought a plane ticket to a remote location, rented a car, bought a gun, drove to a quiet place and ended his life. This amazing boy was gone from this life. All the talent and leadership and love and goodness exited this existence with a single gunshot.

I could take many directions with this topic. I choose to leave it with this: when we see people who are struggling around us, we can jump in and do something to help them with as little judgment and condescension as possible.

[Note: Elder Jones' parents fell away from the church after a while. A contributing factor for the mother was an encounter in a grocery story about six months after Elder Jones' death. The mother encountered another member of the local LDS ward, who asked why Sister Jones seemed so down that day. Sister Jones responded that she was thinking of her son and his death. The other sister responded with, "Isn't it time you got over that?" or similar. Sister Jones stopped coming to church. When our Ben died, we were introduced to a great couple, Ken and Kerry Driggs, who lost their son, Eric, six years earlier while he was serving a mission in Argentina. I remember knowing that this was a couple I could learn from. We love them dearly. I also remember thinking that, with six years having passed since their son died, they would have been able to deal with it and move on. Nothing could be further from the truth. The passing of our sons, Ben, now eight years ago, and Ethan, now four years ago, is very fresh in many ways. I choose to remember that when I deal with others who have experienced loss in the past.]

Just Memories

On my mission in northern Germany, I often wished my mother could see through my eyes. I am not sure why I never wished that for my Dad. I suppose it was because Dad, in WWII, had seen some of the world. Mom always wanted to see interesting things but had little opportunity. It was a pleasure later in life to get to invite Mom to the places we lived. Together we saw Ohio, Hong Kong, Thailand, the Philippines, southern China, and much of southern England.

In Toronto, I was honored to be a young men's leader in the local ward, and I quickly learned to love the two other leaders and all of the boys. We only had about six boys - three sets of brothers. By the end of our two-and-a-half years in Canada I loved these boys like sons and still do. When we were asked to move by my company, I felt like I was betraying those six boys. I have some contact with them still.

When Amy and I moved to South Carolina we moved into the West Columbia 1st Ward, near the Columbia airport and some ten miles from downtown Columbia. Coincidentally, seven or eight additional young graduate-level couples moved into that ward at the same time. Thus commenced an unusual two years. It was a love story. This sweet ward was injected with young couples, little babies and tons of enthusiasm. The ward seemed to adopt us. We felt deeply loved from Day 1. We were given positions of responsibility. LDS wards are famous around the world for welcoming newcomers. But this was something extraordinary. I cannot speak or write about it without becoming emotional. They loved us and we loved them. I remember being asked to coach the young men's basketball team in the youth church league. I enjoyed it so much that I was asked to coach the men's team also. Then I was asked to coach the young women and the women (That is taboo these days in the church, I believe). The funniest part of that chapter was that our ward only owned one set of shirts – a soft purple color. We used those same shirts for the men, boys, women, and girls. After the two years, the ward threw a party honoring those seven or eight couples.

The ward that I grew up in was notorious in many ways. Our ward was the eastern most in Mesa – the old 12th Ward. Our boundaries went for 50 miles and took in an area that was known for low-income families and folks who didn't like to be seen by other people. Most of the stories I tell about the ward should not be repeated often. I learned plenty of bad things that I wish I could unlearn. I will relate one story. It was the norm for the Boy Scouts and their leaders to spend a week at a local BSA scout camp. Each boy should earn at least five merit badges and grow in experience and character. My first year we, as a troop, revolted against our scoutmaster. He seemed to genuinely hate us and we celebrated late into the night when he became ill and had to go home on day 5. Our troop threatened and physically abused some scouts from a large troop (we didn't know how big their troop was at the time) and were, in turn, threatened and hunted for the rest of the week. We hid our troop numbers on our sleeves, as, had the other troop spotted us, it would have resulted in violent injury. As a troop we earned a total of two merit badges (instead of the 50 or so expected of us).

I was to receive some kind of honor on the final evening at a large campfire where all of the scouts at the scout camp were to be assembled. Receiving such an honor publicly would have 'outed' me to the big troop. I was determined not to receive the award. As I pondered my options – feigned illness, disappear for a few hours, etc. – my oldest brother arrived at camp and took me and a friend home early as we needed to fly to Idaho the next morning. I was saved. Such were the experiences in the old 12th ward. I could fill a long chapter with other, similar stories. I still love so many of the people that I knew in the 12th ward.

All but one of the wards I worked in on my mission struggled mightily. They were small and dominated by a small number of families that had been there for a long time. Often fissures erupted in relationships in such wards. Arguments were not uncommon. I remember a one-armed man (he used a metal extension with a hook to replace the arm) regularly using the pulpit or the men's priesthood meeting to remind us that he had been unfairly impacted in life. He was once so agitated that he was shouting 'God is an abomination' as a few of the other men helped him calm down. Missionaries had an opportunity to inject enthusiasm and reason into such wards. New converts also always helped.

World lessons

1995 in Hong Kong. On the harbor.

Introduction

TV and the Internet are practically everywhere and programming content is becoming global and more homogeneous. The relatively low cost of travel makes it easy for us to see other places. The result of pervasive media and cheap travel is a slow, global convergence of norms, fashion, trends and even beliefs. I suppose it will take centuries of connectedness to remove the major cultural differences around the world. I am glad for you and me that it will take that long but saddened for our great-great-great-grandchildren. The differences are the spice in life. Challenges to our natural ethnocentrism are difficult but usually good.

In 1996, while living in Hong Kong, I was on a business trip to Kunming, China. Our company was selling banking automation products to banks. A few of us were to meet with executives from a large regional bank. Our Chinese salespeople needed a corporate executive to state in English that we stood behind our products. I was qualified to be the corporate executive, which meant I was white and couldn't speak Mandarin. When I asked our team what they wanted me to say, they assured me that I could say anything I wanted in English and that they would 'translate' it into Mandarin, meaning they would say what they wanted to say with absolutely no regard to what actually came out of my mouth. Since I trusted them, it became great fun. I talked about how good our company was but also threw in some baseball statistics. We later got the order. But that's not the point of this story. I had arrived in Kunming earlier with several hours to spare. I checked into the best hotel in the city, although I was advised in very broken English that the electricity usually worked 12 hours on and 12 hours off. I settled into my room for a brief rest and turned on the TV. After a few minutes the power failed. Hmmm. What to do for a few hours? I had seen a nice brochure in the lobby and a similar one in my room, advertising their state-of-the-art workout room. I changed into my gym clothes and headed down to the mezzanine level. I couldn't find the workout room there or anywhere else for that matter. After several minutes of looking around, I decided to ask. I approached the concierge in the lobby, held up the brochure, and asked in slow, clear English where the workout room was. The first gentleman, not understanding a word, waved me off and pointed to another man at the main desk. I restated my question slowly. The man said, "No." I was sure he misunderstood and repeated the question again, emphasizing the nice brochure. He again answered with a no. I pressed him one more time. This time he said, "Never have workout room." Now I was confused. "Then why do you have this nice brochure?" I insisted. He responded almost proudly, "Promotional materials", without batting an eye. I wandered off, completely baffled and with that "Doh!" feeling. I still laugh when I think about it and still don't quite get it. Now that is spice.

Feng Shui Part 1

The concept of Feng Shui provided me two neat examples of cultural differences. Feng Shui is a Chinese philosophical system of harmonizing the human existence with the surrounding environment. Near our home in Hong Kong was a stunningly beautiful high-end apartment building, hugging the lush green hills and just up from Repulse Bay beach. The building was light blue accented by darker blues. But it's defining characteristic was a massive rectangular hole which, at first glance, appears simply to be super creative, memorable architecture. But the story went much deeper. In fact the hole was not conceived or wanted by the owners and builders. It is common practice in Chinese culture to have a Feng Shui expert review your location and building plans. The expert, for a fee, advises on aspects from how to ensure the most financial success to how to set up executive offices for peace, comfort and alignment with natural forces. In this case, the expert advised the owners that, much earlier, a dragon had been buried in the mountain behind the proposed building. One day the dragon would awake and would immediately want to get to the ocean. If the building were there, the dragon would be confused, not get to the ocean and that would be a very bad thing. The architects, knowing that the expert should not be argued with, devised the apartment building with a hole in it. It was much more expensive to build. But it had to be done that way.

Another twist to the story came a few months later when I was having dinner in Seoul with several Korean colleagues. As we sat sharing stories, I told the Feng Shui apartment building story. The

Koreans laughed unusually hard after the punch line. After they calmed down, one of them summarized their feelings by telling me that 1) Koreans were not so dumb as to believe in that kind of thing and 2) that a Korean dragon would have been smart enough just to go around the apartment building.

Feng Shui Part 2

As the CFO of our Asian business, I was tasked with finding us new office space in Hong Kong. After weeks of searching, we found a great place in the Wanchai district at a reasonable price. We committed to the contract and had architects draw up plans for our two floors on the 23rd and 24th floor. The plans dealt with the expected issues – ingress and egress, toilets, break rooms and executive room placement. The last item mattered to me, as I wanted an office overlooking the Hong Kong harbor. The plans included ideal office placement for me and the two more senior Chinese executives in our office. Before fitting out the building we knew we needed the blessing of a Feng Shui expert. The three of us met him and his sons on the naked 24th floor and took him through the plans. He seemed uneasy as he wandered around the floor. After several minutes of pondering he told us that everything was fine except that the executive offices needed to be moved to the hill side of the building and away from the harbor side. He said that the prosperity and money would flow to us from the harbor and that the prosperity could only be garnered if our executive doors faced the harbor and were always open.

In a great cultural quirk, one of my ethnic Chinese colleagues, also wanting to sit by the harbor and having been educated in England and the USA, asked the expert how much money it would take for him to change his mind (I think his line was, "Would an extra $10,000 make it any different?"). Our expert was deeply offended and stormed off. We moved the offices for my two Chinese colleagues to the mountain side of the building to align with the expert's guidance. I stayed on the harbor side and asked the two to be sure to bring me the prosperity and wealth as they received it. In turn, I promised that I would soak in the view of the harbor and the South China Sea and tell them about it. By the way, my colleagues dared not defy the Feng Shui guidance as our employees would have certainly learned about it and would have expected poor company performance from Day 1 and many would have likely resigned, knowing that they were in a risky and perhaps cursed business.

Lo-Pa-Chut

We landed as a family in Hong Kong in early January of 1994. We took up residence in a lovely hotel in the Central district, as we had not previously decided where to live. So, on day two or three we visited a few potential apartments (almost no one lives in a single family home in H.K.). We were all still struggling with jet lag. With our family of six and with Ethan in his manual wheelchair, we looked quite a sight as we crowded our family into each taxi and the wheelchair into the trunk.

H.K. taxi drivers, almost all being native Cantonese speakers, are generally barely sufficient in English. Some are fluent but most drivers struggle with anything beyond the basics. Our first family taxi experience was trying as our driver spoke little English. We managed to get him to the first address. As we climbed in to find the second address I had trouble communicating with the driver. I tried verbally three times. I showed him the piece of paper I had. He couldn't understand me and the English writing did not help him. He let me speak to the dispatcher in the hopes that the dispatcher's English was better. The driver kept saying a few phrases over and over again. One sounded like "Lo Pa Chut" and another sounded like "Gwoddy, gwoddy". All this time the kids were putting up with the dissonance in the car – all the talking by the driver, the dispatcher, and me. Atley, who was five and a half and who seemed the most jet lagged, was sitting on my lap. As I was sitting directly behind the driver, Atley was very near the back of his head, perhaps just a few inches. She seemed half-asleep and uninterested in the discussions. But, after several minutes of the confusion and the overly loud shouts of "Lo Pa Chut" and Gwoddy, gwoddy" from the driver into his radio, she had something to say. She raised her head and looked right at the head of the taxi driver and said, "Mister, they don't understand a word you're saying!"

I laughed and have a laughed a hundred times about it since. What must have been going though that cute little five year old head? She was being thrown into a foreign culture and was dealing with it the best way she knew how. That experience was one of hundreds from the previous and ensuing years where my little family was thrown into various cultures. I enjoyed sitting back and watching Amy and each of the kids take it in. I was so pleased with their expanded worldview. After we moved back to the States, I could especially see how different the kids were from others who had not been subjected to similar experiences. Amy and I have never regretted all the moving around, primarily because of the rich experiences and deep friendships we enjoyed.

[Note: We settled on an apartment on the 17th and 18th floors of the Manhattan Apartments in Tai Tam, around the corner from Stanley. The views from our front windows and balcony over the South China Sea were spectacular. The view out the back windows of the rising mountains was equally stunning. We had about 1,600 square feet. Our monthly rent for the apartment, which was covered by my company, was $13,000. Yep, 13 grand. Not a typo. Several times as Amy and I lay in bed we mused on how I could possibly add enough value to my company to justify that kind of expense.]

Get in Line in Asia

In my experience, queuing, or standing in a line, is a concept fundamentally understood by Americans and not at all by the average Chinese. If we Westerners arrive third in a line at a bank or ticket counter we don't crowd ahead in the line. We respect the order in which we arrived and established a presence. Generally speaking, the Chinese don't. You have to sharpen your elbows and defend your turf right up until the time you are serviced. It frustrated me no end in the first year but I adjusted. I even had fun with it later on. As Amy and I queued up to get our tickets and check our bags on a flight from Phnom Penh to Hong Kong, we found ourselves in a quiet little line. I noticed that there was one person in front of us and one Chinese man behind us. That was it.

I intentionally left a space - of only a few feet - between us and the man ahead of us. Then I kept an eye on the gentleman behind us. He took the bait. He could not stand the empty space between the first guy and us. He started to twitch, he violated my personal space rule by practically hugging me from behind and, finally, he just stepped around us, thereby improving his position from third to second. It had been a long day (that's my excuse) so I grabbed him by the shoulder and guided him back behind us with a scowl. In the few minutes before we were called to the ticket agent I even let the space gap increase, knowing that I was torturing the man behind me.

Littering and Other Bad Habits

I guess it was in the 60's and 70's that we Americans decided that littering was very bad. The Chinese have not received that memo yet, even in westernized Hong Kong. (Note: Singapore is the exception. They understand clean there. If you don't believe it, just drop your chewing gum, which is contraband, on the sidewalk. You will be arrested, fined and possibly have your butt caned.)

We were signed up to host a few American sailors in our home for a meal whenever a U.S. ship came into port with time for a stay. Sailors also had the option of signing up. Only the serious sailors with a desire for a home cooked meal and good conversation signed up (the others were either busy on board the ship or were only interested in wine, women, and song). On each occasion we peppered the sailors with questions of where they had been, what they had seen and what they had learned. When asked what each sailor did aboard ship, I always expected answers like 'I land planes' or 'I steer the ship'. But the answers were never that. One said he was the manager of the convenience store. One stocked and cleaned the bathrooms. One ran the brig. I guess when an aircraft carrier has 7,000 people on board it truly is like a city and needs every occupation imaginable.

On one occasion a sailor talked about his role in helping move all of the accumulated garbage from their ship to a local ship in each port with whom the U.S. Navy had contracted to remove and appropriately dispose of refuse. They said that, the day before near Hong Kong's harbor, they had transferred all their garbage to a Chinese scow of sorts, watched the scow steer perhaps a quarter mile away and then watched as the Chinese deckhands dumped all of the U.S. garbage to the bottom of the deep blue sea, sea, sea. The sailor said he was only mildly surprised, as he had been told this was the custom. We - the U.S. Navy - couldn't just dump the garbage. That would be criminal. But we could pay a fee knowing well that the garbage would still end up littering the South China Sea.

As our family dined in a fast food restaurant in Hong Kong I noticed a state of the art trash bin. It had different slots for recyclables, food, glass, and other. I believe there were four slots. Upon further examination I noticed that, under the four slots, there was only one great garbage can. Everything from all four slots ended up in the same place. And I suppose all of it ended up at the bottom of the sea at some point.

A Scooter, the New Sign of Upward Mobility

On a business trip to Indonesia, I found myself surprised at the abject, begging-level poverty in Jakarta. It was especially notable since my colleague host and I were being driven in a new Mercedes with a nice Blaupunkt stereo system. As beggars and children merchants surrounded our car at every stoplight, I was told to keep my eyes straight forward as faces pressed against our windows at literally every light and traffic pause. In the afternoon, during another drive, I noticed a family on a scooter. I had seen a million scooters and a million poor Indonesians that day but this combination re-grabbed my attention. As I recall it was a family of six or seven on the scooter. Dad was driving with Mom right behind. One child sat of Dad's lap, one stood on the gas tank holding the handlebars along with Dad. Mom has a child on her shoulders and there was at least one more behind Mom holding on to something. Dad wore a ripped T-shirt, old shorts and ragged sandals. And he was the best dressed of the lot. I felt terrible for this family and for this country. As I riveted my gaze on this family, my Indonesian business colleague, Widiono, noticed and asked what I was thinking. I said, "What a poor family. I feel so bad for them".

He looked at me like I was from outer space and quickly responded, "But it's a brand new scooter!" The point was 'hey, buddy, this is a middle class family'. In fact, having a new scooter was a sign of upward mobility.

As the two-day trip continued I learned a few other things from Widiono. He addressed the concept that

Indonesians and indigenous Malaysians were stereotyped as lazy. He said it was true and why shouldn't it be. In their part of the earth it is never too hot or too cold to build extravagant homes and shelters or to worry about buying cold weather clothes. The earth naturally provided more than enough fruits and vegetables without any extra cultivation so why plant. Diligence, he argued, was an unfortunate by-product of Europeans and other cultures for having settled in the wrong locations.

The Little Girl in Green

On my first visit to India, I was impressed, as most people are, at the unending string of people. With 1.2 billion people, there are humans seemingly everywhere. And most of them seemed to be very poor and devoid of much emotion or motivation. Garbage is everywhere. Nothing seems planned. [Note: To be fair India is making significant improvement on many fronts in the 21st century.] Moving from meeting to meeting in New Delhi, I was being chauffeured by our local Finance leader, George. Beggars roamed every street. As opposed to other poor countries I had visited where most poor street dwellers were hocking something, so many in India were simply begging. George instructed me never to give anyone anything since begging in India is a racket - organized and planned. He assured me that rupees given to a poor woman would be snatched from her hands seconds later by her groomer. There are even stories of people maiming women and children to make them more effective, more sympathetic beggars. It was a hard experience. Whereas I had seen handfuls of beggars in my life, now I was seeing literally thousands every day (it started as I exited the airport so it was early and often).

At one stoplight there must have been roadwork or extra traffic. We stayed stationary at the light for about five minutes. Sitting right outside George's window was the prettiest, saddest little girl, perhaps eight years old. She was in a green Indian outfit. She sat in the median begging but not aggressively. She looked at George and me with sweet but sick eyes. Tears, I have always assumed from some infection, ran down from the corners of her eyes. She begged us non-verbally for some financial assistance. George had his usual steeled look. I wanted to help the girl but remembered George's advice. Five minutes can be a long time. Somewhere during that little eternity George must have experienced a change. Just before we drove away, George rolled down his window and passed the sweet girl some rupees. We drove in silence for several minutes before continuing our previous conversation.

As Poor As It Gets

I have been to Africa only once. It was a weeklong trip to the Ivory Coast (since renamed Cote D'Ivoire) and then to Niger, one of the poorest, least visited countries in the world, and then just a few hours in Burkina Faso. My company was working with the Niger government on the most basic of automation processes. It was something akin to the Social Security system but more rudimentary. The goal was simply to assign a number to everyone in the country so they could number them. The estimates of the population of Niger varied widely as there was no reliable source of information. [Note: The project was cancelled a few months later when the sitting government was ousted in a coup d'état, which included the assassination of the Prime Minister.]

I have several memories of the otherworldliness of the three days in Niamey, Niger. A wild camel or two roaming the inner city, the lack of infrastructure in the city, the people bathing and washing their clothes in the Niger river, the musty, dirty smell of the hotel, the tour of our host's home and the opportunity to meet his four wives and his parents (who lived in a tepee-like structure a block away).

At our main government meeting, the Interior Minister finally arrived late to the hotel meeting room where over 50 of us had been waiting for 90 minutes. He said, "Let's start with a 30 minute break". It turned out to be a 60 minute break.

[Note: One morning in the hotel lobby, I sat with a Cypriot work colleague as we waited for our ride to the government building. He grabbed my arm and said something like, "See that. That is what is wrong." I looked and asked what he meant. He pointed to a small group of four or five men sitting together. He explained that the speakers were Islamic leaders and that they were proselyting and recruiting adherents of Allah. He said, "Islam is very busy. The Catholics are doing nothing. The Greek Orthodox are doing nothing. Only Islam and you Mormons are trying to grow your religion. At this rate the world will be ruled by Islam someday."]

Romantic Notions

Germanic and Romantic cultures differ. When we were living in London, I traveled regularly to continental Europe. One week I was in Vienna for meetings. After meetings one day a colleague and I were walking back to our hotel. We stopped for a red light. Despite pushing the appropriate button we could not get the pedestrian crosswalk sign to give us a green light. Several green and red traffic lights came and went with no opportunity for us to cross. My colleague, Richard, and I were joined by a small local family, who also wanted to cross. Realizing that the light must be broken, and that traffic was fairly light, and after waiting a few more minutes, Richard and I decided to work our way across the road despite the red pedestrian light. As we got half way across I heard shouting. Turning, I saw that the parents in the little Viennese family were still standing there and that they were not happy with us. Being a German speaker I caught it all. They said we were law breakers, stupid, and bad examples to their small children. We moved on.

A week or two later almost the same situation developed for Richard and me in Madrid, Spain. This time, however, after one cycle of the pedestrian light not turning green, the little Spanish family walked across the street, dodging cars as they went. Richard and I stood and watched. As the family reached the other side I saw both the mother and father turn and look at us. Their looks said, "Hey, people, you're gonna be there all day. Traffic is light enough, what are you waiting for?"

One has to be ready for disparate cultures, even in the same time zone.

I Love All These Places

Lest anyone believe I dislike or devalue any of the cultures I have encountered, let me say that I have deeply enjoyed every country I have lived in or visited. I have lost my ethnocentrism.

I have developed lasting friendships in every place along the way. Despite the different cultural heritages I do believe we are all children of the same God. I see confirmation of that when I recall the caring, even loving relationships that I have with people from all religions and cultures.

I was born in the USA. I have lived in Germany, Canada, Hong Kong, China, and England.

Some of the things I love about Germany include: chocolate, landscapes, mountains, seas, punctuality and trains. I love the people, their recognition of prior sovereign sins and the resolution to avoid them in the future, and their resilience. I love their bakeries, their Christmas markets, Lederhosen and Dirndls, their rich tradition of music, literature and thought.

I love Canada because of its gracious, kind, good people. I believe the Canadian culture is a generation or two behind the U.S. in that it is less pessimistic, less loud, and less sarcastic. I admire Canada's love for the outdoors (I mean, who else has a leaf for a flag?), their national anthem, Hockey Night in Canada, and the Labatt Briar (yes, I even got into curling).

I love Hong Kong for its buzz, creativity, and pace (we moved from H.K. to London and it took me six months to get used to how slowly elevator doors closed in the non-H.K. world). I love its buildings, mountains, bridges, and tunnels. Oh, my goodness, do I love its food. I love that it is so accessible to the rest of Asia. I love the people and their desire to move forward, get ahead, and be reasonable at the same time. And I loved the Hong Kong Sevens (yes, I got into rugby).

I love the United Kingdom. I love the people, the history, the culture, and the castles. I love its neighborhoods, the Home County of Surrey where we lived, the roads and rails, Scotland, and Northern Ireland. I love the cathedrals, the Squares, the theatres, and Lords (yes, I got into cricket).

I have visited Mexico, Argentina, Brazil, the Bahamas, Japan, Korea, China, Taiwan, Macau, the Philippines, Singapore, Malaysia, India, Indonesia, Australia, New Zealand, Tahiti, Cote D'Ivoire, Burkina Faso, Cyprus, Ireland, Norway, Sweden, Finland, Denmark, the Netherlands, Belgium, France, the old East Germany, Switzerland, Austria, Hungary, Liechtenstein, and Italy.

What a grand planet we live on – beautiful, varied, and full of overwhelmingly good humans.

The Unfortunate Trajectory of the USA

Although I love the United States more than any other country, one of the saddest lessons learned from spending more than a decade outside the United States was about our dear homeland. After being gone so long, I could compare the U.S. to itself ten years earlier and also to the other countries where we lived. Both comparisons were disappointing.

The USA we returned to, after having missed the 90's, was louder, ruder, more cynical, and less kind. That was most visible in our TV ads but also visible out in public.

There is a term used internationally - the 'ugly American'. Amy and I watched as time and time again we, as a country, earned that moniker. In restaurants, in parks, in airports, it was easy to spot the Americans on holiday – generally too loud, too assuming, too demanding. I have pondered on why that is. It is complex and must include aspects of us being the only remaining current superpower, of us having had so much success in war and industry, and of us having conquered our own nation through waves of war and expansion. But can this excuse us? I think not.

While not a new trend, our litigiousness increased in the 90's. We are more litigious than any country in the world. I have read that we have 5% of the world's population but 50% of the world's lawyers and 90% of the world's lawsuits. If those numbers are even close to true it is a problem.

With 5% of the world's population we consume 25% of the world's energy. We are, collectively, the spoiled rich kid. We need a punch in the proverbial mouth from time to time, to be reminded not to take our position for granted or to flaunt it.

I have a solution. Every 18 or 19 year old in the country should spend at least six months in a lesser-developed country serving in an orphanage or similar place. We would make the world a better place in the places where the kids serve. But the greater change would be in the hearts and minds of the American kids themselves. They would care a little less about whether they had the right designer jeans on and be thankful that they can afford jeans at all. They would not take running water, flushing toilets, hot water showers, and functional sewers, or the rule of law, for granted.

Rules to Live By

Europeans don't get why most Americans had a problem with Bill Clinton sleeping around. Americans don't get Speedos on European men. Americans don't get why so many Asians smoke four packs a day. Europeans don't understand why we Americans think the sun shines out of our ears. I once heard John Cleese say that one difference between the English and Americans was that, when the English host a world championship, they usually invite other countries. It's true. What are we thinking? Isn't it enough to be NBA champions or the champions of our national baseball league? Do we need to claim that we're the world champions? I cringe when I hear it, especially in this day and age when our clear supremacy in basketball and baseball is very much in question.

When we lived in London, my cheeky English colleagues would pepper me with jokes like, "What is the difference between America and a pot of yoghurt? The answer: "If you leave a pot of yoghurt out for 200 years, it develops a culture". My retort to that was that I was sure they were very proud of their global empire which now stretches all the way to Belfast. ☺

After having served a mission for the LDS Church in Germany for two years as a young adult, I had a good inkling of the cultural gaps that exist in the world. After all, having a very hairy-armpitted German woman answer a door wearing a tank top and holding her arm behind her head, thereby offering a clear view into the massive tuft of growth thriving there, was a clear reminder for this

American boy that I wasn't in Kansas anymore. So by the time our little family secured our first international posting back in Germany, I was ready with words of wisdom for my sweet wife. We applied them in Germany and again in Toronto, Hong Kong and London. The advice was simple and had two parts. First, pretend we're moving to another planet. We won't breathe the same air, speak the same language, or use the same currency. We will have nothing in common. Then, if we happen to find something in common with our own culture – like breathing oxygen or watching CNN or eating food – then that was a bonus. Secondly, with regard to the differences, focus only on the things that are *different and good* rather than the things that are *different and bad*. In Germany, focus on chocolate and castles and yoghurt. In Toronto, focus on the less cynical, less jaded mentality of the average Canadian (as compared to Americans).

The Politics of Entitlement

Politics is a tough subject. Let me weigh in on one topic only.

I come from conservative stock. I generally vote Republican. I like the idea of small government with as little intervention and control as possible.

I want to understand key political issues but I find it very difficult to find a balanced view of any political issues. Every source seems to be hard left or hard right or has some lobby-backed agenda. So I end up confused.

The one issue I have dedicated the most thought to is the historical progression of social benefits. Here is my super simplistic view.

When the U.S. was founded, families or individuals were on their own. They took care of themselves with the help of family and church and neighbors. The government funded a military and a central bank and a skeletal government infrastructure.

That continued until the 1930's when the first social programs were introduced. Then, in the 1960's, for the first time, a person who was not elderly or disabled could receive need-based aid from the federal government. By 2012 there were at least 80 federal need-based programs costing taxpayers over two trillion dollars. In eighty years we have gone from no social programs to 80 programs costing $2.1T. That is the largest item in our budget.

And yet the U.S. remains the only major industrial nation without a uniform national sickness program. With the current Democratic leadership and the trending from around the world, there is plenty of pressure to keep moving in the social direction.

I am torn. I believe with every fiber that simply giving people things creates dependence and entitlement and laziness. I also believe that, if a government finds itself unable to pay for its programs and wants to stop, recovering from or retracting such perceived entitlements on a large scale results in massive unrest and even violence. I also believe that, while people are generally good, they will also often take advantage of programs. I have found my own behavior disappointing when it comes to taking something for granted and then pushing back when it is rescinded, even when I know it should be stopped or taken back.

The better idea is to tie needs-based assistance to some form of payback. Get welfare because you need it and then pay it back once you're on your feet. I have not yet seen that work in a government setting.

On the other hand, I hate that we have uninsured, uncovered children. It is not their fault that their parents are deadbeats or incompetent or unstable or out of luck. It seems like a country with as much affluence as we have should be able to care of its children.

So, all of that to say this: I don't know. But I do think we should change any needs-based social benefit so that the recipient has an obligation to pay it back. But, as a pragmatist, I don't see us taking benefits back or even introducing a payback system. Politicians who preach restraint are not re-elected.

We are creating an ever-larger group of people who believe that government should provide for them. The burden of those programs will be unsustainable at some point. Then all hell breaks loose. The 'entitled' section of society will be looking to government to feed and sustain them. When they don't get fed, they will get angry. And instead of channeling that anger into self-reliance I fear they will extract what they need from others.

Perhaps I am too cynical. I hope I am wrong but fear that I am right.

Just Memories

At the end of our two-and-a-half years in Toronto, I had fallen in love with the town, the country, my LDS ward, and my colleagues at NCR. Even pondering leaving hurt. I remember one particular warm June evening. I had taken a customer to an NHL playoff game at the old Maple Leaf Garden (the Maple Leafs won 6-0 against the Blues and the place was electric). As we left the building and walked further downtown, we encountered hundreds of people exiting two great Broadway shows (Joseph and the Amazing Technicolor Dreamcoat, and Les Miserables). After we got through that, we ran into the reveling Blue Jays crowd. The Jays had just won an extra innings game, were selling out every home game and setting Major League Baseball attendance records, and working their way through a season where they would win their second consecutive World Series. I remember thinking 'I love this town'.

During our London years, the Concord airplane was still flying. By this time the Concords, flown only by BA and Air France, were getting old and were only flying in and out of Heathrow in London, de Gaulle in Paris and Kennedy in New York. There was mounting pressure in each place to stop them flying in and out as the noise was tremendous. A Concord left Heathrow twice and I always stepped outside to see the awesome sight of the bent-nosed Super Sonic Jet as it left town. It announced itself with a sound that felt like at least five times the noise of a normal jet. A friend of mine flew it once from NYC to London. He timed it all. He said it took 3 hours 11 minutes to fly to London and an hour and 57 minutes to drive across London to his home. The Concord has ceased flying. Who knows when we'll see a commercial craft that fast again?

Early in my career at Cisco, I attended a Finance group meeting in Barcelona, Spain. It was memorable for two reasons. The hotel that we stayed in was new and beautiful. It was owned by Saudi royalty. The royals must have been visiting because there were plenty of security men in black suits with sunglasses and the little curly radio wires that ran from the back of their collar up to their ears. Any slight disturbance in the hotel was immediately squashed. An overly loud child in the lobby would be ushered outside with a parent, for example. It got a little annoying over the three days we were there. On our last evening there, we were returning from a group dinner. There had been an award ceremony of sorts and I had been given a prize of snorkeling gear – a mask and flippers. As we exited the bus at the hotel and prepared to enter the hotel, I got an idea. I quickly put my snorkeling gear on and entered the hotel. I tried to make the flippers on my feet as loud as possible as I landed each foot on the marble floor. I got the desired response. Only a few steps in I was confronted by two very large security thugs who made it clear that I would be removing my ocean clothing immediately. I don't often have a rebellious streak in me but my colleagues and I had fun with that one.

The other experience was much better – at least for me. As a team building event our group divided into teams and played various competitive games in the hotel's swimming pool. One game involved each 10-person team removing a ball from the pool. The ball sat in a fixed position about 6 feet from the edge. The rules prohibited anyone on the team from touching the water. Hmmm. We were given some ropes and other gear. We quickly figured out the pathway to success – we had to harness one person, connect ropes to that person's harness, and then slowly let them lean out over the pool to grab the ball. A man from our team volunteered to be harnessed. We had a team leader. The rest of us connected and manned the ropes – four of us on each side at different angles. It was hard work. Holding the heavy body back as it leaned out over the pool required much effort from each of us. After a short while we were sweating and looking down, fully focused on our task and the chants of the team leader ("OK, let him down another inch or two", etc.).

In retrospect, we had made a serious error without knowing it. The harness had a front and a back. It was not obvious and we strapped our buddy in with it on backwards. The only real difference in the front and back of the harness was that the top seatbelt-like strap on the front stopped around mid-chest while the top fastener on the back was clear up around the shoulders. So, with it on backwards, the top strap was now much higher up on our colleague's chest. In a relaxed state, that was no big deal at all. In a taut, stretched-out position with ropes pulling from all angles, the harness tended to ride up a little on the torso of the person in the harness. The more pressure, the more it rode up. So, as we were nearing the point where our friend could reach the ball, all of the rope-pullers were nearly spent with effort. At the same time the harness had pulled up far enough to begin to impact the throat area of our friend. We were all grunting and cheering as we neared what we

118

thought would be a glorious victory. Meanwhile the harness had moved up further and our harnessed colleague was not able to breathe. Our team leader finally noticed that he was red-moving-to-purple in the face and shouted for us all to drop our ropes now. We weren't sure whether he had retrieved the ball or there was a problem but we all sensed the urgency of our team leader's cries and dropped the ropes. I looked up just in time to see our pal drop unconsciously into the pool, followed by our team leader, then the rest of us jumping in to save and resuscitate him. They carted him off to a hospital for overnight observation. He had multiple bruises on this throat. He recovered quickly and was fine in a couple of weeks.

OK, I have to admit that it is this moment when our friend realized that something was wrong that makes me laugh every time. I picture him realizing what was happening, trying to warn us but being unable to. As his face goes red, we all stay focused on the prize as he then loses consciousness and plops into the pool. Had the outcome been worse for him, I do not believe I would still find it funny. But, when someone, including me, has an odd, painful experience that is, in the end, not permanently debilitating, I find it deliciously funny. Maybe that's just me.

Marriage and Family Lessons

The handsome couple. December 29, 1981

Introduction

OK. This will hopefully be as close as I come in this book to bragging. I am so pleased and proud that so many people, through the years, have commented on how good they feel in our home. The amount of unprovoked complimentary comments leads me to believe it is uncommon. They usually mention peace, a feeling of love, and/or a sweet spirit.

I am so glad that is true. Since we're not much for faking it or putting on airs, I suppose there is something to it. I give credit primarily to Amy for creating that peaceful, loving environment. All of the kids and I have contributed as well.

I do not claim to be an expert on marriage or family life. The assets that I possess which a make me capable of doing well in this area are: 1) I had great examples in my mom and dad, 2) I married a great gal, 3) I believe I have an uncommon natural ability to love, 4) I am driven to succeed in this area, and 5) I have a pretty good sense of humor.

There are two quotes from deceased LDS leaders about family life that I love and that capture my feelings perfectly.

David O. McKay said, "No other success can compensate for failure in the home."

Joseph F. Smith said, "God bless me not to lose my own. I cannot afford to lose mine, whom God has given to me and whom I am responsible for before the Lord, and who are dependent upon me for guidance, for instruction, for proper influence. The

Lord help me to save my own, so far as one can help another. I realize I cannot save anybody, but I can teach them how to be saved. I can set an example before my children how they can be saved, and it is my duty to do that first. I owe it more to them than to anybody else in the world."

If, as I believe, families can be together forever, then we might as well get started on a positive note down here in this life.

Quality Time Is A Myth

Early in my career I had a manager at work that preached the idea of quality time at home. He said that, even though we couldn't be at home much, if we focused on maximizing the little time we had, we could have a happy home. At first it made sense. As time went on I felt he was using it as excuse to be at work nearly all the time and to lay off all parenting and marital responsibilities to his wife. Perhaps coincidentally, perhaps not, he was separated then divorced within three years.

Nothing replaces quantity time. Only time spent with a spouse or children tells them loud and clear that they matter to you and that they are loved. Once people feel cared for and loved they will trust deeply enough to open and share their heart. With a shared heart relationships can flourish.

I know there are jobs and circumstances where time is simply not sufficient. In such cases we all have to do the best we can. But it is folly to purposely minimize time at home with the argument that whatever time spent is 'quality time'.

Good Advice For Marriage

The Mormon prophet, Gordon B. Hinckley, who is a favorite of mine, was once asked the secret to a happy marriage. He gave a textbook response about shared work, prayer, trust and other good things. The interviewer then asked Marjorie Hinckley, his wife, the same question. She responded, "Lower your expectations." She was a hoot.

Another Mormon leader once said that we should enter marriage with our eyes wide open, then close them slightly. The same man said, "Some of the most clever things you ever think of should remain unsaid." That is especially true when it comes to your spouse.

Amy has always been able to look past my shortcomings and encourage me. She picked me, as I picked her, and she truly lives by the traditional vows of 'for better or worse'.

Set Your Own House Rules

As the years have flown by, Amy and I have settled on a few unwritten rules that have made our lives happier. Some are obvious and some strange but they work for us. Here are a few:

Don't go to bed angry. Talk it out. Or, if the issue is too hot to handle right then, agree - together - that it needs to be talked over tomorrow.

Don't go to bed with a dirty kitchen. I can't even explain that one but it has something to do with feeling like there is order in the world.

Make no major financial decisions alone. That one is a no-brainer.

Have no TV in the bedroom. I am sure we are dinosaurs on this one but it has served us well. Also, have no TV's in the kids' bedrooms.

Ensure that all PC's and TV's are in open, heavy-traffic locations. There are enough bad media influences that parents need to be able to keep an eye on the screens.

Care For Your Own Children

I have a loved one who once penned a poem that made it clear that he believed that his mother did not love him. I ached for this good person who struggled mightily with his place in the world and his self-image.

At the other end of the spectrum, I have always loved to be home when our kids get home from school. Almost every time they enter the house they greet Mom or call for Mom. It is their security blanket. When they are hurt, they want mom.

Your children, during their childhood, will never love or need anyone more than they need their mother. Amy is a talented lady who could do plenty of good outside the home (she does that now but I am referring to getting a W-2 for her efforts). But we have always tried – and been successful to this point, thank goodness – to allow Amy to be at home to be there for the kids.

As disclaimers, I know that it is not possible for many mothers to be home, from a financial perspective. In those cases the kids will likely understand the sacrifice. I am also not throwing this all at the feet of mothers. Fathers play a huge role. And fathers can even be successful Mr. Mom's. But I cling to the traditional notion that there is no one like mother to be the primary homebody.

No one will ever love your children as much as you do.

A Wider Lens

After Ben finished his Marine training and before he headed out on his mission, I brought him along with me to Monterey, California, where I was attending a strategic leadership offsite (we called it SLO – bad name). We agreed he could hang out, go to museums, take a whale-watching boat trip, etc. He only attended one meeting with me (I snuck him into an hour long presentation by Coach K, Duke's basketball coach) but he did have opportunities to meet several of my colleagues. It was good for him to put faces to names after I had talked about these good people through the years of my employment with Cisco Systems.

Something very unexpected happened. Several of my friends who we met took the time to spend a few minutes with Ben, probe about his life, and look him in the eye. Then, without being paid (I swear) they told Ben how much they loved and respected his dad. In more than one case they told him I was one of their few favorite people in the world. Ben took all of this in with a smile.

But a day later I could see something changing. He was looking at me through a different lens. He respected me more. More than once over the next month he referred to those interactions and how much my colleagues appreciated me. He cocked his head when he said it, as though it were hard to believe.

Now, Ben and I already had a great relationship. We loved and trusted each other. It's not like this was rehabilitating our fractured relationship. Not at all.

But it apparently added a dimension, one that he had never seen.

I was surprised but grateful for all this. It's nice to see your kids respect you more. I have pondered over the years if it could be – or should be – replicated. It would be disingenuous to 'set it up'. I guess it happens if it happens.

But I have come to the conclusion that we need to put our kids in positions to receive feedback on us from other, trusted sources. They need to have their lens widened. They need verification that the 'old man' is not crazy. Too often we can be one-dimensional for them. They can view us as out of touch, harping on the same things.

Having my kids work for friends and neighbors has been one way to allow for that to happen.

Humor

During a youth basketball game, a church basketball game, Ben let loose with a four-letter word. I was working the clock at center court at the time. There were about 100 parents and friends watching the game. I looked across the court to see Amy's dumbstruck face. I was dumbstruck as well. I think they gave Ben a technical foul. They might have tossed him, I can't remember. In any case it obviously fell to me to have a chat with Ben that evening. Instead of the wrath of Dad being poured out on him, I said something like, "I have never heard you swear - ever. So the first time I ever hear you cuss is in front of 100 people at church. Couldn't you have tried it out on a smaller audience?" We both laughed. Then we easily discussed the issue.

I have found humor to the most effective means of diffusing family tension. It does not solve problems but allows for a chance to pause, laugh at some aspect of it, and then to tackle the problem together.

I have seen people who use humor to permanently skirt an issue. That is not healthy and is not what I mean.

With all the death and disease in our family, our humor can be very black. For example, we intend to take a picture at the cemetery of Amy and I and the twins lying in our burial spots right next to the graves of Ethan and Ben. For some that might be dark. For us it's hilarious.

Laughter, and plenty of it, has been a hallmark of our family.

Parenting

OK. Soapbox time. Show me a four-year-old boy with a Mohawk, a pierced ear or an extra-long mullet and I can predict a difficult life for that child. I have been around long enough to test my theories. My private predictions have a high accuracy rate.

What are parents thinking? If you set your child up at that tender age to be a renegade they will play along. If you are thinking 'how does he know he's a renegade' just watch the child for a while. Other 'renegades' will seek him out, other adults will comment on how different he looks, etc. Soon the child assumes the role of renegade.

Parenting is a tough art. It is so sweet to watch people raise good kids and so painful to watch others spawn kids that will eventually be unhappy, disruptive or worse.

Show me a parent who always take his child's side in an argument and I will show you a future deviant.

Show me a parent who refuses to let a child do hard things and I will show you a child still living in the family basement at age 30, unaccomplished and unmotivated.

Show me a parent who lets their child interrupt them over and over again in social settings and I will show a brat now and forever.

Show me a parent who gives their child a smart phone too early or who gives them private access to the Internet and I will show a child who almost certainly will develop issues with pornography and addiction.

Show me a parent who allows their child to date and pair off too early and I will show you a child who will struggle with sexual issues.

Ok. I'll get off the box now.

The Family Proclamation

The leadership of the LDS Church released a proclamation about the family in 1995. I believe every word. I also believe every word was carefully considered and prayed about. Here it is:

WE, THE FIRST PRESIDENCY and the Council of the Twelve Apostles of The Church of Jesus Christ of Latter-day Saints, solemnly proclaim that marriage between a man and a woman is ordained of God and that the family is central to the Creator's plan for the eternal destiny of His children.

ALL HUMAN BEINGS—male and female—are created in the image of God. Each is a beloved spirit son or daughter of heavenly parents, and, as such, each has a divine nature and destiny. Gender is an essential characteristic of individual premortal, mortal, and eternal identity and purpose.

IN THE PREMORTAL REALM, spirit sons and daughters knew and worshipped God as their Eternal Father and accepted His plan by which His children could obtain a physical body and gain earthly experience to progress toward perfection and ultimately realize their divine destiny as heirs of eternal life. The divine plan of happiness enables family relationships to be perpetuated beyond the grave. Sacred ordinances and covenants available in holy temples make it possible for individuals to return to the presence of God and for families to be united eternally.

THE FIRST COMMANDMENT that God gave to

Adam and Eve pertained to their potential for parenthood as husband and wife. We declare that God's commandment for His children to multiply and replenish the earth remains in force. We further declare that God has commanded that the sacred powers of procreation are to be employed only between man and woman, lawfully wedded as husband and wife.

WE DECLARE the means by which mortal life is created to be divinely appointed. We affirm the sanctity of life and of its importance in God's eternal plan.

HUSBAND AND WIFE have a solemn responsibility to love and care for each other and for their children. "Children are an heritage of the Lord" (Psalm 127:3). Parents have a sacred duty to rear their children in love and righteousness, to provide for their physical and spiritual needs, and to teach them to love and serve one another, observe the commandments of God, and be law-abiding citizens wherever they live. Husbands and wives—mothers and fathers—will be held accountable before God for the discharge of these obligations.

THE FAMILY is ordained of God. Marriage between man and woman is essential to His eternal plan. Children are entitled to birth within the bonds of matrimony, and to be reared by a father and a mother who honor marital vows with complete fidelity. Happiness in family life is most likely to be achieved when founded upon the teachings of the Lord Jesus Christ. Successful marriages and families are established and maintained on principles of faith, prayer, repentance, forgiveness, respect, love, compassion, work, and wholesome recreational activities. By divine design, fathers are to preside over their families in love and righteousness and are responsible to provide the necessities of life and protection for their families. Mothers are primarily responsible for the nurture of their children. In these sacred responsibilities, fathers and mothers are obligated to help one another as equal partners. Disability, death, or other circumstances may necessitate individual adaptation. Extended families should lend support when needed.

WE WARN that individuals who violate covenants of chastity, who abuse spouse or offspring, or who fail to fulfill family responsibilities will one day stand accountable before God. Further, we warn that the disintegration of the family will bring upon individuals, communities, and nations the calamities foretold by ancient and modern prophets.

WE CALL UPON responsible citizens and officers of government everywhere to promote those measures designed to maintain and strengthen the family as the fundamental unit of society.

The Von Ellsworth Family Singers

There was a period – in the Hong Kong and England years – when our little family was sought after from time to time to sing. The best few years were when Ethan was between 10 and 14, when he was young enough to threaten and young enough to think that singing with his family was still cool. When he was 12, say, Ben was 9, Atley 7, and Emily 5. At those ages they could all hold their own. Ethan was the only one who struggled with the music. He usually found a note he liked and stayed with it – Mr. Monotone. The other three had nice, clear voices and did a pretty good job of projecting. Atley was always the first to have a song memorized and understand the dynamics of the song. Our largest audience was probably an LDS stake event in Hong Kong where a few hundred people were assembled.

Once, in England, we were asked to sing at an LDS ward event in a neighboring ward. We practiced a cute Christmas song - The Friendly Beasts. The lyrics are below. We all sang the first and last verses together and each of us was to sing an animal's verse solo. Each child memorized a verse. I'm sure each child heard the other verses so often that they could sing most of them. Atley memorized all of them. Ethan was to be the first - the donkey. For some reason he got stage fright or whatever and sang a mixture of his and Ben's camel verse – but mostly Ben's verse. Ben was always very bright and caught on what was happening and that he had just had his verse stolen. And he didn't know the donkey verse well enough to get through that. So, when came his turn, he mumbled his way through the song so that we ended up with two confusing donkeys and nary a camel.

Ethan was mildly amused. Ben was very unhappy that Ethan had facilitated his looking like an idiot (at least is his opinion). Over time we all had a good laugh. After that I remembered to prepare for the worst on stage.

"The Friendly Beasts"

Jesus our brother, kind and good
Was humbly born in a stable rude
And the friendly beasts around Him stood
Jesus our brother, kind and good.

"I," said the donkey, shaggy and brown,
"I carried His mother up hill and down;
I carried her safely to Bethlehem town."
"I," said the donkey, shaggy and brown.

"I," said the cow, all white and red
"I gave Him my manger for a bed;
I gave Him my hay to pillow His head."
"I," said the cow, all white and red.

"I," said the sheep with curly horn,
"I gave Him my wool for His blanket warm;
He wore my coat on Christmas morn."
"I," said the sheep with curly horn.

"I," said the dove from the rafters high,
"Cooed Him to sleep that He should not cry;
We cooed Him to sleep, my mate and I."
"I," said the dove from the rafters high.

"I," said the camel, yellow and black,
"Over the desert, upon my back,
I brought Him a gift in the Wise Men's pack."
"I," said the camel, yellow and black.

Thus every beast by some good spell
In the stable dark was glad to tell
Of the gift he gave Emmanuel,
The gift he gave Emmanuel.

Your Zipper's Down

Although Amy has a beautiful voice and a great ear for music, she is very unassuming and tends to shy away from a microphone or a spotlight. She is a stereotypical alto in the choir - very pleased to blend but uncomfortable having others hear her solo voice. I am quite opposite. My singing voice is average. But I am not just referring to actual singing and stages but rather any endeavor in life. I will give it a try.

Being ready to be on the stage of life has its pros and cons. Amy and I reached an agreement early in our marriage that allows for protection from major embarrassments. We agreed that we would always tell the other - abruptly or rudely, if necessary - if one of us was on the proverbial stage of life with their proverbial zipper down. While we generally encourage each other we know we have a trump card to say 'Stop now before you regret it big time'.

As I developed "1856" The Musical I remember having these amazing experiences with the creation of the songs. And although I was pretty convinced the songs were beautiful, I was never fully ready to put them out there until I passed the 'zipper' test with Amy. She loved them. That's all I needed to know. Amy has my back.

Business lessons

My Japanese colleagues and me in Tokyo, 1989.

Introduction

Two months after joining a major American corporation as a financial analyst I was asked to spend six months as the support person for a high-level task force re-evaluating the company stance on a very important subject. This was my first job after a youth full of dairy and farm life, a two-year mission, and a university education. Being so junior, I was excited by the prospect of working with many of the top officers of the company. I expected to be blown away by the power and insight of these highly paid visionaries. After all, only months earlier I had completed my last International MBA class on case studies of how successful business executives nimbly and proactively solved major business problems. And, after all, these people had been entrusted with the management of a multi-billion dollar business.

Only weeks into the project my opinion of these executives had not only dropped, it had plummeted to near zero levels. My bubble was burst. The fabled American boardroom lost its luster for me. Such a large gap between my expectations and what I found cannot be explained in simple terms. But let me try.

Many of these executives were so caught up in themselves and their own pride and supposed abilities that they were not interested in others' views, even if those views were based on more current and relevant experience.

The structure of big business and the multiple layers of management had beaten any risk-taking behavior out of them. The resulting hesitance to progress the business was appalling to this wide-eyed novice.

Every comment from the bigwigs carried multiple meanings. Every executive had multiple agendas. Everyone had their camp.

This experience and other similar experiences through the years have led me to a few conclusions:
- In any large global enterprise, anyone armed with an MBA or similar degree can contribute very little, move from department to department, schmooze with a few key mentors, and, within 15 years, have a director title and make $100,000 a year or more with great benefits and retirement funds.
- It's no wonder that most big companies move so slowly as they are filled with risk-avoiding, path of least resistance, politic-your-way-to-the-top leaders.
- Many senior executives get to the top by neglecting the other aspects of their lives – family, church, and hobbies. The result is a one-dimensional person who is usually plagued by stomach-eating family problems.
- Few of the senior executives seemed capable of running their own small business.
- There are exceptions – truly amazing people who taught me much and whose influence continues with me.

The Second Rule of Entrepreneurship

Years of observation and experience have led me to establish a few rules for anyone wanting to start their own business. Rule #1 is pretty obvious – you should have a product or service that people love. But Rule #2 is also very important.

Rule #2 – The Dearness Rule - Extract money from people to whom the money is not dear. In other words, your revenue should come from people who have a ton of money or who are spending someone else's money.

Here's an example that I use to highlight the Dearness Rule. In fact it helped crystallize the importance of the Rule more than any other experience. One of our precious Mormon historical sites is Nauvoo, Illinois, on the banks of the Mississippi River. It was an important early headquarters for Joseph Smith and the church. The church built a beautiful temple there. It was later destroyed. Joseph became a martyr while living there. The church moved on from Nauvoo in 1846 and moved HQ to the Salt Lake City area in 1847. Now, after about 150 years of having little to do with Nauvoo, the church has returned in full measure. The temple has been rebuilt (Google it - stunning). The church has purchased and restored dozens of buildings. There is a buzz around Nauvoo, especially in the summer. It is a hidden American treasure, partly because it's not close to anything.

Our little family visited Nauvoo in the early 90's, before the temple was rebuilt. There were still enough people visiting, however, that it was crowded on the summer days when we were there. I noticed that there seemed not to be enough motel rooms. Neighboring towns were at least 20 miles away. There were a few B&B offerings and one nice family motel. But surely one or maybe even two additional family motels could flourish in Nauvoo for several months of the year. I pondered the ideas for days. The law of supply and demand would be in favor of the idea. Land would be cheap. I was confident that the numbers of Mormons flocking to Nauvoo would only increase year after year.

Then it hit me. Before you know what hit me, you also need one more piece of information. People of Jewish descent and Scots are stereotypically cheap. They have nothing on us Mormons. We come by it honestly. With large families money is always tight so we look for bargains. So what hit me was a daydream - a nightmare - really. I pictured myself as the owner and manager of a Nauvoo motel. I realized that good and well-intended LDS families would fill my motel, would haggle about rates, would stuff more people into each room than makes sense, would trash the pool, and use all the towels. At the end of the nightmare I was losing patience and losing money. I abandoned any ideas of investing in a motel in Nauvoo.

I have a brother who wanted to change career direction and open a nursery, selling flowers, plants and bushes. I weighed in that if he was going to sell primarily to individuals, forget it. While that part might bring the most happiness, he had better get a business clientele to form the largest piece of his sales. Cater to local motels and offices. They are often not spending their own money. You get the idea.

A random LDS note: I have created or helped create music and drama. Two of the projects are musicals and one is very much intended for the LDS market ("1856" The Musical). I never created "1856" to make money but it is nice to recover some costs. That is hard in the LDS community. Not only are we Mormons cheap but that extends, for some reason, especially to the arts. I have realized over time that, even though the LDS community has examples of extraordinary talent, it is never fairly compensated if that work is primarily directed at the LDS audience. I am unable to name any artist (music, drama, painting) who has been able to be a successful primary breadwinner for an extended period if their work is created for LDS consumption. LDS artists only thrive when their work crosses over LDS lines into a more mainstream audience. As a result, all LDS-centric art is created and put into a market that will not compensate the artist for its creation or allow for re-investment in the next round of art. Something feels wrong with that model.

Downsizing

My role was deemed redundant and I was laid-off by Cisco Systems after 14 mostly great years. Cisco decided that it had too many people. The separation package was good. Getting meaningful things done at Cisco had become hard so I was not heartbroken. But no one likes to be told for any reason that they are not wanted. And I dearly miss so many of the people who I have come to respect and, in many cases, love. So there is some lingering emotion there. But, thankfully, it is manageable due to an important lesson I learned many years ago.

I also spent 13 years at another large company, NCR. For the last several years there, we downsized the company each year due to challenging business conditions and questionable management. I went through the agonizing process of letting good and great people go mostly because we did not have enough work to do. Each year the reduction in force (RIF) was executed slightly differently and I was able to see differing approaches. If a caring, well-managed company determined by itself where fewer resources were needed, that was the best recipe. The recipe and the results got worse as the company was 1) less well-managed, 2) in a hurry and 3) invited external consultants to help drive the RIF. So, unfortunately these days, when a company is doing a RIF, they are usually in the position because of poor management, they are normally in a huge hurry and they almost always use consultants. So I came to the conclusion that there is little correlation between letting people go and letting the right people go. It bore out at Cisco as I watched many valuable folks shown the door while many less valuable people (in my opinion) stayed in place.

It is sad but true.

[Note: My admin assistant for most of the Cisco years is a saint. I love Joyce Howard. She has gone through all of my life's trials and triumphs over the last decade plus. She managed my schedule and many of my movements. Amy and I once came across an intersection of two roads named Amy's Way and Joyce's Way. We took a picture at the crossroad because that's how I lived my life – a combination of Amy's way and Joyce's way.]

Alcohol

During my stay in Canada, our division leader was moved to another country and we inherited a man who had recently been working for our company in South Korea. I liked him a lot when he was sober. He was very intelligent and had gathered much experience. We ended up travelling together to every major Canadian city. We laughed plenty.

But we learned he was often drunk or otherwise impaired. We learned later that he was transferred out of Korea because he had "drunk all the booze and slept with all the women" in that country. The transfer to Canada was a last ditch intervention. Our president in Canada was an excellent man. I suppose he volunteered to give this man one last try.

His antics soon became legendary. Our division was the break-fix group, full of kind, old technical men who were managing large groups of young technical men. While I was there a man celebrated 52 years with the company. He had started as a 13-year-old apprentice in Scotland and moved to Canada later. A lady, who worked for me, was a daughter-figure to the older management team, ensuring that they completed all the right reports and played by the rules. The guys loved this woman, call her Jane, and were protective of her.

Once, at a management team offsite meeting, after a few drinks, much of the team sat around a fire pit telling stories. The division leader, let's call him Jim, was quite drunk and ruled the floor. His jokes became increasingly lewd and vulgar. It would have been unpleasant for this group of men even if Jane had not been there. But Jane's presence made them even more uncomfortable and embarrassed. When one would quietly urge Jane to go away or would begin to leave themselves, Jim would require that they stay. Finally one was brave enough to ask Jim to tone it down. Jim jeered at him. Then another said something, specifically asking Jim to speak more gently in front of Jane.

Jim then dropped a horrible line, which will forever stand as a monument against alcoholism. In front of all of us, including Jane, he yelled, "Oh it's alright. Jane is so freaking ugly that she knows that I just think of her as one of the boys!"

Jim was finally fired a few months later after he propositioned two senior HR women from our company in a hotel elevator.

It Takes All Kinds

In 27 years of working for large corporations I ran into all kinds of people. They make me shake my head and laugh. I have changed some of their names.

Larry extended his trip to Asia by 10 days and did not let his wife know. Even better, it was only after a full week that his wife bothered asking where he was.

Ian freaked out. He left the Hong Kong office, flew to the Philippines, rented a car, drove it to his ex-mother-in-law's for a visit and then gifted her the rental car. The woman didn't understand why, a few days later, Hertz came and took her new car.

Erbay was famous in the company for working very hard, including early and late. One night around midnight, after a dinner with customers, another executive and I headed back to the office in London to get our own vehicles. We decided to pop by Erbay's office and leave a note that, for once, we were there working and he was not. As we walked across the dark floor we noticed that his light was on. As we entered his office, we saw not only Erbay, but also his entire family. Erbay had his wife and two kids doing various work tasks at midnight on a Friday night. He said they had been out to dinner and that they all agreed that helping him finish off a project or two was a good way to end the evening.

Ed was an older, crusty Canadian, always ready to provide comic relief. Once we stood at urinals next to each other, taking care of business. I started to talk negatively about a lady employee who was notoriously hard to work with and quite manly in some ways. As I started to talk he shushed me, pointed to the men's toilet stalls and commented, "Shhh. She might be in one of the stalls." A couple of his funniest stories are not printable.

Jose loved to talk about software. Any time we discussed small software start up companies, he referred to them as run by 'Daddy Gupta, Mama Gupta, some baby Guptas, and a dog.' I found Jose when I was down as his constant funny banter always lightened my spirits. I was always partial to the colleagues who made me laugh.

Our company president at NCR was a smug, condescending sort. Once, in a meeting, the presenter, who was a large man, suggested we break for lunch. Without even looking up, the president said, "No. Keep going. You can afford to miss a meal or two". When a few senior people looked at him oddly, he added, "What? It's obvious."

Buckingham Palace

During our three years in the London area, I worked for NCR Corporation. For the first year and a half I was the CFO for the UK and Northern Ireland with an office in downtown London. I was the right-hand man for the CEO, Malcolm, and was considered the #2 person in our 1,500-person organization. Large companies are usually political in any case but perhaps more so in the U.K., which is still quite class and level conscious. More junior employees deferred to me more often than I was comfortable with. I sometimes thought, "If you could see me at home you would not be practically bowing to me now". Luckily my direct reports in finance were strong, self-assured folks who had no trouble treating me like a friend and a peer.

One of NCR's lines of business was fixing retail, financial or computing equipment. The maintenance was large and lucrative. Most of the contracts were with large retail and financial institutions but we did business with any company that needed our services. One of our smaller – but more important – accounts was with the Royal Household, fixing computing equipment at many of the Royal properties like Buckingham Palace, Windsor Castle, and others. I met with the computing manager for the account twice at Buckingham Palace. One of those experiences typified the feeling that we often show more deference and respect for people in authority than they often deserve or want.

Our NCR driver, Brian, drove me to the front gates of the Palace. He drove a navy blue Jaguar with a license plate that read 'NCR 1". Now, there are always a few hundred tourists milling around the front gates of Buckingham Palace, hoping to catch a glimpse of the Queen or other important people. Usually, when Brian drove me somewhere in London, I let myself out of one of the back doors. This time, as we pulled up to the gates, he insisted that he open the door for me, casting the illusion that someone very important was coming to call at the Palace. I stepped out in a nice suit with a dossier under my arm, stepped up to the security gate and stated my business and that I had an appointment with the IT manager. After my credentials were checked, they ushered me past the red-clad guards and their guns and poofy headgear and into the large, frontcourt. I was now on a long red carpet that led to the doors of the Palace. It was somewhere on that carpet that I realized that I was the talk of the hundreds of people who were pressing against the yards and yards of extended gates and fencing. I sneaked a peek and could see gesturing and hear people wondering out loud about who I was. As I entered the front door to the Palace, I snuck a last look to see all eyes on me.

I was then ushered into the basement and met with the small team of people who discussed things like whether the annual maintenance rate for printers should go up or not, whether there had been 31 or 32 billable repair calls last month, and so on. As I exited the Palace an hour later, again with all eyes on me, I thought how underwhelmed the tourists would be if they knew what I had been doing. As I walked down the red carpet and into the waiting Jaguar (with Brian standing by the opened door with a very official look on his face), it was all I could do not to wave like a beauty queen just to extend the illusion a few more seconds.

I remember that story when I am tempted to hold someone in higher regard than they might deserve. Whoever it is, they probably just cleaned up the dog throw-up at home or took the garbage out. In any case, they put their pants on one leg at a time.

Consultants

I have heard a saying more than once, "If you can't do, teach". Based on my experiences in the business world, I extend it to "If you can't do, teach. If you can't teach, consult." It is a joke but, as with all good jokes, there is a bit of truth in it.

Business consultants charge an hourly or daily fee for their services. The fee is usually exorbitant. The value proposition is that they have consulted with many companies who are experiencing the same set of challenges that you are facing and can, therefore, advise on the best steps to maintain or create competitive advantage. They package their findings and recommendations in stunningly impressive slides.

Senior consultants can be worth the money. But, too often, the efforts of consultants are one-size-fits-all, simplistically formulaic projects done by wicked-smart but extremely inexperienced junior consultants (who were recently hired from MBA programs like Stanford or Harvard or Wharton). Asking a young person to make sense of a complex business issue in 3-4 weeks and then to recommend is laughable. But it happens all too often in Corporate America.

At NCR I saw the consultants come in when the company was struggling. The first analysis I saw recommended that a certain department fire 30% of their people. The second analysis, for a different department with very different issues, returned the same recommendation – fire 30%. As the weeks went by, a few colleagues and I watched with amusement as each project yielded the same result. It was clear that an edict had been given from the top that NCR needed to fire 30% of their people and no logic, by gosh, was going to get in the way of the goal. At the time, I worked in a department that was deemed by all of my colleagues as the best place to be - profitable, efficient, safe. As I saw the 'fire 30%' analyses continue, I wondered if our department of 70 people, which I had hoped and assumed would be left alone, would be hit by the same 30%. Our nervous group was called together one fine day. We received the news that our entire department was being eliminated and that we had 60 days to find jobs or we would all be fired.

Of course. Why didn't I think of that?

Pacific Rim

After three years at NCR, I was made a manager over one employee. From Dayton, Ohio, we helped manage the inventories and accounts receivable for ten countries – Canada and the Pacific Rim. No one was sure how Canada got put into the Pacific Group.

I was given the approval to travel to Asia – my first international business trip. NCR had a tough travel mentality. Everyone at my level flew coach, even on the 14-hour flights, and we were expected to stay in Asia for at least two weeks to ensure that our travel dollars had been well spent. We were also expected to hit the ground running when we landed in a new country.

So I planned a 26-day trip to Japan, Korea, Taiwan, Hong Kong, the Philippines, Singapore, Malaysia, Australia, and New Zealand. I had never seen any of those countries. I had never met any of the managers who 'kind of' reported to me. The experience was invaluable. Telephone calls can never replace face-to-face interaction. Seeing these magnificent countries left a permanent, positive mark on me.

In Japan, the first stop, my heart nearly stopped. I had brought two bottles of Murphy's Oil Soap for a friend in Singapore. On the flight over the bottles had ruptured in my luggage, soaking all of my clothes not only in soap but also in the colors of the shopping bag that the bottles were in. I discovered it as I unpacked and spent almost the entire night washing and rinsing and blow-drying all of my clothes, including suits, in the bathtub of my Tokyo hotel. I walked to the office the next morning in the rain, sure that my suit would start bubbling up in bright colors as I walked.

The manager in Tokyo, Ukai-san, was a dear old man. We talked late into the evening on my second evening there about many things. In WWII his Dad was a fighter pilot. Ukai-san's dream was to reach age 15, get trained as a fighter pilot and become his dad's protector and wingman. His dream was wiped away when, as a 14-year-old, his leg was severely damaged when U.S. forces bombed the munitions factory he was working in. Then, only three weeks before WWII ended, his father died when his plane was shot down.

On the first morning, Ukai-san introduced me to the 50 people on his team. We did calisthenics together. In his broken English he introduced every person. He told me, in front of everyone, that morale was an issue. He said that, since business had not grown much over the last decade, he had not been allowed to hire anyone in over 10 years. He said it created a stagnant environment. At the end of each sentence the team would all bow slightly and smile and let me know - with a soft 'yes' or 'hai' or just a nod - that they agreed with everything their boss said. Finally Ukai-san said that, because of the situation, all of his best employees had left to find employment elsewhere and that he was left with all the crap (his word was a little stronger). Again they all smiled and nodded agreement.

In one way or another each country was new and interesting. After 26 long days I was able to fly home and be reunited with Amy and our three little ones.

26 days was too long to be gone. The kids had all grown and looked different. I felt like I had missed out. They took a few days to warm back up to me. Amy had assumed some of the household duties normally reserved for me and seemed hesitant to give them back. Our communication was poor for a few weeks.

The next trip, six months later, was 'only' 21 days. Dumb me.

Just Memories

My second role at NCR was in Corporate Consolidation Accounting. It was called the group where no one wanted to be but everyone wanted to be from. The inference is that the hours were horrible but you learned a lot. There was a 40-day period, due to a quarter close accounting period being followed by a year-end close, where I was never outside in the daylight hours. I probably averaged 14 hours a day, 7 days a week. The department had a rule that no resignation letters would be accepted in the two-week period surrounding quarter closes. We could not be counted on for sane thought during that period. I recall being invited to a 'year-end is over so let's get together' department party. I was at the end of my rope at that point. I responded to my boss's boss that the last people on earth I wanted to spend more time with were my current colleagues. He understood.

My 27 years at NCR and Cisco have allowed me to see a few mega-shifts in corporate culture. When I started in the late 80's, Corporate America was very much male-dominated. There was plenty of bad and mean behavior. [Note: Things continue to shift through the decades. I recall a story about NCR's early days, in the 1880's, when the CEO would publicly set a fired employee's desk on fire to send a message.] That has shifted dramatically in most companies. The rights of individuals are respected much more now.

Life Lessons

As a teenager with life ahead of me. Left to right: Rowan, me, Dorne, Keller

Introduction

Perhaps more than your average Joe, I am a people watcher. Just taking life in - with eyes and ears wide open - has been a major source of input for my own life. There is a saying that goes something like, "The fool learns by experience. The sage learns from other people's experiences". So watching, learning, and applying is a good model.

But nothing can replace our own personal experiences in many of life's arenas. We have to get in the game, be active, experience this life and world.

Back during the go-go days of the Internet when new companies and new applications were springing up daily, it was common for investment and capital firms to invest in new ventures. It was important to hire a CEO who could help the company succeed. It was said, at the time, that British investment firms would not hire a CEO who had failed in a previous start-up venture and that American venture firms wouldn't hire a CEO who hadn't failed at least once. The right answer probably lies in the middle. In all of life's ventures we need to be smart enough to make mistakes and learn from them but also smart enough to avoid every mistake possible.

This chapter captures a few of my life's lessons learned from both watching and doing.

Grand Canyon

In 2010 Camden and Atley, Brigham and Emily, and I trained for a Grand Canyon Rim to Rim trip for a few months. We put in many miles on the streets and hills in the Phoenix area. The plan was to hike on May 20/21. We would all walk the 21 miles from the south rim to the north rim, where my nieces, Carli and Daryl Hundley, would pick up Atley and Emily and shuttle them back to the south rim and wait for us boys, who would turn around and walk the 24 miles back to the south rim (24 miles instead of 21 because it's common to take a different trail up to the south rim). That would be Rim-2-Rim-2-Rim, the Big Kahuna, 45 miles, over 10,000 feet of descent and the same ascent. And Rim-2-Rim is a huge accomplishment, too, as most people never walk that far in a day, let alone the steep climb that is involved.

We slept at a motel at the south rim, started walking at 6 a.m. and had a wonderful day hiking in the Grand Canyon. Down the South Kaibab 7 miles to Phantom Ranch, then 7 more on the flats to Cottonwood Campground, and then the beastly 7 miles up the north rim. Walking that far is not easy and takes a toll on the body. We fell a little behind schedule. Up the hill we spread out a little and the last of us arrived at the north rim to Daryl and Carli just before 7 p.m. We did it! We celebrated and talked and ate yummies that the girls had brought us. We boys decided not to hike back due to the hour and some nagging injuries. So all seven of us piled in the pickup and drive the 3 hours back to the hotel at the south rim. It was a great hike and a great day. We'll have wonderful memories of it for a long time.

So we had a great time but I had had my heart set on the Big Hike so it nagged at me for the next few days. Camden and I tried to find a time when the two of us could go back up (Camden has done it before but he was willing to self-inflict the necessary pain to hike it with me) but there was no time that worked anytime soon. I knew that hiking it alone was not the smartest thing but I also realized I wanted to get it done while I was in such good hiking shape. And it was gnawing at me. So I proposed to Amy that we go up for Memorial Day, that Amy and the kids play at and around the rim while I take the 24 or so hours to do R2R2R. I was surprised when Amy agreed – she knew it was a little crazy but that I was obsessed and likely just to wake up one day, drive to the rim and start hiking. She wanted to be there at the rim to positively ID my body when they found it.

So we went. Amy dropped me off at the trailhead at 4:30 a.m. and I started walking soon thereafter. Down, across, and up, up, up. I got to the north rim about 1:30 p.m. but I was much more spent than I had been the weekend before, probably because I kept a faster pace, was in a hotter sun, and hadn't recovered fully from the week before. But there were no wonderful nieces or pickups waiting for me. I was a good boy about hydrating and eating. On the way back down, I reached Cottonwood in good enough shape but was feeling the beginning of cramps in my calves. Each mile seemed twice as long.

There was a little drama after that. As I left Cottonwood a camper asked if I had seen the smoke and fire further down the canyon near Ribbon Falls.

Then other hikers, coming the other way, told me about the huge amounts of smoke coming from the fire and advised me to turn around and get back to Cottonwood. That was not high on my list so I kept going. The smoke got very thick as I got to the fire (which was on the other side of the river) and affected my eyes but not my breathing. Then I was past it. I got some great video of the fire and smoke. About a mile later a helicopter flew over on its way to the fire. Then a while later it came back, circled me a few times, then landed near me. I was most concerned that they wanted to evacuate me for safety reasons. If that was the proposal, I was pondering running away from him or at least arguing vociferously that I was pretty determined to finish the hike. Luckily he only wanted to know what I knew about the fire. I told him I know it was burned out and was no concern and that he could find hikers at Cottonwood that knew how it started. With that he left and I got back to hiking.

I was at Phantom around 7 p.m., left Amy a voicemail from the pay phone, got some water, got off my feet for 15 minutes, then got back on the trail. I got over the river bridge, hiked the two miles along the river and turned up Bright Angel trail as darkness fell. I decided it was time for a headlamp when I tripped and fell in a few inches of water while crossing a creek. From then on it was just me, my headlamp, a lot of dark and a trail that just goes up. For the last 8 miles I never saw another hiker. Those silent, dark miles were actually a nice time to reflect and be thankful for the opportunity and for many other things. Devils' Corkscrew, Indian Garden, 3 Mile, 1.5 mile, then finally the top at 12:15 a.m. – exactly 19.5 hours. My ascent was better and stronger than I had expected – no cramps, no ideas of stopping. I believe the lack of sun made a big difference. Amy insists she prayed me up. I am sure it played a part.

Ironically my most tense moment of the trip came after I had reached the village at the South Rim just after midnight. I was walking down a lit sidewalk towards my meeting point with Amy and came face to face with the two largest bull elk I had ever seen. For a moment I thought, 'Sheesh, I survived 45 rigorous miles in a tough environment and now I'm going to be gored to death outside the El Tovar Hotel'. In about a second I realized that bull elk on the hotel lawns were probably more like pets. I waved as I walked by them.

Amy and the boys had a good time while I was in the canyon. They watched the IMAX Grand Canyon film, ate good food and even took a small aircraft flight over the canyon.

The feeling of accomplishment was huge. 45 miles in less than a day with so much up and down is not easy. The Canyon is amazingly beautiful and changes its look every 15 minutes, it seems. I repeated the hike in 2012 and hope to do it every few years.

Family Trips

I can think of nothing that builds family unity and common memories more than family trips. We had always been fans of family trips and had great opportunity to use our international postings as jumping off spots. During our time in Toronto we took a 26-day cross country trip across the U.S. and bits of Canada. From Hong Kong we spent a week in Thailand and a few days in Hawaii. From London we spent two weeks in continental Europe and several great trips in England. Some of these trips are worth reporting on.

Euro Disney - From London we wanted to spend a day at Disneyland outside of Paris. Amy and I planned out every detail. We decided that we would leave our home outside London early in the morning - like 3:30 a.m. early - and arrive at the park in time to enjoy the day after traveling with the van to the border then driving the van onto the Eurotunnel train and enjoying that experience, then driving the last few hours to Paris. We packed the van the evening before. At 3 we awoke and I carried the sleeping kids one at a time to the van where we laid them in makeshift beds. And off we went. The kids woke up to enjoy the train. Everything went as planned. As we pulled into the Disneyland parking lot, the kids were excited. They got out of their pajamas and into their play clothes. As they were trying to put the finishing touches on their wardrobes, we all came to a stunning realization: we had not packed shoes for any of the four kids. Oops. What to do? After a few minutes of considering options, I came up with a plan. Each of the kids stood on a blank piece of paper and Amy traced their foot. I encouraged them to be patient and play games in the van while I jumped on the METRO subway, found a French shoe or department store, bought some shoes and returned. My French vocabulary consisted of no more than 50 words and did not include store or shoe. But luckily my two years in Germany had taught me how to 'talk with my hands and my feet' (as the Germans say) if required. I figured out where the METRO station was, how to buy a ticket, and where a store was in no time. Walking into the department store with the foot sketches remains an all-time memory for me. The ladies in the shoe department caught on quickly and soon I was back at the van with shoes. Atley's were a bit tight but otherwise the shoes all worked well.

Germany - We spent two full weeks on the continent and visited Germany, Austria, Switzerland, Liechtenstein, and France. We visited old haunts from my mission days and enjoyed the spectacular scenery in Alpine Europe. We took an overnight ferry from England to Germany. We followed our one vacation rule: eat ice cream every day. We saw so many things. The kids ranged in ages from 15 down to 8. Of the hundreds of things that could have been memorable, the kids primarily remember the naked guy at the hotel pool in Aschaffenburg, Germany and the two naked women in the pool in Goslar.

Berlin in 1985 - Before the fall of the Wall, I completed a six-month internship in Frankfurt as part of my Master in International Business degree (MIBS). Our family consisted of Amy, Ethan and me. MIBS planned an event in Berlin. It coincided with my mother coming to visit so we rented a car and drove to Berlin. In those days Soviet Union and the East Bloc were real and scary. The Berlin Wall and the Iron Curtain were serious reminders of the Cold War and the different ideologies of East and West. The roads into Berlin from West Germany were actually transits through Communist East Germany. Just driving into East Germany and the transits, which they controlled, gave us all a feeling of dread and, candidly, evil. The East German border guards were bland and dour and angry. I remember arriving in West Berlin and taking three or four full trips around the Siegessaeule (a roundabout with a beautiful, tall gold statue in the center) while I tried to read the map for the right direction. I remember the bus trip into East Berlin and the East German border guards using ground mirrors for under the bus and searching the bus very carefully on the way out of East Berlin to ensure no one was escaping their fair country. I recall that much of East Berlin was still rubble 40 years after WWII whereas West Berlin was bright and shiny. Mostly I remember getting a speeding ticket from East German police on the transit on our way from Berlin to Munich. I saw a flash of light in the woods and warned Amy and my Mom that we might be stopped. Amy, who was pregnant, desperately needed to find a bathroom. Sure enough, around the next bend two police cars with unfriendly officers motioned us over to the side of the road. I was fluent in German but was not sure if that would serve me well in this case so I played it by ear. The police officer's words are etched in my memory forever. In German he said with a complete deadpan, "We have speeding laws in our country. From 1-10 kilometers over the speed limit the fine is 50 DMark. From 11-20 kilometers over the fine is 80 DMark. From 21-

30 kilometers over the limit the fine is 100 DMark. You were driving 31 kilometers over the speed limit. For this we have no law. We are determining what to do with you." Yikes. I believed that meant one of two things. Either they wanted an excuse to put us in jail for a night or two or Mr. Commy Police Officer wanted to shake me down. I suspected and hoped for the latter. I opened my wallet for him and showed him all of my money - about 150 DMark (about 60 dollars then). He decided that would be enough. Literally shaking, I drove away and told Amy and Mom the story. I recognize that a younger generation might not get the gravity of that experience but it was high drama with the Evil Empire.

Across the Country - in 26 days we put 6,540 miles on our Dodge minivan in 1992. From Toronto we made our way down through Michigan, Illinois and then west. We sat in a Taco Bell when a near-tornado ripped the town apart. We saw church history sites in Illinois, Iowa, Nebraska, and Missouri. We went through the Rockies and on the California beaches. We memorized every song Raffi ('Baby Beluga' is a hit) and Sharon, Lois and Bram ever wrote. We laughed and argued and played. We were attacked by meat bees at my mom's cabin in Strawberry, Arizona. As I recall, I screamed like a big girl. We were able to spend time with extended family.

Lake Powell - we spent a few days with my sister's family on a rented houseboat on Lake Powell in 1995. We also rented a ski boat and a jet ski for a day or two. I have never seen more stars in the heavens than I did while lying on the roof of the houseboat late at night.

Thailand - In the summer of 1994, while living in Hong Kong, we took our family and my mom to the Laguna Beach Club in Phuket (pronounced Poo-Kett), Thailand for a week. It was the first real luxury vacation we had ever taken. We were on a perfect white sand beach. The local Thai people were accommodating like only Asians can be. The food and fun was all part of the package. Each night at dinner there was a different ice carving at the main table. The resort had its own baby elephant, Saiphon, which the kids could sit on. The Kids Club entertained our four kids, who ranged in age 11 to 4, during the day. The TV in the room had bootleg, pre-release movies - another Asian specialty. Almost all of us took a turn at flying high above the ocean with a parachute attached to a speedboat (the local boys would climb up maybe 10 feet above our kids on the parachute strings with no safety devices of any kind). Amy and I escaped for 36 hours to spend a night on a tiny island retreat. The swimming pools and slides were fantastic. The trip home produced a memory for me that testifies of the innovativeness of the wonderful people of Hong Kong. For some reason one of our return flight itineraries was different than the rest. I convinced Amy to fly alone where she could have some peace. So my Mom and I and the four kids, with Ethan in his manual wheelchair, flew home together. DragonAir did a good-enough job with the wheelchair lifts. The kids were tired enough to travel pretty well. When we landed in H.K. we ran into a long line to get through immigration. That is not uncommon but, with a large family of little kids and an aging grandma, it felt like we would have to settle in for at least an hour of line standing. A local airport employee, who spoke broken English at best, attached himself to us to help us get through it all. He informed us that Ethan and his chair would have to go through a different, much shorter line. That would get two of us through quicker. I needed to push Ethan and lift him as needed so off we went, leaving my mom and the three little kids with the helper. Ethan and I cleared the line in five minutes. We watched through large plate glass windows from the other side of immigration. Soon the helper carved the three kids out and took them through a shorter line. Apparently children with no parent could be taken to an 'Unaccompanied Minor' line. That left grandma in the long line. I could almost see the wheels turning in our helper's head as he and mom stood there in that long line. As my mom tells the story, after another few minutes, he came to her and said, "Stay line. I be back." After a minute he returned, pushing a manual wheelchair. He urged her to get into it. She argued back, saying she was fine and strong and didn't need a wheelchair. Then they met eyes and she understood. She sat in the chair, He wheeled her to and through the short line. I will never forget the broad smiles on their faces as he rolled her over to me. She jumped up. We all had a good laugh. Our friend saved us at least 30 minutes.

Hawaii, Christmas 1994 - At the end of 1994 we took the family 'home' to Arizona for two weeks. To break up the trip we decided to stop in Honolulu for two nights. The flight from H.K. to Hawaii was eventful in that our seats were not all together. We had four together and two singles in different parts of the plane. We quickly worked out that Ethan, with his handicap, needed to be with us. Emily was 4 and needed to be with a parent. Either Amy or I would feel like a slacker if one of us took a single seat. So we realized that it was eight-year-old Ben and six-year-old Atley that should go solo. I took them to their seats, introduced them and our situation to their immediate seatmates. I got much appreciated 'we'll look after them' looks from the seatmates. We checked on them a time or two during the six hour flight but had our hands full as well. So they were pretty much on their own. I figured Ben would be fine but Atley could be a handful. Atley was and is, let's say, busy. When the plane landed, I fetched Ben first. According to the man by him, Ben had been perfect, playing video games and engaging in conversation. When I got to Atley's seat I knew immediately that I was going to get a very different report. The 50-something lady on one side of her drove daggers through me with her eyes. I could tell she would kill Atley and all of her relatives if she could. The pretty 30-something girl on the other side of Atley had an unforgettable look on her face. It seemed like the face of someone who had just ridden the world's craziest rollercoaster about 20 times in a row – enraptured by the experience but ready to get off. Her eyes were aglow and tired at the same time. Her hair was mussed beyond repair. She had lipstick here and there. Her seat looked like a bomb went off – magazines, toys, activity books and food. Atley said she had a new best friend.

I also learned that Amy's jetlag is not to be underestimated. At the local motel, I knew Amy was tired so I unpacked the rental car, asking only that she keep an eye on the kids, who had already opened the motel room sliding door and were heading toward a swimming pool. I returned with more luggage to find the kids playing at the edge of the pool unaccompanied and Amy as good as passed out on the bed. Gone.

Before Ethan died he asked us to take the twins to many of the places we used to live if possible. We took that quite seriously. It coincided with our daughters marrying. So we have built a treasure trove of family trips starting in 2007 that form an important part of the foundation of our relationships. That is obvious to me as we seem to relive some aspect of one or more of the trips every time we get together. I have noticed we laugh a lot when reliving our trips. Here is a rundown of the trips along with a highlight or two from each.

Havasupai - In 2007 Amy and I, Camden and Atley and Emily hiked Havasupai. (Brigham was not in the family yet. We left Ethan and the twins in the care of others.) Google it. It is a 12-mile hike one way through desolate national park and Indian reservation lands. At the end of the journey is an Indian village, a river full of waterfalls, swimming holes and the most beautiful light blue water imaginable. Amy was not sure if she was up for the trip. As secluded as it is, there is a daily helicopter service out of the canyon and Amy retained the right to use that if she wasn't confident in her ability to trek out. The 12-mile return hike with a light pack is made more difficult by being uphill. Two days of play and sleeping in sleeping bags also adds fatigue to the mix. We had a blast. When the time came Amy barely decided to hike. I was proud of her but also mindful that I might be carrying her the last few miles. After a dinner at the only restaurant in the village, we started. The first 10 miles are only slightly uphill, following a dry wash, then the last two miles are very steep. Emily is a great hiker. Atley is a plodder. Camden stayed with Atley. So Emily asked for permission to go faster. We let her go but asked her to wait at the bottom of the canyon wall (just before the last two mile climb). She apparently did not hear that part. So when Amy and I and Camden and Atley reached the bottom of the canyon, Emily was not there. I was not worried at all, assuming she had gone on and that we would find her at the top in the parking lot. Amy, less familiar with the path than I, and in possession of a healthy dose of a mother's fears and intuition, decided that Emily might be in trouble of some kind. Leading up to that point, Amy had been quite fatigued, had questioned her decision to hike out, and was deeply concerned about her ability to get up that steep canyon rim. All of that changed in an instant. Up she went. She beat me. Emily was fine. We were all fine.

Havasupai 2007

San Francisco - Later in 2007, we all went to San Francisco for a few days. Brigham was still not in the family yet. We remember the sights, Chinatown, and mostly the food on Pier 39. On Pier 39 we ate fudge, crepes, donuts, cookies, clam chowder, crepes (not a typo, we hit some stations more than once), and ice cream. While eating our clam chowder we watched an overweight man at the Mrs. Field's cookies collapse of an apparent heart attack. We watched as paramedics worked on him. It did not deter us. I think we moved from there to a second round at the crepe store.

London - The first time we were fulfilling Ethan's request to get the twins to our previous haunts was a trip with all of us to London. We took the twins in their manual wheelchairs. It was nine days of tiring joy. We stayed at a flat near Hyde Park. We saw many of the sights in London and also visited Windsor, Stratford-upon-Avon, Warwick Castle, and Canterbury, and also took a large ship across the English Channel to Calais, France. We enjoyed LDS experiences like seeing the place that Camden's great-great-great grandmother first heard the gospel preached (Speaker's Corner in Hyde Park) and very coincidentally attended a meeting with and getting to speak with Dieter Uchtdorf of the Church's First Presidency. We visited the home where we lived in Surrey. We watched 'Wicked' in the West End. We felt especially good about delivering on our promise to Ethan.

Warwick Castle, England 2009

Midwest and Toronto - In October of 2009, we went to the Midwest and into Ontario. There is much LDS history in the Finger Lakes region (Palmyra) and in the Cleveland area (Kirtland, Hiram). We loved the fall colors and the significance of the history we were remembering. Before the two married couples arrived in Cleveland, Amy and I and the twins had come earlier and spent two days around Toronto and Niagara Falls. In Toronto, we reconnected with dear friends and went to the top of the CN Tower. In Niagara, we stayed in a high-floor suite in the Embassy Suites overlooking the falls. Wow.

Disneyland - At the end of 2009, we all went to Disneyland. We froze but that kept the crowds away.

Grand Canyon - In May of 2010, the two young couples and I hiked the Grand Canyon. See the separate entry for that story.

East Coast - In the summer of 2010, Amy and I and the twins spent two weeks on the East Coast enjoying Boston, New York, Philadelphia and Washington, D.C. The young couples joined us for the four days in New York. We loved the history. As a total group in New York we watched 'Lion King' on Broadway, strolled Central Park, went to the top of the Empire State Building, saw the new building starting to take shape at Ground Zero, went to the Battery and Ellis Island, and even took a helicopter ride around South Manhattan. We stayed near Times Square and enjoyed the vibe.

Disneyland and San Diego - at the end of 2010 we all went to Disneyland. This time it was soaking, cold rain that kept the crowds away. I remember Atley's boots sloshing through the rain puddles. It was memorable. Then we went to San Diego, where the highlight was the brunch at the Hotel Del Coronado. We figured we should see how the other half lives for an hour or two.

Redwoods - in the summer of 2011 we took a trip to the Redwoods in Northern California. The twins and I drove up. We spent over five hours at Desert Center with hundreds of other cars and trucks because some yahoo's load of hay caught on fire and the officials decided it was best to let it burn itself out right in the middle of the westbound lanes of I-10. Amy and the couples flew into Eureka once we got there. We found the Redwoods enchanting and awe-inspiring. Of all of the places we have visited I find myself wanting most to return to the Redwood forests and spend a few days hiking there.

Crescent City, California 2011

Disneyworld - thanks in large part to the Make-A-Wish Foundation, we all spent a week near Disneyworld as part of Colby's Wish. We stayed at the Give Kids The World Village there and were consistently inspired by the sweet volunteers who work there. Many come from all over the country to spend a week or more dishing ice cream or bussing tables. The parks were, as always, magical.

Yellowstone, Rushmore - in the summer of 2012 we spent 10 days taking in Four Corners (for about five minutes as they were closing), Flaming Gorge, LDS handcart sites in Wyoming, Mount Rushmore, Yellowstone, the Tetons, and Utah. The entire trip was very enjoyable. In our first hour driving in Yellowstone we ended up in a stack of 10 or 20 cars. The hold up was a massive buffalo bull standing right in the middle of the road. We later came to understand that was quite common. After a few minutes the lead car determined that he could slowly drive around the bull and move along. The others followed. Our family was driving in our two vehicles – Amy and I and the twins in our minivan and the couples behind us in our pickup. As I drove very slowly around the statue-like buffalo I realized I would be only feet, inches perhaps, from the bull's backside. I felt an urge, one of those inexplicable things, to smack it on the bum as I drove by. I was stopped by a few things: would the bull react, were there cameras trained on me somewhere, would the many bystanders disapprove and report me. It wouldn't be much fun getting tossed from Yellowstone in our first hour. Exercising great restraint I managed to keep my arm inside the truck. As we rolled by another 20 feet I looked in my rearview mirror just in time to see Camden smack the bull on the backside as they drove by it. The smack was followed by the bull kicking the pickup and at least one bystander 'tsk-tsking' Camden from across the road. That was the end of it although we were slightly on edge for the rest of the time in the park. It went beyond that, actually. When we were pulled over in central Utah for speeding a few days later we joked, as the officer approached the car, that the long arm of the law had finally tracked down the buffalo smackers.

Tombstone, Bisbee - In December of 2012, without Camden and Atley but with Amy's Mom and my Mom, we spent a day or two in Tombstone and Bisbee in southern Arizona. Emily, who was pregnant, had a rough night and ended up in an emergency room and ended up going home early with Brigham. She was OK in the end. The rest of us enjoyed the history of the old Arizona towns. Among other things, we learned that Tombstone the mining town, at its most glorious in the 1880's, had about 10,000 people (which made it the largest U.S. town between Chicago and San Francisco), of which several thousand were prostitutes. Zoiks. Several funny jokes could follow here but what we read and heard there makes them untellable. Almost all of the prostitutes, called Soiled Doves colloquially, ended up deeply troubled, drug-addicted, alcoholic, diseased beyond reason, and suicidal. The oldest profession is not a good one.

Disneyland - we went to Disneyland again in June of 2013 right before Colby had a major back surgery.

General Conference - for the October 2013 LDS Conference we went to Salt Lake City. We were missing Brig and Emily and Little Ben as Brig's second year med school classes would not allow him to miss the Friday and Monday that we took off.

One-on-One Trips

I don't remember where we got the idea but while we were living in London we decided to pair off, one parent and one child, for trips. It would provide an opportunity for focused 1:1 time. We were making good money so we decided that the child could pick the location as long as it was in the U.K. or Europe and the total time commitment was no more than 3 days.

We had great fun with the trips. In addition to seeing some fun things, the main goal of meaningful discussion and memorable shared experiences was accomplished. Amy went with Ethan to a U.S. Air Force Base in the U.K., with Atley to Paris to see friends and sightsee and with Emily to Vienna to see friends and sightsee. She didn't get away with Ben until we moved to Virginia she and Ben went to Disneyworld.

Ethan and I went to Paris. We were picked up in the company Jaguar car by our driver, Ken (we took Ethan's manual wheelchair). We went first class with the Eurostar train to the center of Paris. We stayed in an average hotel and just enjoyed the sights and foods. Ethan was always about the food. Years later he was still talking about the Greek food we bought from vendors on the streets of Paris.

Ben and I went skiing in the Alps in Austria. It was his first time skiing. The little town we stayed in was straight from a postcard. Ben picked up any sport quickly so we had a great time. We got a speeding ticket. Ben knew I was fluent in German but was still impressed that I transacted the entire ticketing procedure in German with the local police.

Atley and I went to Scotland and enjoyed Loch Ness. We took the train, stayed the first night in a B&B near Inverness, and then camped the next night near the Loch. The next day we went horse back riding along the shores of Loch Ness, always looking for the monster and enjoyed a boat trip on the Loch where sonar was looking for Nessie.

Emily and I also did not get to go before we moved to Virginia. She and I went to Las Vegas. Sounds odd, I know. We stayed at the MGM and had plenty of fun at the M&M store, the Rainforest Café and other family friendly places. We also had great conversations on the long flights.

In each case we have been able to relive those trips together for years and years.

We have continued the tradition but on a much smaller scale due to the difficulty of travelling with the twins' wheelchairs. Every half-year or so we pair off and go get dinner. Once Cade and I dropped Amy and Colby off at In N Out Burger and we went to Five Guys. The main point of these outings is to have meaningful conversation. Cade and I are both serious about our food. We ordered and waited for our food amidst some unimportant chitchat. Once the food came we dug in. At the end of the meal we realized that we had not spoken one word during the entire meal. We laughed all the way back to In N Out to pick up Amy and Colby and have laughed about it often since.

Coaching

I have always loved sports. As the kids grew up it was logical for me to be involved with coaching their youth sports teams. I coached each of the kids at least twice in T-Ball, basketball, softball and baseball. For two years in London I was also the commissioner of the sports program.

When the kids were a little older, in Virginia, I coached Ben and Atley in their 7th grade basketball teams. At that age the kids can be coached. I tried to find the right balance between playing to win and playing to have fun. It as clearly more fun to win and the kids responded to the coaching.

Ben's team was made better by the fact that I chose the father of the best player in the league as my assistant coach. The son comes along with the dad even before the draft. The boy, Steve, was Ben's best friend and his dad was a dear friend of mine from church. So I wasn't being a complete pig. (Once, in Hong Kong, I ended up with an assistant coach on Ben's 3rd grade basketball team who was the Asian General Manager for Haagen Dazs. I thought I had hit the jackpot. We got ice cream for us and the boys exactly zero times. It was very disappointing.) We competed well and were among the three best teams in the league but not a clear favorite. We sailed through the tournament, winning the final by 39 points. It was fun to be with Ben and the other boys.

Atley's team was different. Girls are different. They had a team song. We were the Starzz and our team song, devised by the girls, finished with something like "double the Z, I said double the Z". The girls each became dear to me. They tried so hard. Atley had a sweet little lefty shot but did not have a good feel for the game. Of the eight teams, we were perhaps third best well behind the top two in talent. We worked on some things in practices and the girls responded. When the tournament time arrived, we won a quarterfinal easily, then somehow won a semifinal, which I had expected to lose. The team we would meet in the finals had beaten us by at least 20 points in each of the two round robin games. We put in the best strategy we could formulate and hoped for the best. The girls played like crazed little maniacs. They seemed to respond to the larger crowd and the seemingly high stakes. We played neck and neck until we were down by 2 points with 7 seconds to play. We had the ball in the backcourt, therefore needing to get the ball inbounded, drive the court and put up a desperation shot. Odds were heavily against us. We drew up a play that had our little playmaker, Chrissy Smith, receiving the ball and driving up the right side of the court, right in front of my coaching position. The girls executed the play well. Quick little Chrissy got around some full court pressure and dribbled up near me at half court with two or three seconds to go. I yelled at her to shoot. This little girl, perhaps 70 pounds, launched a 50-footer from the hip. From my position I could see that it had a chance. The ball sweetly banked off the backboard into the basket just as the buzzer sounded. I remember jumping around like we had won the NBA Finals, hugging each girl and their parents. Mindful of the idea that we might be over-celebrating a 7th grade school league final, I was comforted by the fact that everyone in my view was doing the same, even people not connected to the team. Most of the girls were crying tears of joy, as were some of their parents. The stands, maybe a hundred people, went crazy. I was so proud of those girls.

That experience has always reminded me of the power of sport, of effort, of overcoming, of teamwork. It reminds me that I love to teach and coach.

My Basketball Life

I grew up with four older brothers. Behind our home on the dairy we had a full court basketball court. We played every chance we could. Being the youngest I had to learn to get my shot off over their long arms and tall bodies. I learned to get around them with quickness. I made some progress on being tough when shoved to the ground. I had some natural talent. In addition to having a good shot, I also had good court awareness and could get open shots for other players.

As a result I was the best 3rd, 4th, 5th and 6th grade basketball player around. For several years I didn't play anyone in my age that was better. That begins to create dreams in a boy whose father was a sports-first kind of guy. I could see myself excelling at a good college and playing in the NBA. Then, during middle school years, I was arguably the best player on our school teams. I was not the tallest but was the best playmaker and the team revolved around me. At summer basketball camps I often caught coaches talking about me amongst themselves in glowing terms.

I had excellent freshman and sophomore years, still in the vein of 'best playmaker'. The second half of my sophomore year was probably the best school basketball I ever played. I played with confidence, ran the team and scored plenty.

Everything looked promising. A new high school opened and I was part of that. Then the dreams unraveled. My junior and senior seasons were basketball nightmares. At the heart of the problem was a lack of confidence brought on by my own insecurities and a coach who was focused on calling out what each player had done wrong. I learned that some people are best motivated by being praised for the good things they do. They then want to do more good things. Having their errors pointed out perhaps motivates other people. They then want to prove they can do it right. As with most things I am sure there is a full spectrum ranging from 'folds like a flower when criticized' to 'thrives under criticism and pressure'. Unfortunately at that time in my life I was a 'folder'. I began to recognize it, tried to correct it, and hated that it was so. But nothing helped. Each time I got on the court I was mindful of having the coach focus on my errors. That made me nervous and self-conscious so I made more errors. It became a vicious cycle. I still had enough skill that I was useful. I was often the first man in off the bench. I had some good streaks. We had a very good team. But I knew I did not have the faith and confidence of the coach. Once one of our guards was suffering from a stomach flu. For several trips up and down the court the player, a dear friend of mine, practically begged the coach to pull him out so he could recover for a while. I was the obvious substitute in that situation. Each time the coach yelled at my buddy to be strong and hang in there. That was perhaps when I hot rock bottom. I was less useful than a limping, moaning, ready-to-throw-up-at-any-point point guard.

Watching my shot go in- I think.

I knew I needed to toughen up. Time, perspective and experience have mostly closed up that character weakness in me. I consider myself tough enough for most situations now. I have faced down bullies and naysayers and difficult situations and come through.

I deeply believe that most people will improve, thrive and exhibit more positive behavior if they are praised rather than scolded. Years ago I took a three-day course on management. It was an excellent course. At the end of the three days, the instructor said. "If you only remember one thing from this course it should be this – you can be a great manager if you find people doing the right thing and thank them for it". That belief has been at the heart of my management, coaching and, most importantly, parenting style.

[Note: Ironically, the social side of my high school basketball career was as positive as it could be. Coincidentally, or not, it seemed to me that the very best people in school were on the basketball team with me. We created strong friendships, supported each other and have done so through the years. High school basketball brought me great life lessons and great friends. The lessons were painful as most of the best lessons are.]

[Another note: As my senior basketball season went on, I think I began to make some progress on my 'toughness' problem. I tried to care less what my coach was thinking and more on what was the right thing to do. I tried to support my teammates - we had a very good team - and think a little less about how I was feeling. Candidly, I was never quite sure if it represented progress or resignation. But it got me through it. In the divisional playoffs, we faced my old high school in a do-or-die game. The winner moved on and into the state playoffs while the loser went home. I had a very good game, one of only a few that season. I tied for top scorer, as I recall, and helped us win the game. I remember the coach praising me. I didn't care. The article in the newspaper the next day talked about how "Craig" Ellsworth led the Toros. I didn't care about the typo. I suppose that was progress.]

Heart Attack

I had a heart attack on May 1, 2009. In many parts of the world May 1 is called May Day. ☺ In retrospect, the only warning sign I can connect was the day before the attack when Atley and I walked the 3-mile hike up and back to the Wind Cave at Usery Park east of Mesa. We hiked at midday with light cloud cover but probably 93 degrees and both of us found it harder than usual. I had unusual tightness across my shoulders and chest but thought nothing more of it, as it seemed to go away as we hiked down and went on our way.

Amy had travelled to Utah for LDS Women's Conference so I was alone with the twins and took off work to care for them. All had gone according to plan until Friday afternoon. I lay down for 30 minutes and awoke at 2:30 to get the twins off the school bus. Only seconds after standing up I started experiencing pains in my chest. The pains intensified and the symptoms almost immediately spread to numbness and tingling across my chest and down my arms and also to sweating and clamminess. The boys' bus was a few minutes late so I had about 10 minutes of significant pain while waiting for them. On a scale of 1-10 the pain was about a 7 and I didn't know what was wrong. It was probably only a few minutes before the possibility of it being a heart issue popped into my head only because the symptoms seemed so classic for a heart attack. But I tried to dismiss that thought as alarmist and focused on trying to hold still and determine what was wrong.

That was made harder by me needing to get the twins off the bus. I walked down the driveway once, got the mail in a daze and wandered back in, agitated that the twins weren't there yet and that my ability to get them off the bus was waning. I lay down on the couch, hoping for relief and waiting for the sound of the school bus. The pain remained at 7 and the other symptoms continued. The bus finally came. I opened the garage door and Cade, who could still walk a little, walked in the house. I walked halfway down the driveway, motioned hello to Richard the bus driver, and pushed Cade's manual wheelchair back into the house, which Colby was trying unsuccessfully to push towards the house with his power chair. All this time I was on the verge of panic as I had found that any activity significantly upped the symptoms. So I told Colby and Cade that I couldn't help them get settled as I wasn't feeling well. I grabbed the phone, half expecting to need to call 911 any time but hoping for relief, and lay down on the couch. After another few minutes of pain, I called the twins to me and explained that I was not doing well at all. I asked if they knew the address to our house and asked them to call 911 if I fell asleep and they couldn't wake me. (Two funny asides: 1) When I explained the tingling down my arms, Colby said "I get that sometimes at night, too" and 2) when I told Cade I might have to go to the doctor to get treated, he said" Can you get it all done in time to go the school carnival at 5:30?")

As the minutes went by, the pain level fluctuated between 5 and 7 but it remained scary. I was close to dialing 911 several times. I called Emily somewhere in there and let her know I was unwell and might need her to run home from the nearby salon, where she was working as a receptionist. By 3:30 I was surer that it was heart-related and I was still hurting a lot. I tried Ed Hancock (friend, home teacher, doctor) and Billie Bollwinkel (friend, nurse) unsuccessfully. I was wondering who could help and realized I also needed priesthood support. I called our LDS Bishop, Tom Larsen, who immediately came and gave me a blessing and insisted I call Debra Barton (friend, nurse). After telling her the symptoms she wondered why I wasn't in the hospital. I told her I would think about it. A few minutes later she was at the door, ready to watch the boys and insisting that her husband, Bob, drive me to the emergency room. Emily had also arranged to come home right then. I didn't fight Debra's plan although I wanted to. The pain had gone from 7 to 2 right in line with the priesthood blessing, which promised me immediate relief from the symptoms. So, again, the typical male brain entertained the idea that I was overreacting, that it was something small and was now over with. But I agreed to go with Bob Barton to Banner Baywood. On the way there I was feeling even more reticent, since the pain level was no more than 1 and I was feeling much better. I wondered when and if I should call Amy in Utah and decided not to since I had no idea if I was overreacting and I was sure she was having a great time. We arrived at the ER around 4:30.

The ER admitted me fairly quickly (I guess chest pains gets you to the front of the line). Bob stayed with me the whole time and Bishop Larsen joined us later. They did multiple EKG's, chest X-rays, and blood work. The first two were unhelpful but the blood work showed very high cardiac enzyme levels (Troponin) that were proof enough that I had had a fairly large heart attack and had dome damage to my heart. All this time my pain levels were no higher than 2 and were near zero for a while. The ER doctors, in consultation with the specialists behind the curtain, decided I needed to go the Banner Heart Hospital which is literally connected to Banner Baywood. I was told the cardio doctors would decide whether I needed an angiogram to assess and hopefully fix the damage next or if a treadmill test would make more sense as a next step. Unknown to me the evidence was clear enough to them that they had already scheduled the angio for noon on Saturday. I did not learn that until 11 p.m. or so. Hospital time runs slow with tests and processes and paperwork so that I was in my bed at Banner Heart (BHH) around 10 p.m. In the meantime I knew it was serious enough that I should call Amy with real news. Bishop Larsen called her for me. She rearranged her schedule to get home as early on Saturday as possible.

Atley and Lisa Heath (Atley's mother-in-law) arrived soon after I got into my room at BHH. They were a great comfort. By this time I had an IV line, plenty of poke holes from shots and bloodletting, and a full set of body stickers that allow for taking an EKG. Lisa left and Atley stayed the night, sleeping on the floor as the chair did not recline much at all. During the night the pain jumped up to 3-4 and made me very uncomfortable. My sleep was, therefore, poor. I remember thinking how weird it was to be literally having a heart attack while lying there and I was eager to get to the operating room at noon to sort out what was really wrong. In the meantime Emily and Brig were great at home, clearing off their schedule, taking the boys to the carnival and taking great care of them.

Before 7 a.m. Lisa was back to visit and then to take Atley home to shower and pick up Amy at the airport at 9:30 a.m. The morning for me was spent preparing for surgery (they call angioplasty a procedure officially...not sure what the difference is between a procedure and a surgery), which included a shower, new gown, and more tests. Amy arrived around 10:45 after getting home, seeing the boys and Emily, and driving to BHH. Getting her there was a great comfort to me.

About noon they took me down to the operating room. Three nurses came together and were a team in support of Doctor Ambrosia. In the OR they prepped me, deadened an area near the groin, put me on a drug in the IV line that knocked me out about halfway, cut into my leg and major artery and did their thing. That included going up the artery into the heart and combining that with imaging devices hovering over my body that provided the picture for the Doc. He found 100% blockage fairly high up on the most important of the three heart arteries (called the Left Anterior Descending). It was close to a point they call the Widow Maker. I was apparently helped slightly and perhaps saved by an enterprising heart that tried to create other paths around the blockage. The blockage was in a bad spot also because the artery turned downward there and it was apparently like working inside a corkscrew. But Doctor Ambrosia figured it out, ballooned it and then stented it. He apparently found that the right artery had about 20% blockage in one place but he deemed it OK and that it could be handled with diet and drugs. They showed me a replica of the stent they used. It was 24mm (apparently one of their longer options) and looked a lot like a ballpoint pen spring to me, but covered with mesh. I slept through much of the procedure, which lasted about an hour, but awoke occasionally to watch the monitors with the team. I remember them discussing that they found the problem easily and that the solution was a little more complex than it should be because of the corkscrew turn. Amy was in the waiting room during the procedure and had a good chat with the Doc afterwards, where he explained all that had gone on.

I was back in my room at 1:30 or so. For the next 11 hours I was expected to lay on my back with my right leg fully extended and flat. With a sore back and my normal wiggles, that proved hard. At about six, after they were sure that my blood had thinned enough, Lisa, the excellent nurse with no inside voice, removed the catheter out of my leg/groin. She had Casey and Lauren assist and what I thought was a very minor thing turned out to be fairly major. I hadn't thought through that they had infiltrated a very major artery to perform the procedure and that pulling out of it also disrupted the system. The concerns were around bleeding and stabilization of the blood flow, blood pressure and heart rate. So, as Lisa pulled the catheter out she told me she had to push down very hard on my incision for 20 minutes. As she started that, I went dizzy, my blood pressure went down, and my heart rate went up. It was about 10 minutes before I was somewhat back to normal, which was a little scary. All the while Lisa was pushing on the incision.

Between 1 p.m. and when I went to sleep at 10 or so, I had visits from family and friends. Then another six hours of lying flat. I dozed at 10 while Amy tried to sleep on a foldable bed that she borrowed from a friend. At midnight the nurse checked me, made me stand up, and I was then free from my restrictions. I slept well enough although there were interruptions for vitals measurements.

On Sunday morning, the hospitalist mentioned that we might be able to leave later in the day. Subsequent discussions with nurses and Doctor Spadafora reconfirmed that. Everything seems to take forever in a hospital. We were finally discharged about 1:30 p.m. with instructions and prescriptions.

I went through a heart attack checklist with multiple doctors and nurses. I had only one of the usual normal indicators. I wasn't old (49), I had little family history of heart problems, and I stayed away from alcohol and drugs. But I was a fat boy, weighing in at about 235 when 200 made more sense and I paid almost no attention to the food I ate. Two hours before the heart attack I had eaten a 'double-double animal style' burger at In N Out, which I washed down with a chocolate shake. I joked that the blockage in my artery might have been an onion. A few months later, after some pleading by Amy, I did commit to losing weight. I lost 50 pounds in four months with Medifast and have kept half of it off over the last four years.

All of the medical professionals who dealt with me were excellent. They were caring, thorough and forthcoming when they could be. My favorite remark was by the lady hospitalist. When I asked her if my Troponin enzyme score was high (the higher the reading the more obvious that a heart attack occurred) she said, "I've seen higher but they all died".

Fremont Football

I only played one year of organized football. Dairy life meant no Pop Warner. I also missed out on Little League and other youth sports leagues but do not remember feeling deprived at all.

I played starting cornerback and third-string quarterback for the Fremont Falcons on our 9th grade team. I weighed 115 pounds. I played well enough as I loved to hit and was naturally athletic.

But it was a disaster season. We lost every game. Our coaches were satanic ☺. OK, not quite satanic, but close. Our head coach proved to be an exceptional line coach later on but this was his first head coaching position and he wasn't great at it. The assistant coach excelled in shouting, swearing and breaking clipboards on players' helmets. He was a world class Greco-Roman wrestler and believed, as cross country runners and wrestlers seem to, that pain is just weakness leaving your body.

We had two-a-day summer practices for ten days before school started. They were hell for me. Temperatures were over 110 for the afternoon practice. The coaches worked us mercilessly. I had consistent nightmares for the only time in my life. I dreaded each new day. I was driven forward by one thing and one thing only – I am not a quitter.

At one point during the season, when we had lost five or six games, emotions spilled over during practices. One player quit the team and then a few more. We reached a point where, of the 60 players we started the season with, only 10 or so had not quit. I remember a practice with fewer than 10 players. It was everything I could do not to quit. I hated it. But I was not going to let my parents or siblings down in that way. I hoped they would cancel the rest of the season. The quitters and their parents complained. The principal demanded that the coach apologize and take the players back and change his behavior. If you've ever been on a team you know that, once the coach's authority has been undermined, a team is rudderless. We played out the string. We lost every game (never even got close to a win, even against Ray, Arizona, which had like 100 people in the whole town, and eventually ceased to exist as it was subsumed by an open-pit copper mine).

During the season I broke my right hand, then my left hand, then ripped the tendons around my right elbow to pieces. I never missed a game. I played three games with a wrapped cast on one arm and one game with wrapped casts on both arms. Needless to say I did not intercept any passes in those games. The horror of the season and the multiple injuries made it easy for me to forego any more organized football in high school.

[Note 1: Fremont was a junior high and included grades 7-9. Only two and a half junior high schools fed our high school. Three years later when my buddies were seniors in high school they won every football game by a landslide. The kids from Fremont were as instrumental in the perfect season as were the kids from the other main junior high. You can draw some conclusions from that about the importance of coaching, a little dignity, and confidence.]

[Note 2: As the third string quarterback I only got in on offense twice, when we were trailing by 50 points in the last minute or two of games. In addition to handing off a few times, I passed the ball twice. My career record was: 2 passes, 2 completions, about 50 yards. Yes, a perfect passer rating.]

[Note 3: Fremont Junior High felt like how I imagined a penal institution would feel during my years there. It had every demographic that predicted trouble. Knives, brass knuckles, fights, and threats were commonplace.]

Parent Fans

My parents were famous in my circles for being 100% supportive of their kids' sporting activities. In my case I calculated that during my junior high and high school careers I had about 130 games or meets. Both Mom and Dad attended every single one, including days when they were ill, games played in Yuma or Coolidge, or days when they had conflicts. Mom always brought snacks for my buddies and me.

They also had a perfect or near perfect record for my siblings. I recall my little sister, Beryl, and I getting into our Halloween costumes and driving the three hours to Yuma with my parents. My folks drove around until they found a nice neighborhood. Beryl and I then trick-or-treated to our hearts content. Then we piled back in the car and drove to my brother's high school football game, where Beryl and I ate Halloween candy and my parents cheered my brother on.

Extra Credit Sports Discussions

My mind goes wandering on all kinds of issues. Sports and religion are probably the two areas that get the most attention from my little brain. Here are two examples of my mad musings on sports.

A great pro football team wins 80-90% of its game (14-2 record, for example). A great pro basketball team wins 80% (65-17). A great pro baseball team wins 65% (100-62). Why does a great baseball team win such a low percentage of its games? I have pondered that great mystery ☺. A great hitter can only bat one out of every nine team at-bats or four times a game. And he can be pitched around or walked. A great pitcher pitches only every fifth day. Compare that to football where Peyton Manning can touch the ball on every offensive play and basketball where LeBron can touch it every play and defend the other team's best player. So, in baseball, the great players contributions can be minimized and the likelihood of winning is diminished and is more controlled by the supporting cast than in the other major sports. Depth matters in baseball whereas the current mantra in the NBA is to have a 'Big Three' and in football it's about the quarterback. I thought you might like to know that.

This next one is deeper and requires some assumptions. I will mention race but it is not a racial discussion in the classic context. We could probably all agree that most of the great NBA players are black. Fine. Whether that is physical or socio-economic is a discussion for someone else. I want to focus on the white guys. Here is the observation: most of the best white (meaning I believe they are

51% white or they look like it to me) basketball players in the NBA are not Americans. In 2012 only four of the top 100 NBA players were white Americans. 13 were white non-Americans. They were Europeans and South Americans and Canadians. They dominate the Americans. And it's not even close. One might argue that there are more little white boys in the combination of those countries and continents but I say rubbish. I believe that most American boys grow up liking basketball and having dreams of being very good at it someday. I also believe that few white boys from Europe and South America do the same. They grow up with soccer. So if you can stay with me on that assumption – that there are as many or more white American boys wanting to excel at basketball than there are in the rest of the world – then we need to figure out why so many more non-American white boys get to the NBA and excel there as compared to Americans.

Here's my theory. White American boys grow up watching and trying to pattern their games after black American stars. That kind of game often involves quickness, leaping ability, and dunking. By the time these kids are 20 years old, their approach to the game is not suited for their capabilities. Watch a white (or black) European or South American and you are likely to see a player adept at passing, positioning, shooting, and rebounding – basic and fundamental basketball skills. The European kids are learning these things in programs that highlight their potential early and fund them from the time they are 14 or so. So, you fathers of promising, young, tall, white American kids, get your boys to Europe if you want them to succeed in the NBA. Or have them watch plenty of film of great fundamental players like Larry Bird or Bill Russell or Paul Silas.

A Little Rusty

Although I was spared the experience of having close family die in my youth, there was one traumatic death during my youth.

I was 11 years old. Upon turning 12, I would become a Boy Scout in our LDS-sponsored troop and be able to participate in campouts and outings. I looked forward to it. To my disappointment the troop scheduled a 50-mile bike outing on April 1, 1972, three days before my twelfth birthday. I lobbied my parents and leaders for an exception to go but was denied. The Scouts went without me.

On the afternoon of April 1, I was working on the Chandler dairy, not remembering that my boy friends were having an adventure. The afternoon was interrupted by a phone call to my Dad, informing him that one of the Scouts, our neighbor, Rusty, had been hit and killed while riding his bike on that outing.

Rusty was a year older than I. He was also a dairy boy, his Dad operating a dairy a half-mile away. A year makes a big difference at that age so Rusty and I were friends but were not extremely close. He was a great kid with unlimited potential. Despite not being close, I remember going to my bathroom at home and sobbing while curled up in the fetal position in my shower stall. I suppose my sobbing was a mixture of sadness for Rusty and his family and the realization that people die. That was a new idea for me.

As I have been told the story, here is what happened on that fateful bike trip. Near the end of the fifty miles, the boys needed to cross from one side of the road to the other. Rusty saw the boy in front of him cross the road and look back at possible oncoming traffic. Rusty knew that the boy, therefore, had the information Rusty wanted. "Any cars coming?" Rusty asked. "Two. Then you can cross", came the reply. So two cars passed, Rusty crossed and was hit and killed by a third car, one that the first boy had not seen.

Although that accident occurred more than 40 years ago, it still affects my life - positively - today. There have been dozens of occasions when I have been smart enough to verify something for myself instead of taking someone's word for it. In some cases it has paid large dividends. Thank you, Rusty.

A Prayer of Gratitude

As a child I was taught to pray to my Heavenly Father. As a believer, I still pray regularly. One of the most meaningful experiences I have had with prayer was accepting a challenge from some forgotten teacher or church leader. The challenge was to extend my personal prayers and dwell only on the things for which I was thankful.

I have done so many times now, spending up to an hour in quiet prayer, reflecting in great detail on the people and things that have blessed my life. The power of the experience lies in going beyond the normal things that we think of first. Here are a few examples from my life of relatively obscure people and experiences that I was reminded of only because I took the time to ponder, for which I am deeply thankful:

My second grade teacher, Mrs. Young, was exceptionally sweet and let me know that I was loved.

My most influential and powerful missionary companion was only my companion because President Schreiber asked him to extend his mission by a month. Most of my meaningful lessons learned occurred in the five weeks I served with him.

Being raised on a dairy was a blessing in a myriad of ways.

During the potentially dangerous middle school years, I seemed to have a protective hand over me, removing me from danger (physical, sexual, emotional) at crucial points in time.

My early April birthday usually coincides with the arrival of spring in the desert, full of orange and yellow flowers and mild temperatures. My local part of the world is beautiful on my birthday.

A business trip was surprisingly cancelled on December 1, 2005. I was, therefore, home with Amy when we learned that Ben died instead of being in a hotel somewhere.

My ninth grade Seminary teacher, Brother Cuthbert, was funny, dedicated and taught me, by his example, a great deal about being a man.

I could add hundreds - perhaps thousands - more. I am thankful.

Giving

While Amy and I lived in Provo, we received an anonymous check for $100 as Christmas neared. I never learned who sent it. I have never forgotten it.

There is something great about doing something good for someone else and not taking credit for it.

Once in a Sunday School class I attended, the teacher said, "Anonymous acts of service are great. I have given hundreds of acts of anonymous service through the years." Oops, I thought to myself, you just made them un-anonymous and lost credit for all of them. So I will not report on our giving.

But there are two practices I will share. The first we learned from the book that Kurt Warner, the ex-NFL quarterback, wrote. His family (and now ours), when they are out at a restaurant, picks a family and quietly arranges with the waiter or waitress to pay for their bill. Out of the corner of one eye you get to see the waiter inform the family that their meal was paid for by someone else in the restaurant. The reaction is always priceless. The family is surprised, pleased, and thankful. Then they spend five minutes looking around the restaurant trying to determine who their benefactor was, ascribing kindness and generosity to every table they look to. The waiters are always as pleased as we are. It's a win, win, win.

The second is simply to ask yourself (and ask God) every day: who needs my help? Just that little query, I have found, makes me mindful of those around me, and also seems to plant ideas in my head.

Great People

I have met some great people through the years. Some are so extraordinary that I want to tell you about them. I will change their names in every case.

Phil seems to be everywhere he is needed. He is a member of our local LDS ward. Most members in the ward have one or more 'Phil' stories. A typical Phil story goes like this: 'I got a flat tire and needed help. Phil drove up, changed my tire, and got me on my way'. He brings the widows' newspapers and garbage cans in. He includes those who are regularly excluded by others. He anticipates situations somehow. He is embarrassed by any recognition. He is the Good Samaritan.

Mark was my friend in Ohio. He married at an older age and thereby missed out on the opportunity to have his own children. He thought of others first. He always had good advice. He was a calming influence. I remember a couple, down on their luck, coming into the LDS chapel looking for some money for gas. It was easy to see through them. They wanted money for drugs or booze or both. Mark talked to them, encouraged them with a few words, gave them $50 and wished them well. He had a tear in his eyes when he came back in. He was teaching a Sunday School lesson once when a fellow in the congregation, who was mostly inactive in church and needed prescribed drugs to keep him stable, burst into the classroom screaming. At first I thought Mark had organized the intruder as part of the lesson. It became clear that the man was out of sorts, though, when he started using every 4-letter word in the book. Mark looked as calm as a summer morning. He spoke softly to the man and asked if he could talk to him outside. By the end of the story, Mark took him home, got his drugs into his system, and got him settled into bed.

Alex is a joiner. He was secretary or treasurer or member of many civic and church groups. He used the word 'joiner' to describe himself. I had never heard it before in that context. I asked him why. Nonchalant he said that he likes people and likes to help.

Ellen was an American schoolteacher at our kids' school in Hong Kong. She was sweet and kind and good. She took our two young daughters under her wing, giving them small things and inviting them for games and chats at her house.

Roland was the first person we met in our LDS ward in West Columbia, South Carolina. He was a volunteer greeter and took it seriously. His southern drawl and charm and his sweet smile impressed us immediately. He soon became our local bishop. He and his equally good wife and their two teenaged children adopted us. They loved us in word and deed. We loved Roland's southern sayings - things like, "That was some fine country eatin'!". He would sing songs like "Have a Little Talk With Jesus". He housed us when we needed a place for a couple of nights. He and his wife took care of us when we were ill.

There are so many more. I have been surrounded by truly great people.

Pickup

When my oldest sibling turned 16, my parents bought a new car for him to drive. It wasn't portrayed as his car but only he drove it. The car was the very low end of the cheapest line of American-made cars. Thus started a trend of buying a new car for each child. With each child the cars got more expensive. My folks were not rich but were doing well enough on the dairy. My dad loved continuing the trend. Mom thought it was unnecessary. By the time I was ready to turn 16, cash was short for my parents. I suppose I didn't know the extent to which they were hurting but I must honestly say I might not have cared. There was a trend to continue and I had been thinking for months about which car to buy. I narrowed it down to a 280-Z or a Chevy Pickup.

Mom, by this time, was sick of the trend and tired of me obviously not appreciating that this represented a real sacrifice for my parents. She made a few demands of me leading up to buying the car that I grudgingly complied with.

I decided on a 1976 Chevy Silverado. We actually went to the dealership and ordered the pickup the way I wanted it a few months before my 16th birthday. The colors were Rosedale Red with a large swath of Santa Fe tan. I wasn't allowed to get either 4-wheel drive or cruise control because mom knew I would kill myself with either one of those. We ordered very cool wheels and tires and got a 4-barrel carburetor that gave the 350cc engine a little more hop.

When it came it was like a dream come true. It came on March 19, 1976. I still remember March 19 like it was the birthday of a loved one. It was the coolest looking pickup in town, I thought. Everyone commented on it.

There is a saying, "What we obtain too easily, we esteem too lightly." That saying could have been invented for me. I am sure I voiced appreciation. I was deeply thankful. But I did not want to know or think about what sacrifices it meant for my mother. I did not learn to service the pickup like I should. I never offered to earn enough money to take over insurance or even gas costs. I was insistent that, while I was away for two years on my LDS mission, the pickup be covered and stored so that no one else was using it. I was a spoiled brat.

The good news is that I did slowly realize what a brat I was and I see it now for what it was. I did recover a little. I held on to that pickup for 15 years and took reasonably good care of it later on. After those 15 years, Amy and I gave it away to a good family whose daughters needed basic transportation to and from high school. I felt good about leaving it there in Ohio.

[Note: I learned that lesson well enough that our three healthy children all drove absolute junkers to school.]

My 1976 Chevy Silverado

Popularity Never Was A Test of Truth

I had an exceptionally good peer group in high school. They helped keep me on a good course. I am forever thankful for them.

The group a year younger than us seemed to have more than its share of difficulties, including alcohol and pregnancy. What made the difference? It is certainly complex but I believe that one key factor was a need by the younger group to feel or look popular. Whereas my buddies had no trouble looking 'square', the same did not seem true for the younger class. The irony was that my group of buddies was seen by many as the most popular group in school. They set their own trends and direction.

I have heard that popularity never was a test of truth or goodness. I believe it, especially as it applies to social trends.

Leave the No-Doz Alone

Part of my Master in International Business degree was a 6-month internship with a German company (Degussa) in Frankfurt. Amy and I had our oldest, Ethan, by then. Ethan was two-and-a-half years old. The internship with Degussa was a real treat. They treated me so well, even offering me a job 'anywhere Degussa does business' after I graduated (I had an offer in hand from Degussa USA in New Jersey when I decided to take a better offer from NCR Corporation). We traveled as much as our scant student finances would let us - we were living off student loans and a small monthly stipend from Degussa. My mom visited us for a while and we traveled with her to Berlin, and Austria. At the end of the internship, in February of 1986, we returned to the U.S., flying People Express. They were a super-cheap fare airline and went bankrupt a few years later.

We were probably a pitiable sight as we worked our way through airports. We had nine large suitcases. Amy was pregnant with Ben and I asked her not to lift anything heavier than her purse. Ethan was heavier than a purse. So I had nine bags and a two-year old to move each time. The Newark airport was particularly hard. Amy and Ethan were to fly from there to Columbia, South Carolina, where they would stay with dear friends for a few days. I was to fly to Phoenix via Los Angeles, retrieve my pickup (which we had left there during our time in Germany), and drive back to Carolina as quickly as possible. In Newark, Amy and Ethan were both feeling the effects of jet lag and Amy was unwell. I literally dragged two suitcases forty yards, fetched two more, etcetera. Amy stayed with the forward bags while I tried to keep my eye on the rearward ones. Ethan was whimpering and Amy wanted to throw up. As I recall we had to go from one terminal to another connected terminal. We moved our little family and the bags perhaps 500 yards, 40 yards at a time, two bags at a time. I must defend my sanity here. First, People Express did not have bag-sharing arrangements with other airlines. That's why I had all the bags. The airport was full of people so there were no carts to be had. And I couldn't afford a skycap. So we slogged onward and finally got the bags checked and Amy and Ethan to the right gate.

I remember feeling bad that I was so glad to say goodbye to Amy and Ethan. I would miss them for the next few days but I knew they could rest on the plane and that the Berry's would take great care of them in Columbia. Mostly I was just glad to say sayonara to those heavy bags.

Once they flew, I caught a delayed plane to L.A. Its late arrival meant that I missed the connector to Phoenix and had to sleep in the airport on a bench that night. A nice homeless man slept near me. He made his meager living collecting baggage carts and shopping carts and collecting the deposits for each one. I recall him chastising himself repeatedly for using that day's revenues on a meal at McDonalds. He said that if he had used the same money for a loaf of bread and a pack of bologna he could have eaten for a week.

I was on the first shuttle the next morning. My folks picked me up and we had a lovely day together. I set out at noon the next day on the 2,100-mile trip from

Phoenix to Columbia. I planned to take four days to get there. I drove only eight hours or so on day 1 as I got started late. From the motel I called Amy. Things were not going well in South Carolina. Amy and Ethan and the entire Berry family had a stomach flu. Amy did not ask me to hurry home but I felt compelled.

I started driving at 7 a.m. the next morning and did not stop, except to get gas, go to the bathroom and grab food every few hundred miles. I drove the 1,700 miles straight through in about 32 hours. In Alabama I was so tired that I bought and took No-Doz for the first and last time in my life. By the time I got to Augusta I was so jittery that I was unsure if I could get from the gas pedal to the brake pedal in a reasonable timeframe. Luckily it was good freeway roads and good weather all the way. When I arrived on the evening of day 3, I was so worn out I slept for 16 hours. I was of no use to anyone there. As hard as it would have been, I probably should have stuck with the 4-day driving plan.

[Note: I passed and was passed by a specific car several times while driving across Texas, Louisiana, Mississippi, and Alabama. The single male driver held a book on the steering wheel, obviously reading as he drove. I was able to see his progress as I passed him each time. Audio books seem like a safer option.]

Just Memories

During my teenage years, my Dad owned or co-owned a few ranches in Idaho. I was able to spend some or most of four consecutive summers in the little town of Carey, Idaho. With a population of about 500, it was a Mayberry of the West. Everyone knew everyone else. Any news traveled fast. It seemed like one person died unexpectedly each year. Life rotated around school and church and farming. I made great friends. The lifestyle was different enough from my now-suburban lifestyle that I cherished the differences. The sheriff was a deputy named Dude. If he caught a local youngster speeding, instead of issuing a ticket, he took their license and told their parents. A big night out was cruising main, which was a one-mile stretch with exactly zero lights and one stop sign. Sun Valley, with all its glitz, was 45 miles and worlds away. Kids drove legally at 14. I drove illegally at 14 since I was not an Idaho resident. My mom ended up coaching our young men's softball team for a while as our previous coach disappeared with his family in the middle of the night (the FBI was looking for him). I lost my car keys at the bottom of Silver Creek and miraculously found them at the bottom of the rushing creek with the use of goggles. Carey was like stepping back in time and I liked it a great deal.

A different friend from Mesa accompanied me to Idaho each summer. One friend, Darrell, agreed to help me meet a pretty girl one evening in Sun Valley while we were ice-skating. The plan was for Darrell and I to skate near her and for Darrell to bump me slightly into the girl so that I would be forced to make contact, apologize, and then strike up a conversation. Everything went according to plan until the 'slight' bump, which turned into a large shove. I knocked the girl and her three-year-old sister over. We went sprawling across the ice. I picked the girls up and apologized but the conversation never really got started as the pretty girl needed to tend the large bump on her little sister's head. Another friend, Pat, had never driven before. Once, I needed to get a tractor from point A to B at our ranch. After driving Pat to the tractor, I instructed Pat on the basics of driving our Chevy Suburban and jumped on the tractor. As we neared the house, I drove by the house on the tractor toward the barn and motioned Pat into the house driveway. He was going too fast, took the turn into the driveway on two wheels and finally came screeching to halt inches before hitting the garage. He explained later that a large roll of paper towels had rolled underneath the brake pedal. He stomped on the brakes with both feet until the paper towels finally yielded their shape. He did not drive again that summer.

The long trips between Arizona and Idaho and then from Arizona and Utah made for some unforgettable memories. As a young BYU student, the drive from Provo to Mesa usually started after school around 4 or 5 p.m. and ended bleary-eyed in Mesa at 3 or 4 a.m. On one such trip, a friend and I stopped for gas in southern Utah around midnight. I went around back of the gas station to the public bathroom and entered. In my tired state I didn't see a half-inch lip on the doorstep. I hit it as I stepped forward, tripping and falling at the same time. As I fell, my head hit squarely into the small of the back of a man who was standing at a urinal relieving himself. I crumpled to the ground and rolled away. He grunted and worked hard to maintain his position at the urinal. I don't remember much after that except that my friend and I laughed for the rest of the trip. On another trip from Idaho to Arizona when I was sixteen, two friends and I stopped for gas and snacks late at night in Salina, Utah. The attendant was fast asleep at a desk. We decided to have fun with it. We quietly gassed up, took a fan belt that I needed and an 8-track tape that I wanted and then calculated our bill. We then woke him abruptly, described our activities, paid him and left. We expected to see him sit up, embarrassed and determined not to let it happen again, but as we drove away we could see him lean back in his chair for another nap. Another friend and I were driving to Idaho in a roundabout way from California when we were 17. In the middle of the night in Nevada we decided we were too tired to drive any further that night. We pulled off with the intention of sleeping in sleeping bags in the bed of my pickup. As we exited the freeway there was a sign that gave the name of the road or exit. It was 'Devil's Gulch' or similar. We stopped for a minute, the hair stood up on our impressionable young arms, and we decided to drive on. We ended up stopping in a large town an hour to two later. I think it was Wells, Nevada. We were so tired that we stopped and parked in the first parking lot we saw and quickly went to sleep in the back of the pickup. We were awoken just before dawn by a police flashlight. We were in a bank parking lot and I guess we were not very welcome.

As a freshman at BYU, I had only been there for a few weeks when I got what I thought was a great idea. Several of us decided it would be good to travel to Mesa for our high school's Homecoming events. We were struggling to find enough seats in vehicles and enough money for gas to make the trip. My idea was to buy a used car, use it for the trip, and then sell it at some point in the future. I went to a local used car place and explained that I needed a cheap large car. He showed me cars in the $1,000 range. I clarified that it needed to be really cheap. He said he had a car or two in the $800 range. Still too expensive, I said. He then understood and took me to a car that he said I could have cheap as it didn't really run and he planned to scrap it later that day. Now we're talking, I thought. He sold me a 1969 baby blue Ford Station wagon for $120. Nine of us loaded it up a few days later and planned to head south. The wagon had its issues, to say the least. I liked that the key was replaced by a push button and that I could toggle a switch and the radio would get huge reverb. And it was huge. That's where the good stuff stopped. It got about 8 miles per gallon. It lost oil like it was allergic to it. And sometimes it would quit for no apparent reason. I replaced the battery, topped off all fluids and hit the road. We drove to Arizona, gassing up and singing and praying as we went. In Flagstaff, about 400 miles into the 600 mile one-way trip, I figured I'd add oil. I added five quarts before I got it to the right level. Anyone who knows cars is laughing or crying reading this. An engine only takes about 5 quarts. I had run it dry in 400 miles. I'm sure the pistons were screaming for relief. By the time we had returned to Provo, I had added 10 total quarts of oil and ran out of gas twice, both times literally as I rolled into a gas station. A week or two later I put in an ad in the classifieds to sell it. I gave full disclosure on the issues. I found a mechanic who was sure he could fix it and that he had found the bargain of the year. I sold him the wagon for $220. I saw it parked the next week in the Marriot Center parking lot, where it then sat for at least two months.

The mother of these Utah or Idaho to Arizona stories for me was in December of 1979. I had just finished my first semester at BYU and was eager to drive quickly home to Mesa for the holidays. I was traveling with twin girls from Mesa. They were sweet and good and naïve. We were in my pick up and it was full of luggage and other things. We left at 4 p.m. and hoped to get home around the 4 a.m. We knew a storm was dropping snow in southern Utah but knew it was planned to get worse. So we hoped to get through on bad but not horrible roads. In central Utah we hit the first of the storm. The paved roads soon behaved like iced-over dirt roads. On the 55 MPH road I was pressing my luck going 25. The snow was driving hard and visibility was poor. The drive to Kanab that usually took 4 hours took almost 8. My nerves were frazzled as we hit Kanab. We gassed up and ate. I was spent but we were so pleased that it was only raining in Kanab. I didn't really trust the twins to drive but, hey, it was only rain and I had to get a midnight nap in. So I asked one of the girls to drive the hour to Page, Arizona while I slept. She agreed. I got in the passenger seat and immediately fell sleep.

I was awoken about 30 minutes later by screams from the twins. I woke up just in time to see us drift off the road into a mildly-sloping ditch in the middle of a snowy winter wonderland between Kanab and Page. Anyone who knows the route know it's remote to an extreme. It was now 2 a.m. or so. Hmmm.

What to do? My rear-wheel-drive pickup got poor traction in snow. But I got out and tried for over an hour to dig enough snow out around the tires and replace it with a tarp and some dirt, hoping to get traction. Nothing worked. The snow was driving hard, visibility was poor, and the temperatures were in the 20's. I was actually getting quite concerned. The twins were an emotional wreck so I decided to keep calm. In the hour I worked on the back tires not a single car had come by in either direction. I decided that I would need to try to get help from the next car in any case. As I then continued working around the back tires, I looked up once and saw headlights coming the Page direction. They were a mile off. Since it was impossible to drive very fast in the conditions, I knew I had a few minutes so I put my head down again to work. I looked up a minute later to see taillights. That's when the entire experience began to get a little eerie. No one - I mean no one - turns around on the road between Page and Kanab at 2 in the morning in a snowstorm. Weird. So I went to work again. A minute later I looked up again to see headlights. This time I fixed on them and didn't let them out of my sight.

As the vehicle neared I got into the middle of the road and waved my arms. The driver of the Jeep stopped. I could tell he was a little drunk. His passenger was extremely drunk to the point of being incoherent. After explaining our situation the driver kindly agreed to help. The 4-wheel-drive Jeep would come in handy as pulling my pick up out would not be easy. He made his passenger move to get the tow chain that was under the passenger side seat. The buddy moaned and whined the whole time and I could see that he had wet himself. It all added to the

226

surreal atmosphere. The twins were beside themselves with fear and concern. It was while we were positioning the Jeep and attaching the chain that I understood the headlights, taillights, headlights story. The driver explained it in slurred speech, full of every curse imaginable and the occasional guffaw. He said he was driving along when they hit a patch of ice that spun them around. He got his bearings back and kept driving, only to see a sign a mile or two later that showed the mileage to Page, from whence he thought he was coming. That's when he knew he was going in the wrong direction and turned around again.

As I knelt near the front of my pickup I pondered exactly where to connect the chain. It would have been easy to hook it up to the bumper and much more difficult to attach it to the axle. I finally decided it was worth the effort to get to the axle so that took a few minutes. My hands were frozen solid. Now we were ready to get us out. In my pickup with him ready to go in his Jeep, I shouted for him to take up the slack of the chain. "Take up the slack" must have sounded a lot like "Hit it!" because that's what he did. He hit the gas hard. When he got the through the slack it jolted hard on us in the pickup. The Jeep's traction held and we literally bounced three times as we came out of the ravine and out onto the road. The girls again were screaming. I was so glad I had hooked to the axle. Hooked to the bumper, the Jeep would have pulled it right off.

Once we got the chain unhooked, I thanked the kind man over and over. We then drove slowly to Page. When we finally got to Flagstaff around 7 a.m. we were stopped by a wall of police on the freeway south of the city and informed that a freeway bridge has washed away north of Phoenix and that we had to turn around and go back to Flagstaff. So we drove the hours more in snow, detoured through Williams and Wickenburg and arrived home around 5 p.m. In the meantime a few people had been killed after driving their car into the river where the bridge had been. One incorrect news report had described the vehicle as a pickup so, by the time we arrived home, some loved ones wondered if we were dead.

Regrets

As far as I know, I have never done anything felonious. I generally try to be good in the Christian sense. And yet I have enough regrets to fill pages. They are almost all related to injuring the feelings of others to whom I should have been more kind. I remember having a birthday party as a six or seven year old. I received a gift of two used, tiny metal cars from a neighbor boy. As I recall, I quickly responded with something like, "These are dumb." or "I don't like these cars". That is the only thing I remember about that party. I wish I could take back that selfish, stupid line and so many more.

I occasionally wonder how much looking back with regret is healthy. I know that it helps my resolve to avoid similar issues in the future. But it also fills me with a melancholy feeling of being less than adequate and of having people that I like, or love, find me wanting. On balance, looking back at regrets feels more destructive than helpful. But I cannot forget.

In some cases I have sought out the people I offended to seek their forgiveness. In most cases I have not. For those who know me I am very sorry if I have disrespected you in any way.

Handcart Lessons

The handcart statue on Temple Square in Salt Lake City, Utah.

Introduction

The Mormon handcart saga has become an important, ingrained part of my life. While working for an American multi-national company near London, England in 1998, I was asked to teach early morning Seminary for the LDS branch in Addlestone, Surrey. I knew it would be a challenge. I'm not great at getting up early and our handicapped son, Ethan, also a Seminary student, needed to be dressed and readied for the day. But I took on the calling with the belief that I would be blessed to survive, and maybe even thrive. I grew to deeply love my ten high school students as we met for an hour Monday though Thursday morning at 6:00 a.m. in a cold porta-cabin behind our small chapel. We froze together, learned together, laughed plenty and had many powerful, spiritual experiences together. I found the course content - Church History and the Doctrine & Covenants - completely fascinating. We studied the origins and doctrines of the Church, the life of Joseph Smith and many other early pioneers.

As I pondered the significance of the sacrifice of the early Mormon pioneers day by day, I was deeply moved by their faith and testimony. While each chapter of church history intrigued me, the handcart pioneers, who had suffered such great loss, were of particular note. My fascination with the handcart companies was deepened by a family connection. The leader of the first handcart company was my great-great-grandfather, Edmund Lovell Ellsworth. The stories of the successes and the struggles of the five handcart companies of 1856 gripped me. I was so deeply affected and their sacrifices remained with me to such an extent that I penned a few poems about the handcart pioneers and the difficulties they endured. [Note: Looking back, I now realize that my method of understanding, memorializing, and coping with particularly meaningful experiences is to write poetry about them.] I don't remember the exact timing of the events in 1998 and 1999, but the few poems turned into several, then developed into a story line for a play, then musical notes and melodies that seemed to stream from somewhere else. Then came characters, stories and a structure of a musical. By the spring of 1999 I had the basics of a musical with original songs and meaning that people, whom I trusted, described as powerful, beautiful, and worth developing and sharing.

In the summer of 1999 we moved from England to the Washington, D.C. area where Amy delivered our preemie twin boys in January of 2000. Their care and the normal workload associated with four other, wonderful children and a profession, replaced most of our waking hours and sleeping hours and put the musical project on the back shelf. In 2001 we moved again, this time back to the ancestral home of Mesa, Arizona.

Then, in 2003, living back in Arizona and sensing a deeply rooted obligation to complete the musical, I re-launched the project. I realized that I needed help crafting complete songs - not just melodies - with piano accompaniment and classical structures, and later would need someone who could produce music and provide rich orchestrations. I was then blessed to find Mildred (Milli) West Wiseman Packard, a talented, experienced composer in Mesa. While I had hoped to find someone to help me craft harmonious, complete songs, I found much more in Milli. She provided invaluable help with music theory, shaping of melodies, crafting and editing of the lyrics, and even editing of the script and fine points of the English language.

Then, with completed songs and a desire to complete the soundtrack for the musical, and ultimately see it portrayed on stage, the next step required someone who could provide orchestral arrangements and also produce the creation of the soundtrack. Milli knew the right person and connected me to Randy Kartchner, an accomplished producer, composer and arranger living in Franklin, Tennessee, but originally from Mesa. Randy was able to take beautifully constructed piano sheet music and turn it into powerful, moving orchestral pieces. "1856" is a large, complex musical project which tested Randy's creative powers. Randy rose to the occasion and exceeded the wildest hopes that I had for the music. The final step in finalizing the soundtrack CD for release and also for the stage production was choosing and recording all the voices and live instruments. Randy worked nearly around the clock to see it through to completion, and also contributed some original music.

With regard to the script and flow of the musical, I turned to my niece, Tawnya Gray, for assistance with script improvement, character development and descriptions, stage directions, review of historical accuracy, a director's notebook, research on period costumes, language and activities.

With the soundtrack and script ready, "1856" was ready for the stage. The premiere production of

"1856" occurred in Mesa, Arizona in 2005. With Lisa Compton, a dear friend, directing an 80-person cast, five performances on the Mountain View High School stage brought the musical to life. Nearly 4,000 people came.

The next summer "1856" returned to the stage with me directing. This time the Arizona cast performed in Mesa at the Mesa Arts Center Ikeda Theatre and then at the Capitol Theatre in Salt Lake City. The 13 shows combined to attract more than 10,000 people and excellent reviews and audience feedback. Audiences spoke of the power of the music and the story. We were also invited by the Church to perform the songs of the show in a reader's theatre style production on Temple Square, which was a powerful experience.

The next year it was LDS stakes taking the stage with their own productions of "1856" The Musical. The first stake to produce it was the Colorado Spring North Stake in October of 2006. Their excellent, stake-unifying production played to a full house for each of their three shows. In the summer of 2007, the Grace, Idaho Stake did a great job and also played for full houses in their three performances. Finally, in July of 2007, the Parker, Colorado Stake did a marvelous job with their stage production of "1856". Each of the stakes performed superbly and added new interpretations. Stake leaders spoke of the power of the message and music and of the unifying power of the production in their stakes. Other stakes have used music from "1856" to prepare their youth for commemorative handcart treks.

Our core production company staged "1856" again in the summer of 2008. We returned to the Capitol Theatre in Salt Lake City and then finished up in Mesa. The cast size swelled to 170 and the quality of the acting, singing and dancing continued to mature. Sandy Stones of Mesa co-directed with me and added professionalism and experience that we had been lacking. Feedback suggests that we had truly hit our stride and that the fast-paced show was exceptionally powerful.

Nearly 30,000 people in four states have seen "1856" The Musical. Reviews and response have been extremely favorable. We have not staged "1856" since 2008 but the musical will play from time to time in accordance with the sentiments of the deceased but beloved LDS Prophet Gordon B. Hinckley, who in 2006 said about the handcart chapter, "What a story it is. It is filled with suffering and hunger and cold and death. It is replete with accounts of freezing rivers that had to be waded through; of howling blizzards; of the long, slow climb up Rocky Ridge...Hopefully it will be told again and again to remind future generations of the suffering and the faith of those who came before. Their faith is our inheritance." We hope to stage it in 2016 and then every five years thereafter.

My journey that began with handcart stories and very clear inspiration in 1998 has now matured and blessed many lives. It has certainly blessed me and my family. Not only have we been able to honor the handcart pioneers but we have also consistently felt the Holy Spirit, testified of the restoration of the gospel of Jesus Christ, and mingled with wonderful people who have become dear and trusted friends.

The stories and life lessons from the handcart saga have remained with me and serve as a continual reminder of the legacy I have inherited.

As we were in the latter stages of creation of the script and soundtrack, we found a few places in the musical that needed improvement or changing. One clear epiphany was that I needed a closing anthem that embodied the overall message of the musical. I pondered and prayed for the right inspiration. It finally arrived at the bottom of the Grand Canyon (Havasupai, actually) as I accompanied our LDS Ward's male youth on a hiking, camping and swimming outing. As I lay on my sleeping bag in the warm afternoon, the ideas and words flowed. In an hour or two I had finished most of the lyrics of the anthem. I had a similarly sweet experience as I sat at the piano a few days later and asked the question I had asked so many times before, "Heavenly Father, if this poem is a song, what does it sound like?" Again, after some thought, a melody flowed. Then with the help of Milli and Randy it was improved and honed. The anthem for "1856", "A Rescue Awaits Us", is my most heartfelt expression of belief:

"A Rescue Awaits Us"

This life is full of trials and the trail is lined with tears.
Our joy is mixed with sorrow as we face our doubts and fears.
The graves in lonely meadows and the aching in our hearts
Will turn to our salvation as we choose the better part.

The Savior who could quell the storms and stop the wind and rain
Allows life's raging torrents to discharge their grief and pain.
Of Saints who pulled their carts through sand, some lived while some died there,
But all became acquainted with his love and tender care.

To reach the peaceful valley, we rejoice along the way
With hope and trust in Jesus through each bright or bitter day.
With sacrifice and sweet submission, selfless charity,
The gospel's light will give us peace and teach humility.

CHORUS
A rescue awaits us though the journey may be long;
And if we bear it patiently in faith, and prayer and song,
With angels round about us leading gently, safely home,
Then Christ the Lord will welcome us and call our souls His own.

Christ the Lord will rescue us and call our souls His own!

My Favorite Review of "1856" – Based on the 2006 staging

1856! The Musical – a powerful account of the arduous handcart treks of Mormon pioneers

Posted by <u>Lawn Griffiths</u> on June 29, 2006 – 9:56 am

America's greatness can be told in innumerable stories of tenacity, courage and endurance. Groups of people with like ideas, such as the Mormons, created their place in the American fabric through their determination and unity. A prime example is the historic quest of the Mormon handcart companies, made up of families who put all their belongings on two-wheeled carts and trudged from a rail line in Iowa City, Iowa, across the plains and mountains to reach their Zion in the Salt Lake Valley of Utah. We took in this summers offering of 1856! The Musical that is being performed through June 30 at the Ikeda Theater at the Mesa Arts Center, 1 E. Main St. It's an amazing and powerful production that could be staged anywhere in America to convey the human spirit and offer yet another account of a religious group's struggles to find a place to practice their faith in the face of persecution. 1856!," with a cast of 140, is special on another level because it is wholly the creative work of Cory Ellsworth, a Mesan, who wrote the music and script, with help of professionals. It was first staged last summer at Mountain View High School in Mesa with a cast of 80. It especially resonated with members of the Church of Jesus Christ of Latter-day Saints who regard the handcart treks as part of their religious heritage. Of course, it comes on the 150th anniversary of that pioneer journey.

We saw the 2005 production, got the sound-track CD and have been playing it repeatedly for a year. So it was with great anticipation when we bought third-row tickets and watched the crisply delivered musical at Ikeda on June 28 (www.1856themusical.com). Smartly choreographed with the sweeping feeling of an epic event, 1856! comes at you with a full experience of what it must have been like to be uprooted and put through the hostile venture on a continent an ocean away. The program notes, Their story is Mormon legend and a national treasure. It is a story that has few rivals in western or American history.

Ellsworth, whose professional work has taken him far and wide, was teaching early morning seminary to teens in London in 1998 when, he said, he found time to ponder the significance of the early pioneers sacrifices and their faith and testimony. This deep respect and reverence soon resulted in his penning a few poems that led to lyrics, melodies, characters and a story line for a musical, he said.

Nearly 3,000 Mormons, many of them immigrants from England, chose to make the journey across the plains with simple handcarts because they lacked the financial means for oxen and wagons. The musical, with scenes set on the docks of England as well as along the American route, captures the deep themes of family bonds, weighing faith and doubt with perseverance and ultimate goals. The story offers a sharp contrast of handcart companies that got the jump on the weather and left Iowa City in order to arrive in Salt Lake well before the winter storms in the Rockies versus one that got off late and got trapped in the storms and lost loved ones. Strikingly moving is the account of how brethren left Salt Lake in November to rescue the distressed company and get them through the last hundreds of miles.

The most moving scene came when family after family watched a child die from the bitter cold, hunger and sickness. Five bodies of girls were laid side by side on the stage while the parents evoked their grief through imagining their hopes and dreams for their children. I couldn't help but think of the musicals creator Cory Ellsworth and his wife Amy whose own son Ben died last December in Argentina in a train accident while on his Mormon mission. So much promise lost. Cory, who directs the play, turns up inconspicuously in several scenes.

The cast is superb, the lighting and staging work are exquisite — and the finale with the full, large cast epitomizes what is great and unique about theater. The quality of the show makes it not surprising that the cast of 1856! The Musical heads to Salt Lake City to do five shows at the Capitol Theatre July 20-22 and 25-26 (www.arttix.org). My bet is this is a production that has legs and will be revived again and again as a piece of the American experience. Catch the show if you can.

The Handcart Legacy

When the Mormon Prophet Brigham Young first viewed the Salt Lake Valley he uttered, "This is the right place. Drive on." He and his small advance group of 142 men and three women drove their wagons into the valley on July 24, 1847 and founded a settlement that became Salt Lake City, Utah. The Latter-day Saints had traveled beyond the boundaries of the United States seeking a quiet place to practice their religion, away from the hostility they had faced in the East and in other countries.

After that small start, Mormon converts from the eastern United States and Europe trickled almost non-stop into Salt Lake and from there into vast areas of the West. From 1847 until 1869, when the continental railroad was completed, much of the journey was completed with wagons, carts and feet.

Nearly 300,000 people came West during those years - many seeking gold, land or a new life. Nearly 70,000 of those were Latter-Day Saint converts. Most of these Mormons were poor and made their way West with limited or borrowed means. Usually that meant becoming part of a wagon train, and driving a team of oxen or cows. Most of the pioneers walked along side the wagon since the wagon was primarily meant to carry supplies, tents and, occasionally, the sick or weak.

Of the roughly 70,000 Mormon pioneers in that period, some 3,000 - less than 5% - used a novel method of travel, the handcart. Much smaller than a traditional wagon, the handcart was meant to be pulled and pushed by people, not animals. The plan was the inspiration of Brigham Young. The key, known advantage was significantly lower cost. The hoped-for advantages, which indeed came to be, were quicker pace (by not having to deal with the care, feeding and management of animals), improved health, and a decreased number of deaths. In 1856, the first five handcart companies rolled west from Iowa City (the terminus of the train tracks from the East at that time) to Salt Lake via Winter Quarters/Council Bluffs, a trail of 1,300 miles.

The wildcards in such trips were weather and disease. While disease was a mostly unmanageable wildcard, the weather under which they toiled was more under the pioneers' control. They could choose when they traversed the long trail. The key to success was to walk the 1,300 miles during the summer months. The cart-pullers would be subjected to the summer heat and the sometimes-violent summer rains and thunderstorms but not to the more worrisome Fall and Winter ice and snow storms that can rage on the trail in Nebraska, Wyoming and Utah at altitudes of up to 9,000 feet. For groups that started in England, the ideal plan called for ship departure in March and departure from Iowa City with handcarts at the beginning of June. The 1,300 miles would require about four months to traverse, culminating in a late September or early October arrival in Salt Lake.

The members of the first three companies left England and Iowa City on time. Totaling about 1,000 people, their arrival in September and early October created a huge stir in the small and still-struggling Mormon community of about 6,000 people [Note: the population of SLC in 1860 was

8,236.] The travelers arrived in comparatively great shape with fewer deaths than previous wagon-based companies. Their success was heralded as salvation for the thousands of converts who still desired to come to their Zion in Salt Lake but who could not afford it. These early companies were met entering the Salt Lake Valley in Emigration Canyon by the local leadership of the Church including Brigham Young and a brass band. Brother Brigham's plan was working.

The emigration of European converts was under the management of Church leaders. They hired agents along the way and gave overall governance for the complex process of moving so many people across an ocean and a continent. One of the many practices they observed was not allowing travelers to embark from Iowa City too late in the season. But, in fact, there were handcart pioneers on the Plains later than desired. Two more companies totaling another 1,000 people, also mostly English converts, started later from England, got fitted out with wagons in Iowa City later, and commenced walking later than was prudent. Much has been written about why these Saints left Iowa City, or rather were allowed to leave, when the risk of weather-related trouble was obviously high. Their early August exodus meant walking until the end of November. Some Church leaders along the path knew about the late companies but Brigham did not learn of it until after the third company had arrived in Salt Lake in early October. On the eve of the Church's General Conference and only one day after the third handcart company arrived, he was informed by returning missionaries who had rushed past the late companies, that additional companies were still on the plains. The Prophet was at first stunned by the presence and sheer number of people on the plains who were at risk and he was also angry and confused at the breech of travel policy. After gathering his thoughts overnight, he used the General Conference of the Church as his platform to call for immediate rescue efforts. Rescue efforts commenced the next day, October 6, with rescuers and wagons heading east.

Early fall storms began in earnest on October 19, 1856. It turned out to be a very harsh fall and winter. The late companies were already short on rations and were dealing with poorly prepared carts. The terrible weather continued and eventually stopped them in their tracks on the high plains of Wyoming around October 23. The companies were a few hundred miles apart and both were in dire need of help. Camped, starving, dying of cold and disease, they were finally found by the rescuers. But nearly 200 of the 1,000 pioneers died. The suffering was unimaginable. Of the survivors many lost limbs or digits and many suffered from at least temporary delirium. The stories of these handcart pioneers are touching and inspirational. By all accounts it is fair to say that, if the rescue efforts had not been so timely and robust, many hundreds more would have died.

As the rescue teams hobbled into Salt Lake escorting and carrying the last companies in early December, the handcart plan euphoria from two months earlier turned to deep sadness. There was recognition by the Saints that they were contemporary with an event that was both tragic and awe-inspiring. Stories of the heroics, bravery, and faith of the walkers and the

rescuers began circulating the next day and have grown as the decades have passed.

Leaping forward, in 1997 the Church of Jesus Christ of Latter-Day Saints celebrated the sesquicentennial (150 years) of the arrival of the first Mormon pioneers in the Salt Lake Valley. The Church organized celebrations and remembrances all over the world. The official slogan was 'Faith in Every Footstep". It was accompanied by a logo that depicted a family bravely pulling and pushing a handcart. A handcart! When Brigham and the first group entered the valley in 1847 – the inspiration for the 1997 celebration - handcarts had nothing to do with that part of history - nothing at all. They entered the scene nine years later and exited the scene permanently four years after they began. Yet the handcart graced the emblem of the sesquicentennial. The stories of the handcart chapter are often mentioned in General Conference talks.

So what did the handcart pioneers and their rescuers do to deserve such attention? The handcart chapter is permanently etched into LDS history as perhaps the most important saga that ever played out since the 1830 founding of the Church. I compare it to the Pony Express. Just as the Pony Express developed into a romantic epitome of what Americans believe they are - bold, rugged, adventurous, task-oriented, daring - despite the fact that the Pony Express operated for only 15 months, so the handcart story epitomizes what is most dear to the heart of the dedicated Latter-Day Saint. The handcart saga features such faith, work, vision, and humanity and encourages such love, respect and awe that it can be held up as high as any other chapter in Mormon history in terms of dedication and sacrifice for a cause – that of the restored church and gospel of Jesus Christ.

And while the handcart story is an LDS story it is also a story that can evoke parochial feelings in any American, any person of faith, or indeed anyone struggling with the challenges of life since most of the lessons are generally inspiring and broadly applicable.

Long live the handcart legacy. It is truly an American and a Mormon treasure.

Edmund The Man

As mentioned, Edmund Lovell Ellsworth, my grandpa's grandpa, led the first handcart company across the plains. Edmund was born in 1819 in New York state. He encountered, studied and accepted Mormonism in 1839 and moved to the church's then-center of Nauvoo, Illinois. He was present and involved with most major church developments from the time of his baptism til his death, including the building up of Nauvoo and the Nauvoo Temple, the martyrdom of Joseph Smith and subsequent power shift to Brigham Young, the exodus and migration to Utah, the missionary effort abroad, the handcart chapter, settling the West, polygamy, imprisonment for polygamy, and, finally, the dedication of the Salt Lake Temple just months before he died.

Edmund served as a missionary in England from 1853-1856. Near the end of his mission he reported a recurring dream to his missionary companion. In it his father-in-law and prophet Brigham Young asked him if he would lead a handcart company across the plains. Weeks later he received a letter from Brigham asking him to do that very thing.

I am amazed by that experience. I love that he had the dream, that it came true, and that he was ready to commit to and fulfill the assignment. I picture him doing all he could to prepare the convert immigrants while in England and helping them all he could on the ship and on the train. I picture him preparing and patiently dealing with his handcart company. Several of the journals from the time record what were viewed as miraculous events that Edmund experienced. I like to envision him walking into Salt Lake with his weathered, happy company, being welcomed by the whole town and led by Brigham and a brass band. Wilford Woodruff, a counselor to Brigham and a future prophet, said, a few days later "When I saw brother Ellsworth come into this city covered with dust and drawing a handcart, I felt that he had gained greater honor than the riches of the world could bestow, and he looked better to me than he would have done had he been clothed with the most costly apparel that human ingenuity can produce. He looked better, I say, than a man adorned with jewels and finery of every description."

Edmund was asked to take two of the handcart girls as his third and fourth wives. One of those girls, Mary Ann Bates is my great-great-grandmother. Being a polygamist was difficult. Being a polygamous wife was likely much harder. Providing for four families was impossible.

Edmund built bridges, fought Indians, and was active politically and, of course, in the church. He ended up having 42 children, with his four families spread across Idaho, Utah and Arizona. He spent four months in the Yuma Territorial Prison for being a polygamist (Yuma High School's mascot is the Criminals because of the Prison heritage). He was essentially poor for his last few decades. He wished he could have provided better. More importantly, he wished he could see his loved ones more often. One letter to his first wife, the 'wife of his youth' as he described her, is heartbreaking in its tone.

Edmund, as an old man living in Arizona, was able to make the arduous journey to Utah to witness the dedication of the Salt Lake City Temple. The temple was 40 years in the making and cost immeasurable blood, sweat and tears. Having it in place and dedicated added credibility to the Mormons. It improved their spirits. It was a nice crowning event for Edmund. It seemed only appropriate that he could then go home and die. The cause for which he sacrificed so much was now on relatively solid footing.

Edmund is buried in a quiet, small cemetery outside of Show Low, Arizona. Rough math says he has well over 10,000 living descendants today. I am happy to be one of them.

THE HAND-CART MISSIONARIES OF 1856.

The original of this rare portrait belongs to Major Richard W. Young. It needs only a glance to tell that the men are a group of stalwarts. The picture was taken in England, in 1855, when the men composing the group were filling missions in Great Britain. The occasion of their coming together was to arrange a plan for dispatching emigrants from the Missouri river to the Salt Lake valley by hand-cart trains. All are now dead. The names of the eighteen men in the group are: Top row, left to right: Edmund Ellsworth, Joseph A. Young, William H. Kimball, George D. Grant, James Ferguson, James A. Little, Philemon Merrill. Second row: Edmund Bunker, Chauncey G. Webb, Franklin D. Richards, Daniel Spencer, Captain Dan Jones, Edward Martin. Third row: James Bond, Spicer Crandall, W. C. Dunbar, James Ross, and Daniel D. McArthur.

A short sketch of each, taken in part from an old copy of the Deseret News, will be interesting:

Edmund Ellsworth married Elizabeth, the oldest daughter of President Brigham Young. He assisted in the management of his father-in-law's business, and built the first flour mill in Soda Springs. He settled finally in Idaho.

250

Mary Ann Bates Ellsworth

My grandpa's grandma was born in Upton on Severn, Worcestershire, England in 1834. She joined the LDS Church in 1855 much to the disappointment of her family. She emigrated to the U.S. in 1856 and became a member of the Ellsworth Handcart Company. She helped pull the first handcart that ever entered the Salt Lake Valley. She became a plural wife to Edmund. They settled in Utah and then Arizona and never saw any of her English relatives again.

She lived a hard life. Edmund was often gone. She moved from the rough environs of Utah to an even rougher place in Arizona. She bore 13 children and raised 10 of them to adulthood.

She was firm in her adopted faith all of her life, never wavering in any way. She raised her family in that faith.

She is buried in the Mesa Cemetery, about five miles from where I live. I stand by her grave once or twice a year and think and speak out loud as though she was listening. I thank her for her faith and determination. Inevitably my chat with her turns into a prayer to my Heavenly Father. I thank Him for her and all those who paid such a terrible price to lay the foundation upon which I stand. I pray for strength to be worthy of their sacrifice and to be a strong-enough link in the chain of generations.

Susannah Stone Lloyd

Susannah Stone was a convert to the LDS Church in England and also became a handcart girl. She was a member of the Willie Company - think cold and tired and starving. She endured it well.

She wrote later, "We waded through the cold streams many times, but we murmured not, for our faith in God and our testimony of His work were supreme. Only once did my courage fail. One cold, dreary afternoon, my feet having been frosted, I felt that I could go no further, and withdrew a little from the company, and sat down to await the end, being somewhat in a stupor. After a time, I was aroused by a voice, which seemed as audible as anything could be, which spoke to my very soul of the promises and blessings I had received, and which would surely be fulfilled, and that I had a mission to perform in Zion. I received strength, and was filled with the Spirit of the Lord, and arose and traveled on with a light heart."

Susannah married a good man, raised 14 children and was strong and faithful in every way. She lived to be 94 years old. Her final comments about the handcart chapter were, "I am thankful that I was counted worthy to be a pioneer and a handcart girl. It prepared me to endure hard times in my future life. I often think of the songs we sang to encourage us on our toilsome journey. It was hard to endure, but the Lord gave us strength and courage."

Susannah Stone Lloyd

Susannah is the ancestor of my son-in-law, Camden

When Camden and Atley have children, some of Susannah's blood will be flowing through their veins. I like that.

[Note: One of the songs in the musical represents the dying words of a good man in a late handcart company. I believe it captures the heart of why good people like Susannah undertook this difficult journey and what they would have chosen as their legacy.]

"As The Angels Come For Me"

As the angels come for me
Father Dear, I beg of Thee
Bless my boys and let them live.
Grant them years to love and give.

Let them tell their precious ones
What in this time and place was done.
Let our faith, our hopes, our tears
Ring with power in their ears.

As I've reached the journey's end
I pray thy mercy to extend.
Bring me home with thee to stay
With my family, Lord I pray.

Be a Bulldog When It Matters Most

Reddick Allred volunteered to help rescue the handcart pioneers. He was 34 at the time and was a veteran of the Mormon Batallion. He departed the Valley on October 7th in company with about 50 men and 20 four-horse wagons hauling 10 tons of flour. When the first storms hit on October 19th Reddick was put in charge of the supplies of flour, some beef cattle, four wagons and 11 men to help guard the supplies. As the leaders of the rescue effort rightly assumed that the handcart pioneers would be in trouble and that the rescue effort would require plenty of resources spread across the trail, Reddick was placed at a location - South Pass in Wyoming - that was nearer to Salt Lake than it was to the furthest handcart company. Reddick held his position and expected to be of use when the advance rescue teams reached him with the struggling handcart groups.

Because the handcart Saints were much further back on the trail than most expected, and because the weather was problematic for the rescue teams as well as for the handcart companies, the rescuers found the handcart companies much later than expected. They made first contact with the Willie Company on October 24th while the Martin Company was not found until October 30th. At the time the first rescue teams met them, the Willie Company was about 300 miles from Salt Lake City and the Martin Company was still around 500 miles away.

Communication up and down the trail was practically non-existent under the conditions. The only possible method of sending messages was with a horse rider. But horses and riders were in short supply and were all needed in the rescue effort. Reddick and the other rescue workers who were positioned at South Pass began to wonder why no handcart pioneers had reached them yet. As the weather turned worse and the days went by, many of the would-be rescuers actually turned back towards Salt Lake, rationalizing that no straggling groups were coming their way, either because they had camped for the winter in Nebraska or somewhere else along the trail or had all perished. In hindsight it may seem wrong-minded or cowardly but, keeping in mind the horribly cold weather and idle time, it is not hard to conceive how even stout hearts would have concluded that they were on a hopeless mission which could even put themselves in peril if not aborted. Several turned back, leaving Reddick with a smaller team to provide help should the struggling pioneers actually appear. Reddick Allred was pressured by those leaving to do the same and abandon his post. He withstood the peer pressure and held his ground, setting himself up to either help with the rescue or, if there were no rescue to carry out, to appear a fool as he straggled back into Salt Lake City.

There was a rescue in progress. The first crippled group of handcart pioneers and rescuers reached Reddick at Rocky Ridge and then South Pass on October 25th. He helped every way he could, dispensing his food, offering encouragement and ably assisting that group and successive waves of stragglers until he then helped the last group limp into Salt Lake City. When the overall leader of the rescue effort, George D. Grant, arrived at South Pass with the last group, Reddick's efforts were somehow already known. When Grant saw Reddick he hailed him with "Hurrah for the Bulldog! Good for hanging on!"

Reddick, the Bulldog, arrived in Salt Lake City on November 30th, 1856, accompanying the last handcart company. He lost his toenails to frost but had stood his ground in the face of ridicule and personal danger.

We Are Our Brother's Keeper

Margaret Kirkwood was determined to gather to Zion in 1856. Her husband and son had died in 1852 and her 19-year-old son, Thomas, was handicapped and could not walk any distance. Robert was 21, James was 11 and Joseph was five. Margaret and Robert knew that they would shoulder the load of pulling the cart, which would include, not only the weight of their provisions, but Thomas as well. James was often responsible for Joseph.

The Kirkwoods were made part of the Willie Company. The pleasant path through Iowa and Nebraska turned for the worse in what is now central Wyoming. Clothing and rations were insufficient. After their rations had run out and the early snowstorms had arrived in late October of 1856, the company was struggling to survive. The advance rescue party arrived with a little food and a lot of encouragement. Still three to five people were buried in shallow graves each day. The few rescuers that now accompanied them pushed the suffering company along, knowing that sitting still would lead to more deaths.

On October 24th, the company took on a large task. They needed to hike 15 miles and could not stop short of their day's target (where water and firewood awaited them). That was a standard day's walk but by this time the company was emaciated with cold and starvation. The trek took them up a set of hills collectively known as Rocky Ridge. Unfortunately, on top of all that, a blizzard hit them in the face as they started their pull that day. The 15 miles, which normally took about six hours, now took at least twice that long for the fastest carts and up to 24 hours for the many stragglers. 15 of the company died within the next 24 hours as the result of Rocky Ridge. 13 are buried in a common grave - sacred ground in my opinion - at Rock Creek Hollow. Those who arrived earlier went back time and again to bring in struggling carts.

The Kirkwoods were not spared the difficulty. While Margaret and Robert pulled and Thomas tried not to freeze, James was given full responsibility for getting Joseph to camp. They lagged behind their own slow handcart. James did everything he could to encourage little Joseph, holding his hand, pulling him as necessary and speaking encouraging words. When Joseph could walk no more, James carried him, alternating positions - over his shoulders, then in his arms. After what must have seemed like forever, James saw the fires in the distance. Their mother was waiting for them. James had long stopped speaking, Joseph noted later. James brought his little brother into the Rock Creek Hollow camp and set him down gently near his mother. James then collapsed and passed away without a sound.

[Note: In the musical, a mother kneels at the side of her child's grave. That scene happened all too often in 1856.]

"A Mother's Voice"

This is a mother's voice,
Soft and sad and low,
Crying for this lovely child

Now gently laid below.
She was sick and she was cold;
Her eyes looked up to me.
I had no answer, no reply.
O, how can such things be?
I had such dreams for her.
Now she's gone away.
I will miss this lovely child.
God, keep her safe for me.

Ask and….. sometimes…… ye shall not receive

Stories of answered prayers are common and faith promoting. Heavenly Father loves His children and wants to answer their prayers. When He does we like to tell the stories. When He doesn't we often don't know how to explain it. We either don't talk about it or perhaps we wonder if we lacked faith.

The handcart chapter may seem to be a case of God not answering prayers. He could have stopped the October snowstorms but He didn't. Why? Does it imply that there is no God, that He didn't care, or that He was unhappy with the handcart companies or their leaders? I believe that none of these apply.

When our oldest son, Ethan, was diagnosed with Duchenne Muscular Dystrophy (DMD) in 1990 it was easily the most traumatic and difficult time of our young lives to that point. We were dazed and emotionally spent as we dealt with the diagnosis, tried to inform and console Ethan and our close relatives and dear friends, talk through the medical options, and gather our spiritual reserves to cope. One of the spiritual aspects of the ordeal was asking our Heavenly Father to heal Ethan, to take the disease away. We prayed and fasted. Many of our family members and ward friends did the same. We read every scripture we could find on healing, read inspirational stories of healings and petitioned God in faith for a miracle. We pronounced priesthood blessings upon his head.

Ethan was not healed. Prayers are not always answered in the way we like. But I believe they are always heard.

I did happen on one scripture that struck me with power. It is in reference to healing. It promised the Elders of the church that they could heal people unless those sick people were 'appointed unto death'. Our Ethan was not appointed to get well. He was appointed to struggle, to learn but also to teach. We were appointed to accompany him and support him.

Prayers are not always answered in the way we expect or desire. Our ways are not the Lord's ways. He knows what is best for us.

Be a Great Team Member

Levi Savage was returning from a 4-year mission to Siam (now Thailand). He met up with the emigrating European Saints at Council Bluffs, Iowa and attached himself to a handcart company.

He was present at a pivotal meeting where the last few companies were deciding whether to push forward to Salt Lake that year despite it being very late and the very real chance of hitting Fall storms, and waiting until the next Spring (which has its own risks as there was not sufficient lodging or food for so many people). As the group discussed the pros and cons, most were in favor of pressing forward and putting their faith in God. Levi asked if he could say a few words. In essence he said, "I share your enthusiasm, Brethren, and God has been good to us. But shall we not safely stay, recover our stamina, and go next year? Brothers and Sisters, wait until spring to make the journey. If we go now, we will likely have to wade in snow up to our knees and shovel at night, lay ourselves in a thin blanket, and lie on the frozen ground without a bed. Some of the strong may get through in case of bad weather; but the sick, elderly, and very young will be led like lambs to the slaughter. We are without wagons and destitute of clothing. The handcart system I do not condemn. I think it preferable to unbroken oxen and inexperienced teamsters. The lateness of the season is my only objection to leaving this point for the mountains at this time."

Rather than being thanked for his heartfelt, balanced comments, some of the leaders in the meeting scolded him for his lack of faith.

He then said, "Brothers and Sisters, all I have said I know to be true; but seeing you are to go forward, I will go with you, will help you all I can, will work with you, will rest with you, will suffer with you, and, if necessary, will die with you."

Brother Levi was then good to his word. As part of the ill-fated Willie Company, he did work and suffer with them. In the worst of the storms with death all around him, and even after the ordeal was over and all of the survivors were safely in Salt Lake City, there is no record of Levi expressing any 'I told you so' sentiment. And dozens in the surviving company recorded his strength and bravery as reasons why so many made it through.

The Cast of "1856" - My Other Family

We have staged "1856" in 2005, 2006, and 2008. I hope to stage again in 2016 and then every five years thereafter. We had about 80 people in the cast and crew in 2005, and 150 in 2006, and 200 in 2008. That makes about 400 people who have contributed heart and soul to 'my baby'. Words of gratitude always fall short of describing how I feel about those sweet people who have helped this story come to life on the stage. They feel like my family. I hug them when I see them. We embrace and look into each other's eyes with a knowing, comfortable, familiar look that speaks of shared, sacred, meaningful experiences.

1856 Cast 2006

Thank you, all you great and wonderful "1856ers". I am tied to you - and you to me - forever.

I look forward to expanding the size of the "1856" family in 2016 and beyond.

Do It Now

When Joseph Smith was martyred in 1844, the mantle of leadership for the struggling church fell to the Quorum of the Twelve Apostles, led by Brigham Young. Brigham's first major task was getting the 10,000 Saints out of the Nauvoo area, where they were under continued threat. The LDS left Nauvoo en masse in February of 1846 and trekked through the rain and mud of Iowa. They had hoped to get to the Rocky Mountains before the cold returned in the Fall of 1846 but that was not to be. They made it only to what is now the Omaha, Nebraska area, still 1,000 miles from their future home in the Great Salt Lake Basin. After a difficult winter, full of disease and death, they moved forward in 1847, the forward group arriving in the valley on July 24th. From then until the train connected the continent in 1869, Mormons of all kinds fought their way along the Mormon Trail, all determined to join with the prophet and the church in Utah.

Using handcarts was Brigham's idea. He felt certain that it would be cheaper and faster than wagons. He was right - as long as they started early enough to avoid weather. Brigham had left instructions for his leaders in England and along the trail about timing. So, when he learned on October 4th that there were still two large handcart companies on the Plains, his heart sank. But then he stood. The very next day, in the General Conference of the church, he said, "Brothers and Sisters, only yesterday we learned of a very serious matter. On this 5th day of October 1856, many of our brethren and sisters are still on the Plains with handcarts at least seven hundred miles away. They must be brought here. We must send assistance to them. That is my religion. That is the dictation of the Holy Ghost that I possess. It is to save the people. I shall call upon the bishops this day. I shall not wait until tomorrow or the next day for sixty good mule teams and twelve to fifteen wagons. I will tell you all that your faith, your religion and your profession of religion will never save one soul of you unless you carry out just such principles as I am now teaching you. Go and bring in those people on the plains and be as speedy as possible. I call upon the people immediately for the help that is needed. I want you to give your names this morning if you are ready to start the journey tomorrow. I want the sisters to fetch in blankets, skirts, stockings, shoes, hoods, winter bonnets, garments, and every description of clothing."

His mantra was consistent from October 5th to December 12th (the day the last stragglers came into Salt Lake City) - bring those people in from the Plains. He sent many of his own wagons. He scolded those who started East but who returned before finding the struggling companies. He wept openly as he visited with each company as they finally arrived.

Brigham sounded the alarm and mobilized a people when the winds were still warm and the storms weeks away. His actions saved something like 800 lives.

[Note: In "1856" The Musical I tried to capture what I believe Brigham's tone was, first, on the evening that he heard that there were still people out on the plains, and, then, the next day in General Conference. Here are the lyrics for those two songs:

"When Will The Sun Rise"

When will the sun rise? When will these tears dry?
When will this darkness give way to daylight?
In this trial and test, when can my heart rest?
When can I see sunrise?

When will the sun set? When will this day end?
When can these burdens leave me forever?
On this endless day,
When I see no way,
When will I see sunset?

We've come this far,
Led by a guiding star
And it has led us safely along to this Promised Land.
With heaven's help so near
We have no need to fear.
Now I see, patient be, while I wait for the sunrise

Sunset or sunrise, darkness or daylight,
Hope is our watchword, faith is our true friend
Come day or dark night, we'll work and we'll fight
Through sunset or sunrise.

"Who Will Go"

It wasn't long ago that we had crossed these plains;
And we have walked this path of trouble, grief and pain.
We've come to gather home and praise God's holy name.

And these dear faithful friends are surely just the same

Who will go? Who will stand and give his name?
Who will give? Who will part with goods and gain?
We are safe. We are warm. They are shivering in the storm.
We must go. We must give. We must bring them home.

MAN IN AUDIENCE

It wasn't days ago that I too crossed these plains;
I know these travelers by faces and by names.
I'm here and free from harm, but I will leave again
To save them from the storm and ease their grief and pain.

BRIGHAM   Who will go?
    MAN   I will go!
BRIGHAM   Who will stand and give his name?
    MAN   I give my name!
BRIGHAM   Who will give?
    MAN   I will give!
BRIGHAM   Who will part with goods and gain?
    MAN   With goods and gain!
BRIGHAM   We are safe. We are warm. They are shivering in the storm. We must go! We must give. We must bring them home.

BRIGHAM   Who will go?
    AUDIENCE   We will go!
BRIGHAM   Who will stand and give his name?
    AUDIENCE   We give our names!
BRIGHAM   Who will give?
    AUDIENCE   We will give!

BRIGHAM   Who will part with goods and gain?
          AUDIENCE   With goods and gain!
ALL   We are safe. We are warm. They are shivering in the storm.
We must go! We must give. We must bring them home.]

Joseph Paur, center middle as Brigham Young. Tom Larsen, front, as a willing rescuer.

Don't Break The Chain

Mary Goble was a 12 year old in the Hunt Wagon Company, which was assigned to follow the last handcart company. The wagon companies were hit with nearly the same issues of fatigue and reduced rations that their handcart friends experienced. Mary talked about her mother bearing a child along the way in a wagon. She tells that her baby sister died 12 days later 'for want of nourishment'. I cannot and do not want to imagine Mary's mother trying to nurse that baby girl, not being able to satisfy the baby with mother's milk as she was not eating enough food to produce milk, and then watching the baby die of starvation. Mary had her legs frozen and nearly lost them. Her mother died in the wagon just days before they arrived in Salt Lake. It was so cold and the company and rescuers all so spent that they did not even bother burying her until after they arrived in Salt Lake. Brigham Young wept when we pulled back the flap on their wagon.

Mary received a prophetic blessing that her frozen feet would improve and be healed. That promise came true. Mary went on to marry, raise a family and live a remarkable life. She is the grandmother of a beloved figure in the church, Marjorie Hinckley, who was the wife of the prophet Gordon B. Hinckley. Marjorie said of her grandmother, Mary Goble, "I know that day will come when I see her. How could I face her if I have not tried to build on the foundation she laid?

Recently I stood at the grave of my great-great-grandmother, Mary Ann Bates, in the Mesa, Arizona cemetery. She was born in England in 1834, converted to the Church as a teenager, and headed to Salt Lake City. She was a member of the first handcart company and later married the handcart captain, Edmund Ellsworth, who was my great-great-grandfather. Edmund was a true pioneer and never wavered. He served several months in a sweltering Yuma prison for being a polygamist. Mary Ann was faithful to the end and bore a strong testimony of the truthfulness of the gospel. Next to her grave are the graves of her son and his wife, George and Caroline Ellsworth. Next to them are their son, Frank Ellsworth, and his wife, Annie. They are my grandparents and held me as a baby and toddler. Frank served a mission in the Southern States. Annie grew up near London, England, converted to the Church as a teenager, was disowned by her family, came by ship to America to join the Saints, and never saw her family again. My father, also faithful, lies in a grave 10 miles from this cemetery, near my two deceased sons. I owe these good people something very special - my faith, my dedication, my work. They created a legacy of faith that is powerful and meaningful and serves as a guiding star for me.

Feelings of the Heart

In "1856" Sarah Parker is the mother of the family which is attached to a "late" handcart company. She is fictional but is a composite of several real women. In the musical she deals with a rebellious son and the death of multiple children. She does so with faith and determination. The women upon whose character she was based showed such strength. As I read their stories I know what I wanted my protagonist to be like. I wanted to include a song in the show that would serve as her anthem and would describe her resolve and her attitude.

I penned the words to the "Feelings of the Heart" and was given the melody. On stage the family is having supper and Sarah gathers her family around her at sunset and sings these words.

"Feelings of the Heart"

There's beauty in a sunset, and there's grandeur in a storm;
There's wonderment in mountaintops and when a child is born.
All these I see, and these are dear. Forbid that they not be,
But greater things that move my soul I cannot touch nor see.

Far greater than a summer rain His love flows over me;
More powerful than lightning bolts His grace has set me free.
The God who gave us flowers and asked the stars to do their part

Has kept his grandest beauties for the feelings of the heart;

Like warm breeze that gently blows through the trees
Wrapped in His holy arms I feel Him whisper peace.

Our God who gave us everything, who loved us from the start,
Has kept His grandest beauties for the feelings of the heart.

Jamie Kay Alston, who has portrayed Sarah for our production each time and whom I love like a daughter, has said that she wants this song sung at her funeral. So do I.

The Vault of Heaven

One of the women upon whom Sarah Parker is based is Elizabeth Horrocks Jackson. Aaron and Elizabeth and their three small children were part of the Martin Handcart Company. Once the storms arrived and the rations were reduced, Aaron faded fast and died next to Elizabeth in the tent. She moved forward. Members of the company were so weak one night that no one was able to pitch the tent. Elizabeth said, "The result was that we camped out with nothing but the vault of heaven for a roof, and the stars for companions. The snow lay several inches deep upon the ground. The night was bitterly cold. I sat down on a rock with one child in my lap and one on each side of me. In that condition I remained until morning."

In addition to being tired, weak and starved, she also became depressed. In that state she had a 'stunning' dream on the night of October 27. "In my dream, my husband stood by me and said, "Cheer up, Elizabeth, deliverance is at hand." The next day rescuers found them. The family was helped into the Salt Lake Valley and arrived on November 30, 1856.

Much later Elizabeth wrote: "I will not attempt to describe my feelings at finding myself thus left a widow with three children, under such excruciating circumstances. I cannot do it. But I believe the Recording Angel has inscribed in the archives above, and that my sufferings for the gospel's sake will be sanctified unto me for my good."

[Note: If you want to read stories of the handcart pioneers, I recommend 'Tell My Story Too' by Jolene Allphin.]

Joy in the Journey

Mary Murray Murdoch died on the plains of Nebraska on October 3, 1856. She was 73. Mary was called Wee Granny, 4'7" and less than 90 pounds. Mary converted to the LDS faith in Scotland at the age of 67. Her son John had converted earlier and emigrated to Utah. Mary was determined to gather and join John in Salt Lake City. John sent money for her passage.

Mary's little, old body gave out, even before hitting the early fall storms. Mary must have known that the odds were small that she could survive the entire journey.

Mary's legacy lies in her final words. Just before dying, she told friends, "Tell John I died with my face towards Zion." What a sermon is contained in those few words.

The Little Man in the Corner May Have Something to Say

Frances Webster and his wife were in the Martin Handcart Company. The story is told of an event from a Sunday School class many years later in southern Utah. Frances is the person referred to as the 'old man'.

"A teacher, conducting a class, said it was unwise ever to attempt, even to permit them [the Martin handcart company] to come across the plains under such conditions.

"[According to a class member,] some sharp criticism of the Church and its leaders was being indulged in for permitting any company of converts to venture across the plains with no more supplies or protection than a handcart caravan afforded.

"An old man in the corner ... sat silent and listened as long as he could stand it, then he arose and said things that no person who heard him will ever forget. His face was white with emotion, yet he spoke calmly, deliberately, but with great earnestness and sincerity.

"In substance [he] said, 'I ask you to stop this criticism. You are discussing a matter you know nothing about. Cold historic facts mean nothing here, for they give no proper interpretation of the questions involved. Mistake to send the Handcart Company out so late in the season? Yes. But I was in that company and my wife was in it and Sister Nellie Unthank whom you have cited was there, too.

We suffered beyond anything you can imagine and many died of exposure and starvation, but did you ever hear a survivor of that company utter a word of criticism? Not one of that company ever apostatized or left the Church, because everyone of us came through with the absolute knowledge that God lives for we became acquainted with him in our extremities.

"'I have pulled my handcart when I was so weak and weary from illness and lack of food that I could hardly put one foot ahead of the other. I have looked ahead and seen a patch of sand or a hill slope and I have said, I can go only that far and there I must give up, for I cannot pull the load through it.'" He continues: "'I have gone on to that sand and when I reached it, the cart began pushing me. I have looked back many times to see who was pushing my cart, but my eyes saw no one. I knew then that the angels of God were there.

"'Was I sorry that I chose to come by handcart? No. Neither then nor any minute of my life since. The price we paid to become acquainted with God was a privilege to pay, and I am thankful that I was privileged to come in the Martin Handcart Company.'"

Deal With Things As They Are

Nellie Unthank, referred to in the previous chapter, was actually Ellen Pucell as a little girl. Ellen's parents converted to Mormonism in England, emigrated in 1856 and were attached to the Martin Handcart Company.

The trek proved too much for Ellen's parents, who died five days apart during the winter storms in Wyoming. Ellen and her sister, Maggie, had their legs frozen. Maggie somehow managed to get to Salt Lake with the use of her legs intact. Ellen made it to Zion but her legs had to be crudely amputated just below the knee. One writer said, "When they took off her shoes and stockings the skin with pieces of flesh came off too. They strapped her to a board and without an anesthetic the surgery was performed. With a butcher knife and a carpenter's saw they cut the blackened limbs off. It was poor surgery, too, for the flesh was not brought over to cushion the ends of the stumps and in pain she waddled through the rest of her life on her knees."

Ellen, now Nellie, married William Unthank and raised six children in southern Utah. The same writer summarized, "In memory I recall her wrinkled forehead, her soft dark eyes that told of toil and pain and suffering, and the deep grooves that encircled the corners of her strong mouth. But in that face there was no trace of bitterness or railings at her fate. There was patience and serenity for in spite of her handicap she had earned her keep and justified her existence. She had given more to family, friends and to the world than she had received."

In Cedar City on the campus of Southern Utah University there is a statue of Nellie, honoring her courage and faith. The statue depicts her, not as an old woman on her stumps but as a young handcart girl with beautiful, flowing hair.

The Blue Angel

Of the rescuers who left Salt Lake to find and bring in the struggling handcart companies, my favorite might be Joseph Angell Young, the son of Brigham Young.

Joseph had just spent two years as a missionary in England and was returning home, accompanying the vast number of LDS converts who were making their way west in 1856. Joseph was part of a small group of returning missionaries and leaders, led by Franklin D. Richards, that zoomed past the late handcart companies in lightweight buggies, hurrying to Salt Lake to inform Brigham Young and to drum up support for a rescue effort. When Brigham asked for volunteers to head east immediately, Joseph was one of the first to volunteer. After all, he knew many of the pioneers personally and had taught and baptized some of them.

In the rescue corps, Joseph was assigned twice to head east in front of the small rescue teams as an advance scout to find the troubled companies. Then he was asked to ride back alone to Salt Lake to keep President Young apprised. Joseph put on three or four pairs of woolen socks, a pair of moccasins, and a pair of buffalo hide overshoes, and then said, "There, if my feet freeze with those on, they must stay frozen till I get to Salt Lake.

Joseph found the Martin Company in dire straits, with five or more deaths every day, all freezing and starving and the company stopped because of the harsh weather. One of the members of the Martin Handcart Company wrote this, "So apparent was the sentence of death written on the expression of some of the half starved men and boys who died, that I could tell how long they would stand the ordeal. One boy about my own age was walking up and down by a large grave I was helping to dig. I read in his face that he would be interred there unless we moved on before two days had passed - we stayed four - he was buried in that grave.

It was at this place that Joseph A. Young arrived as the leader of the express relief party sent from the valleys by President Brigham Young - he rode a white mule down a snow covered hill or dug way. The white mule was lost sight of on the white background of snow, and Joseph A. with his big blue soldier's overcoat, its large cape and skirts rising and falling with the motion of the mule, gave the appearance of a big blue winged angel flying to our rescue.

"The scene that presented itself on his arrival I shall never forget; women and men surrounded him, weeping and crying aloud; on their knees, holding to the skirts of his coat, as though afraid he would escape from their grasp and fly away. Joseph stood in their midst drawn up to his full height and gazed upon their upturned faces, his eyes full of tears. I, boy as I was, prayed 'God bless him.'"

Joseph wept as he saw the struggling companies, did all he could to encourage, and passed out the few rations he had.

Just Memories

There is power in visiting the sites connected with the handcart chapter. From Mormon Handcart Park in Iowa City to downtown Salt Lake City there are several places to visit that educate and inspire. About one site, the then-President of the LDS Church, Gordon B. Hinckley, said, "There isn't much to see here but there is a lot to feel". I say amen to that. Rock Creek Hollow in Wyoming is one of those sweet places. At least fifteen good people were buried there on one terrible, cold day in October of 1856.

Some church leaders have opined that, while we look at the handcart pioneers with love and deep respect, they would look at us with equal or greater respect for the challenges we face today. The inference is that today's struggles, which are less physical - things like pornography and the breakdown of healthy social mores - are more difficult. I get that. But every time I ponder deeply about the sacrifices made by the early members, especially when I am physically very cold, I am glad they did what they did and that it was not required of me.

I have so many great memories of the time we all committed to stage "1856". From 5:30 a.m. practices to late night rehearsals, so many people committed so much time. The shows are no less memorable. It seems every show had its own feel, from forgotten lines to powerful spiritual experiences.

Wheelchair Lessons

Ethan, our oldest, as a part-time missionary at the Mesa
Regional Family History Center.

Introduction

Amy and I have had six children together. Our order was boy, boy, girl, girl, wait a decade, then twin boys. We love each child more than we could ever express and each is a great soul. We have had our share of physical challenges with our children. When people learn our story they usually think we have had more than our share.

As I have said earlier, for my first twenty years, I never had a close family member die. There were no serious diseases in my family. Amy and I have not been as lucky in that way. Ethan, our oldest, suffered from Duchenne Muscular Dystrophy (DMD), and died at age 25. Ben, our only 'healthy' son, died at age 19 in a train accident in Rosario, Argentina while serving a two-year LDS mission. One of our daughters, Atley, is a carrier of the DMD gene and must, therefore, be very careful about how she and her husband, Camden, have children. Atley also has more than her share of aches and pains and some of those issues may be attributable to being a carrier. Our twin sons have DMD, are confined to wheelchairs and will live shortened lives. Our other daughter, Emily, while healthy, has had to watch and to deal with the emotional toll of seeing her brothers and sister suffer, cope and deal with tremendous challenges. That is also true of all the kids. They are all dealing with some version of PTSD (Post-Traumatic Stress Disorder) but the "P" could just as well stand for Perpetual in their cases since it seems ever-present and not going away anytime soon.

When the "Crosses" The Musical soundtrack was completed and the living kids all listened to it, Colby commented that it was sadder than our life really was. I reminded him that the staged play would have a lot more humor than the actual songs but I also got his point. He is right. We have moved forward day by day with plenty of light and laughter, even black humor when that was all that was available. The following pages will show that we have not moped or complained too much. We have certainly not cursed God - just the opposite.

The Diagnosis

It was a normal day at work. The sun was shining through the large window panels. I was involved in my normal routine of meetings, telephone calls and checking inventory and receivables reports. Business was good for NCR. The assets were in control and my career showed signs of promise. Things were good at work. They were even better at home. Amy and I had four lovely children and a solid, loving relationship. We were making a good enough living, we had many caring and cared-for friends in the neighborhood, at church and at work. For the most part, the Ohio summer skies were blue and the breezes were warm.

Early in the afternoon a dark cloud settled in for a long, long stay. As I picked up my ringing office telephone, Amy asked if I could come home. I greeted the out of character question with a, "Probably, but why?" "Dr. Jones, that specialist, called and he said that Ethan's blood test results came back and he says that Ethan probably has Muscular Dystrophy.

Hearing the quiver in her voice and feeling that I needed to be strong when her emotions were frail, I added, "Interesting. I'm sure it'll be OK. I'll come home right now". As I hung up the telephone, I did not yet comprehend the full impact of what we had just discussed. After all, how good was this doctor? How sure was his diagnosis? Other than Jerry Lewis, I didn't know anything about Muscular Dystrophy.

The fifteen-minute ride home was filled with anxiety and full of questions. The only thing that I fully understood was that Amy would need comforting and that Ethan was ill. As I walked through front door, Amy greeted me with tear-stained cheeks and a look on her face that I had seen a thousand times on TV in emergency operating waiting room scenes. She was emotionally spent and scared. I hugged her and held her tight as she cried. It was clear that, for the moment, she only wanted to be held. Her grief seemed so consummate that I was certain she had more information than I. She did. I noticed our blue medical book on the couch.

I had poked fun at Amy many times through the years for having that blue book in the house. It explained practically every sickness and disease known to mankind along with symptoms. It seemed that every time one of the children was sick, Amy, consulting the blue book, ascribed some awful disease to the child. She was seldom right but it never bothered me much as I saw it as an expression of her love and concern for each of the children. I often joked that she always had one of the kids' feet in the grave with that book.

After Amy cried and felt comforted enough to speak, I asked her to fill me in on what she knew. I don't remember the words exactly but, after the conversation, I felt assured that the doctor was capable and that the diagnosis was sound. I began to feel the weight she was carrying. Then we sat together as she led me to the correct page in the blue book and I read what she had read - the medical explanation of what Duchenne Muscular Dystrophy is. This is what I read; "Duchenne Muscular Dystrophy (DMD) is a severe recessive X-linked form of muscular dystrophy characterized by rapid progression of muscle degeneration, eventually leading to loss of ambulation and death. This affliction affects one in 3500 males, making it the most prevalent of muscular dystrophies. In general, only males are afflicted, though females can be carriers. Symptoms usually appear in male children before age 6 and may be visible in early infancy. Progressive proximal muscle weakness of the legs and pelvis associated with a loss of muscle mass is observed first. Eventually this weakness spreads to the arms, neck, and other areas. Early signs may include enlargement of calf muscles, low endurance, and difficulties in standing unaided or inability to ascend staircases. As the condition progresses, muscle tissue experiences wasting and is eventually replaced by fat and fibrotic tissue. By age 10, braces may be required to aid in walking but most patients are wheelchair dependent by age 12. Later symptoms may include abnormal bone development that lead to skeletal deformities, including curvature of the spine. Due to progressive deterioration of muscle, loss of movement occurs eventually leading to paralysis. Intellectual impairment may or may not be present but if present, does not progressively worsen as the child ages. The average life expectancy for patients afflicted with DMD varies from early teens to age mid 30s."

The weight increased and the cloud darkened. My mind raced. The volume of thoughts of past, present, and future generated by my mind was staggering.

When he was born he was so beautiful and strong. Not only was nothing wrong in those days, but he seemed perfect in every way. As a toddler his muscle structure was such that many people commented on his solid, muscled physique. Additionally, his cute, round face, light complexion, bright hazel eyes, and bright red hair made him a center of attention practically wherever he went. In those early years his development seemed right on track.

The first sign of any trouble, but not significant enough to worry about, we thought, came in his third year. We were living in Germany as part of my Master in International Business program. Our living arrangements - third floor with no elevator, using the subway or our feet for transportation - provided great opportunities for walking, especially up and down stairs. Ethan seemed to tire too easily and would occasionally balk at climbing stairs, especially when he was tired and had already walked a great deal. Amy and I occasionally wondered if he was too weak but quickly dismissed any concerns as stairs must be formidable for a little boy, there were no noticeable physical changes, and we did not have any other children to make a comparison.

When he was three, four and five, living in Ohio, we certainly realized that he was slower and slightly weaker that other children his age but, again, there were reasons to believe it was no major concern. He was alert, looked strong, had good hand-eye coordination, and was intelligent. He just ran slowly. And we hoped he would catch up. We reasoned that kids grow and progress in spurts.

By the time he was six and seven, still in Ohio, he was even slower by comparison. He was by far the slowest in this class and he could not jump vertically. We were fairly certain that something was wrong, but had no idea what. He still looked OK. His calves, especially, looked strong. At check-ups, the family doctor could offer no help. Amy and I knew in our hearts that something was wrong although we seldom discussed it. Looking back, I believe our rationale must have been that if we avoided his health issue, it might go away.

Amy had recently demanded that our family doctor refer us to a specialist. It was he who rendered the verdict – Muscular Dystrophy. Thoughts of the future flooded in on us. How much pain would Ethan have to bear? How would he deal with it? When would he be confined to a wheel chair? How would he react to a wheelchair? Other thoughts were noble and, I believe, heartfelt. We sincerely wished we could take this away from him. We wanted to ease his burden. We would have sacrificed our lives and health for him.

As a high school student, I had studied Elizabeth Kubler Ross' "On Death and Dying" and knew that we should have been saying, "It can't be!" or "Why him?" or "Why would God let this happen?" Strangely, I felt no anger and did not wonder why Ethan should go through this. I believe that there is a God who loves us, who wants the best for us but who is ultimately interested in our personal progression. For that reason, He allows us to stumble, suffer and fight through the variety of crosses we have to bear.

As I pondered the situation and sorted through my feelings, they crystallized and dwelt on one thing only - deep love and sympathy for my son on his journey. I wished I could take his place. I wished I could ease all future suffering. I wished I could hold him and never let him go.

During those first few hours of that afternoon of August 8th, 1990 a dark, thick, sickening, suffocating cloud settled over our home and our lives. At that moment, it seemed that the cloud would never lift.

Crosses

'Crosses' The Musical is my attempt at explaining some of the emotions of losing children as seen from the father's, mother's, and children's views. It is also intended to educate and inspire others who are dealing with difficult family health issues. I felt providentially inspired in the creation of the story and the lyrics. The story mimics our own life in many ways but not nearly all. I feel strongly that Randy Kartchner, who orchestrated "1856" The Musical also, was deeply inspired in the creation of the tune and music for each song. You will be the judge of both lyrics and music.

I will go a little deeper in these pages on some of those emotions as there is only so much one can do in a two hour staged play. On the other hand, there is power and emotion brought to bear through the use of music that cannot be replicated in prose so perhaps it's good that that I combine the musical with these thoughts.

I will follow the rough flow of the musical in my thoughts here. The overarching message that I am trying to send with Crosses is that, although bad and hard things happen to everyone, each person has the opportunity to deal with life's hardships in a way that will allow for happiness and fulfillment. It is a choice. It is seldom easy. Just getting out of bed and not harming yourself may be a victory on some days. But life can also be sweet, even in the face of heartbreak.

The Responsibility of Fatherhood

Soon after my mission I met and fell in love with Amy in the summer of 1981. I am still deeply in love. While romantic passion goes in spurts and wanes over the years, my love and respect for her have grown in so many ways. I have watched her weather many of life's hardest experiences with grace.

I loved Amy's face, her form, her laugh, her way (and I still love all those things). She was guileless. She played the piano and sang beautifully. And, most importantly, it felt very right. Depending on who is telling the story, we either got engaged after three days or three months. An 18-year-old Amy went home after our first date and told her mother that I was the man she would marry. On the third date, which was the third day, we talked openly about how we were 'done' as in done looking and committed to marry. I remember being surprised that it happened that way for both of us. We decided to keep it between us for a while, as we would both look silly to the outside world. It wasn't until October 2, six weeks into the courtship, that we made it official with a ring.

During all of that, I don't recall being scared. Perhaps I should have been. A young lady would take my name and be very dependent on me. I had no education although I was working on it. I had no money and no savings and was dependent on my parents' good graces and a great but low-paying job. But I had no fear, only excitement.

I contrast that with learning, about six months later, that Amy was pregnant and that we would become parents in March of 1983. I was scared and felt immense pressure. The idea of being responsible for feeding and teaching our own child was awesome. Our LDS theology teaches that each person is a spiritual child of God. Therefore we were inheriting our spirit brother or sister as a child with the inherent task of raising that precious person the way God would want us to. That added to the pressure.

The fear and pressure only lessened a little over the years. When we raised Ethan the first few months without him passing away, that helped. When he responded to basic teaching, that helped. Now, after 30 years of parenting and six children, I still feel the pressure. I count it as the greatest responsibility I will ever take on. A great LDS leader once said, "No other success can compensate for failure in the home". I believe that.

In the Musical I include the two consecutive songs that describe my feelings about being a father and provider. Here are the lyrics:

"Overflowing"

Can the coast be any clearer? Can the scene be more secure?
Can the road be any smoother? Or the pathway be more sure?

A home, a job, friends and family, little boys and gentle wife.
A family so full of promise. I am loving this sweet life.

Glass half empty? Not for me. Mine is full as it can be.
Overflowing happy. Overflowing that's me.

Can the coast be any clearer? Can the scene be more secure?
Can the road be any smoother? Or the pathway....
Can it be, can it be more sure?

"Let Me Not Lose My Own"

I could praise this glorious day.
I should stand and shout hurray.
Ideally life looks this way.
Why then do I stop to pray?

Caring for these little ones
Has my heart and brain undone.
Can we feed and clothe and care,
Protect and teach this little pair?

Knees buckle, body quakes,
Muscles weaken, heart aches.
Let us not, Lord, fail these few
Souls that we received from you.

Never have we walked this road.
Atlas bore no greater load.
My good wife and I plead now.
Teach us patience, teach us how.

Knees buckle, body quakes,
Muscles weaken, heart aches.
We cannot do this alone.
Let us not, Lord, lose our own.

Take It From Him

When we learned that Ethan was sick and when we learned, many years later, that the twins were sick, we were heartbroken. We were stunned. We sincerely wished we could take it away and would have swapped with them. Which parent wouldn't?

In 'Crosses' I captured one of my emotions in the song, 'Can This Be?' Earlier in the musical the song 'Behold This Boy' captures my dreams for my firstborn son. Contrasting those two songs below will give you an idea of what I was feeling.

"Behold This Boy"

Behold this boy, this daddy's boy!
He'll be my life and pride and joy!
Something great awaits this lad.
And when it comes, he'll thank his Dad.
He'll be like BamBam or Hercules.
He'll prob'ly cure some dread disease.
Maybe a lineman, I don't know,
He might have his own fishing show.
Boy scout, pilot, brave Marine,
Tall and handsome, just like me!
Oozing pure testosterone,
Our son, our child, our very own.

Beth:
Look what we and God have done.
Tiny, helpless, little one.
To be held and loved and fed.
Sheltered, taught and gently led.
He'll be good to everyone.
A kind, respectful, perfect son.

Not too shy and not too loud.
He'll always make his mama proud.
Healthy, strong and full of life,
He'll find his way and find a wife.
Raise a family, find true joy.
That's the plan for this dear boy.

Davey: OK, he can hug and kiss his Mom.
And hug me too… but not too long.
Beth: And he can join the football team
… if his room is mostly clean.
Both: protect his family, confront his fears.
Laugh a lot, and shed some tears.
Make us equal to this test.
Our boy, our child, deserves the best.

"Can This Be?"

Can this be? Am I awake?
My racing heart is bound to break
Dearest boy, dearest boy
Our hope, our life, our greatest joy

No Marines, no family
Am I awake? Oh, can this be?
Shattered dreams, numbing fear
Like a nightmare looming near

Is there a reason for this thing?
Did we or he do something wrong?
It makes no sense. It can't be so.
Perhaps the "why" we'll never know.

This we know, the dreams are gone
And yet we must somehow go on

Darkness, sadness everywhere
I hope not more than we can bear

Amy, the purer and better of the two of us, earned having the song 'Take It From Him' written for her character in the musical. She wished so badly that she could take it away and take it upon her.

"Take it From Him"

I believe that you are there
And that you love and watch and care
I am trying to be good
And do the things I know I should

I don't know why this test came
I'll not ask why or call you names
You may not honor this, my plea
And yet I have to ask. Oh please

Take it from him. Take it away.
Can't we erase this awful day?
Oh, that he were healthy now
I'd sacrifice it all, I vow.

Take it from him. Give it to me.
Take me now but let him be.
I would crawl right in the grave
If, by dying, he'd be saved

Well, that is how I truly feel.
You do with it what you will.
I'll be back tomorrow then
To ask the same thing once again.

In It For The Long Haul

Once the fog lifted we vowed to do everything we could with and for Ethan. What else could we do? The song below captures our feelings and was precisely what we tried to do through the years.

"We Will Walk With Him"

While he is a little boy, yes, we will play and sing with him.
Oh, the good times we will have and, oh, the smiles and glee.
All the places we will go and all the sights we'll see
Glad to be a family, yes, we will play and sing with him.

When he can no longer run, yes, we will slow and walk with him.
Simpler toys and slower games and breaks along the way.
Happy days and busy nights all filled with measured play,
Pleased that we're still going strong, yes, we will slow and walk with him.

When he falls and stands no more, yes, we will hold and carry him.
Roll his chair and comb his hair and shield him from the rain.
Find the good and marvelous and try to share the pain.
We will show him this great world, yes, we will hold and carry him

When he cannot reach his mouth, yes, we will hold his spoon for him.
Dress him, help him, brush his teeth, and do what must be done.
Pray that there are peaceful days and still some time for fun.
We will be there, day and night, yes, we will hold his spoon for him.

When his lungs no longer breathe, yes, we will stop and bury him.
Glad to share his precious life and have him for so long.
Glad we played and seized the day and sang our little song.
Now and then, start to end, we will love and care for him.

People are Good

One of the epiphanies we had was that people are very good. We so often hear the opposite, 'kids can be cruel' or 'people can be so mean'. While I suppose those things can be true we were pleasantly surprised at how positively people reacted to Ethan and his struggles. The poem below was from a real experience. It was awesome!

"Folks Are Good"

He couldn't catch and couldn't run although he did look good.
It's T-ball time, he's five years old, he joined just like he should.
The kids might tease and poke and jeer, their parents just as bad.
We feared for him, they'll tear him up and leave a broken lad.

Sure enough from game to game, the kids and fans saw that
My boy was weak and very slow, could barely swing a bat.
We braced and watched and feared the worst and then the words rang out-
Not words that tore or broke or cut but cheers from round about

Come on, Ethan. Come on, boy. Hey, you can make the play.
Hang in there. We're here for you and we think you're OK.
There! You hit it! Run, run, run! I'll bet you beat that ball!

Oh, so close! Well, that's OK. We know you gave your all.

We were dumbstruck and felt bad that we had feared the worst.
The kids were great, their parents too. So happy I could burst.
Folks are good, the message came and rang both clear and loud.
There is goodness in each heart and goodness in the crowd.

In the last game he reached base, mistakes let him aboard.
And you might have thought he'd won the game, the way the dugout roared.
Then second, third and finally home. They mobbed my little boy.
And cheers rang out from every one while I just cried for joy.

That scene repeats from time to time, and folks always come through.
It's not just him they're cheering for. They'd do the same for you,
Cuz folks are good and want the best and they will help and cheer.
Yes, folks are good, the lesson's learned. I got it loud and clear.

The Grind

Despite our love for Ethan and our commitment to help him live a great life, it was really hard. For example, for the last several years of his life he sat uncomfortably in his wheelchair. His hips were uneven due to a partially botched spine surgery. As a result he asked for a 'hip shove' every few minutes. At night he needed adjusted or flipped or something scratched every hour or so. Throughout Ethan's life Amy and I were the only caregivers 99% of the time so were constantly tired. Ethan was not always pleasant. That led to me penning this poem.

"It's Not Like in the Movies"

Every tragic movie starts with someone sweet and fair-
Talent, beauty, teeth so white and flowing golden hair.
Family, friends and life is good, then sickness lays them low.
The golden one confronts disease and ends up as hero.

He or she is brave and true and valiant to the end.
And they earn their angel's wings. The script perfectly penned.
Wavering and weak-kneed flaws are strictly not allowed.
Formulaic Hollywood and Greeks must be so proud.

It's not like in the movies in a three-part tragedy.
Glamour runs and drama hides when enters dread disease.

Patience wanes and tempers flare, regrettable lines ensue.
Seldom easy, seldom fun when loved ones fade from view.

Endless doctors, drugs, delays in serial nightmare,
Episodic rays of hope are crushed by raw despair.
It's not like in the movies, no Brian Piccolo.
We're sadly in the credits of an awful horror show.

Depression or Something Like It

The first several weeks after Ben died were the hardest of our lives. As hard as learning about Ethan's or the twins' diagnoses was, we still have them with us. Ben was gone to the next life in an instant. Whereas watching Ethan live and die was like the death of a thousand cuts, Ben's death was like one massive, crushing death. It took our breath away and nearly paralyzed us.

In the song, "Stop This Now", in the musical, I used an analogy that I believe works well. In life I have had my share of really bad days. But, as bad as some were, I always felt lessened anxiety or sadness after a night's sleep, even if it was fitful. That streak ended with Ben's death. After a night's sleep, Amy and I would awake to an immediate remembrance of his passing and the acute sadness associated with it. It piled on from day to day.

That is the definition of depression for me - when a night's sleep does not lessen the pain.

"Stop This"

Stop this now.
No more pain.
No more awful, endless rain.
You go on but I'll remain.
I'm stepping off this hell-bound train.

Downs have ups, so they say.
They are wrong.
The downs just stay.

The game is over.
I won't play.
Leave me here and go away.

And every time that I awake,
Expecting peace as morning breaks
The sun just sneers and looks away
And leaves the weight of many days.

Such gloom is wrong, such primal ache.
The heart will give but then will break.
Let me loose.
Let me go.
Lock the door and close the show.

On a more hopeful note, life does go on. Time does have a way of helping and then healing. There comes a day when you wake up and your son's death is not the first, or, perhaps, even second thing that comes to your thoughts. It gets better. You do not love or miss him less but you learn to move through your sadness. As I write this Ben has been gone almost eight years. In ways his death seems like yesterday. It is always more fresh and more painful than I would have expected. But, in other ways, it seems like a few years ago. Our faith is bright. We expect to see Ben and Ethan again and it will be a happy time.

If you are in a position - due to the cards you have been dealt - that morning brings no relief from pain, please hang in there. A less dark day will come. Then a neutral day will appear, and then even a bright day.

Amy

I don't believe that I can adequately describe my love for Amy. From our first few dates, I have loved Amy romantically. But, in addition to romantic love, other forms of love develop that deepen and, in some ways, supersede, romance.

As odd as it may seem, a military analogy may be helpful here. Amy and I have been in the infantry together in a hostile place. We have been in the foxhole of life together. We have dug the foxhole and hunkered down in it when the enemy fire was heavy and shrapnel was flying around. She covered me and I covered her when one of us had to leave the trench for a minute or two. She never opted out, never surrendered with a white flag. I came back from the war having witnessed Amy's behavior on the front lines. I can only bow my head with deep respect when I ponder her battle record.

One of my favorite books is 'To Kill A Mockingbird'. In one scene, the father, Atticus Finch, is defending an innocent black man on serious charges. He performs nobly but unsuccessfully in a very trying situation. Several black people from the town watched the proceedings from the balcony (they were unwelcome in the courtroom in those days in the south) along with Atticus' two children. After the case was lost, everyone streamed from the courtroom except Atticus, who was sad and thoughtful, and the blacks and the children in the loft. Atticus seemed unaware that he was being watched from above. As Atticus finally slowly left the room, the blacks all stood in respect. Atticus' daughter, Scout, or Jean Louise, was too young to fully understand the situation and had not stood up. A kind, older black gentleman prodded her to stand with these words, "Miss Jean Louise, stand up. Your father's passin'."

Atticus earned that. Amy has earned it as well.

"The Woman I Love"

Given me in marriage, she was young and sweet and dear.
Full of dreams inviolate, the path was bright and clear.
Raise a family, love her husband, laugh along the way,
Stumble here, struggle there, but sing and dance and play

Given stones when bread was asked, or so it seemed to be.
Children, loved and beautiful, who suffer endlessly.
Murmur, question, cry a stream, then humbly let it be.
God be God, and she His child eternally.

Inhumane the sufferings be that God allows to rage.
Our reaction to these plagues will make us foul or sage.
Being so, my love has won the battle to be wise.
When the angels come for her she'll rise into the skies.

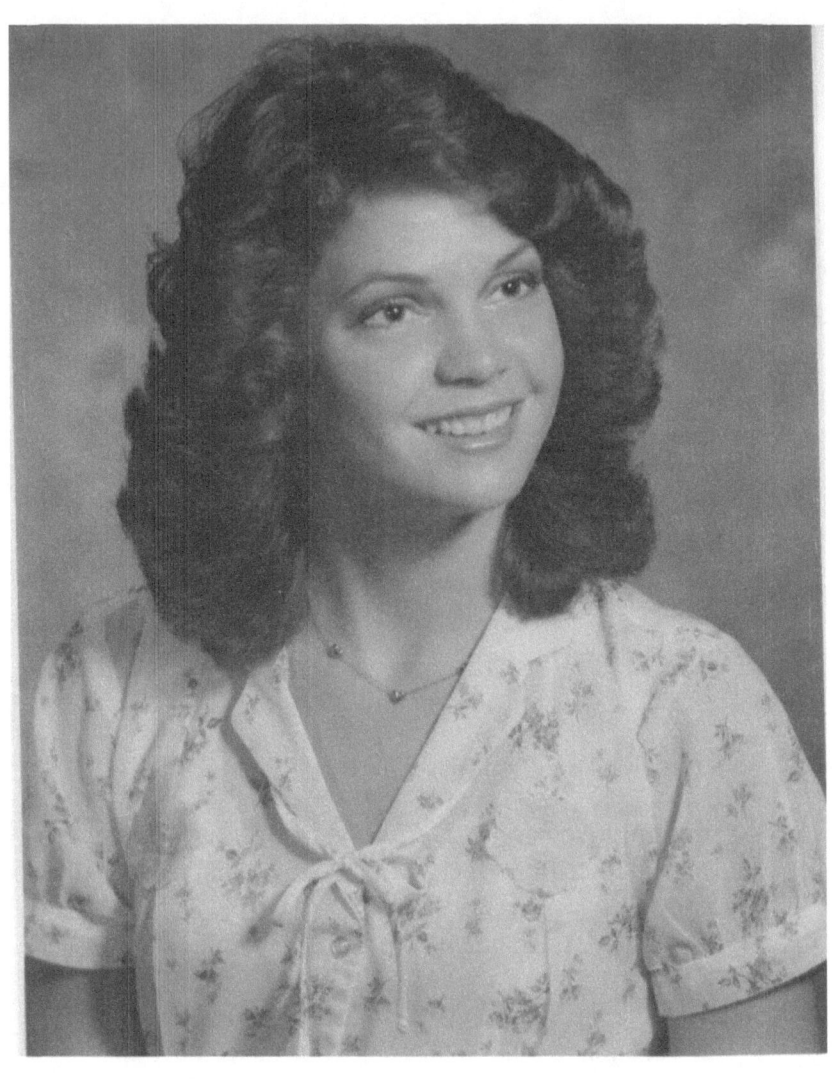

Amy's high school graduation. May 1981

With our grandson, Benjamin Nicoll. 2013

Roses

The following poem reflects how we feel about having had our boys for as long as we did in this life. The poem neglects an even more powerful and important issue and truth - that of the next, eternal life. But I find solace in the message of this poem and song.

"A Rose" (a mother about her fallen son)

Settled in a bed of brown,
Nestled into fertile ground,
Nourished, watered, loved and lit
The rosebush gives its magic gift,

Springs the rose! And all who see
Admire its brilliance, majesty.
Nature's awesome love display!
My rose shines for all its days.

Alas, the days move quickly on.
My rose was here but now is gone.
The petals fall, its time has passed.
Loved and lovely, but gone at last.

Worth the effort! Worth the loss!
Beauty - timeless - worth the cost.
Even now the memory sweet.
I had a rose that bloomed for me.

Uncommon and Wise Perspective

During the creative process of Crosses, I found that it made most sense to have only four characters in the play - Mom, Dad, MD son, healthy son. Since it is mostly autobiographical, it might have made sense to include sisters and more brothers. As the musical took shape I decided that I could make almost all of the points I needed to make with just the four characters.

Since I wanted to stay mostly true to our real emotions and experiences I was put in the position of having to assume or guess or create words and emotions for Amy, Ethan, and Ben. I did so prayerfully. It was not a blank slate. I had, after all, been with Amy though everything. I had listened to her and observed her. The same was true for the boys.

For Ethan I needed to create lyrics that would capture how Ethan felt right at the end of his life. I crafted lyrics and adjusted here and there until it felt like what I thought Ethan would have to say. A few months before he died, Amy and I presented him with the lyrics. I told him I would adjust anything that he thought incorrectly portrayed his feelings. It was an emotional time with our dear boy. Through tears he told us that these were EXACTLY his feelings as he prepared to die. So, below, are some of Ethan's dying sentiments (the last paragraph is the parent's response).

"I Walked"

I had…..
A thousand dreams and maybe two.
And some might that think that none of them have yet come true.
It isn't so. It seems to me
That life is more than bucket lists I've come to see.

I walked alone, I even ran (well, kind of).
I stood and fell and stood again, just like a man.
So thankful for the peace I've known
And for the precious loving ones I call my own.

I saw this life through my own lens.
It wasn't bad, and not so sad, and now it ends.
With few regrets and fewer fears
I'll miss you both, I'll see you soon, now dry your tears.

(Parents sing)
Goodbye for now, you precious one.
Oh what a gift to have and hold you as our son.
We seal you up to God above
And send you there with loving care and all our love.

Joy and Pain

The analogy in the song, "Joy and Pain" is one that I have seen played out with babies numerous times. A tranquil baby, lying on the floor, is approached by a sibling or other loved one, who engages the baby in games of one kind or another. The baby laughs and squeals. After a while the baby is over stimulated or overly tired or even hurt and begins to wail. The parent intervenes, comforting the baby and restoring order and thinking, "If we had left the baby alone everything would still be OK."

I apply that to all of us in life. Would life be better if the hills were low and the valleys not very deep? We would never know the exhilaration of climbing to the pinnacle of a large mountain or the danger of working our way through a dangerous valley. One opposite, say joy, could never be understood, if one had not experienced its counterpart, agony.

"Joy and Pain"

Precious baby lies content not wanting any more.
Brother comes to tickle him and roll upon the floor.
Giggle follows giggle, our baby's all aglow.
Playtime ends. Brother turns to go.

Baby's stimulation ends. He quickly wonders why
No one there to entertain, he screams and wails and cries.
Was the baby better off in peace upon the ground?
Or giggling then crying out in one eternal round?

Why is pain so close to joy? Why does happy walk with sad?

Why are mountain peaks near valleys? Why do castles turn to sand?
Even out the landscape, Lord, it's not so hard a task.
What's that you say? OK, I know. I just thought I would ask.

Stand

There are a few words that are more important than others. 'Remember 'is an important word. Another word I have come to believe is as important as any word is 'stand'.

In the days after Ben died, loving friends and family helped us in so many ways. The help was deeply appreciated. But I also became aware that those earthly angelic helpers were also watching our family and especially Amy and me. How would we respond? Were we angry or depressed? Would we be able to attend the funeral, let alone speak at it?

I recall a strange emotion overpowering me in those days. It was one of a sacred obligation to stand and represent and be. I felt that Ben would want me to practice and be loyal to the truths we had been taught and believed as it pertained to trials and the purpose of life. I knew my family was looking to me to do the same. I knew it was time to walk the talk. And, luckily, I did not have to fake any of that.

As I stood to address the large audience at Ben's funeral, I felt like, in some odd way, that I represented every father of a missionary, every loving father, every faithful Latter Day Saint. As I said things like, "God is in his heaven", "There is nothing wrong here" and "No foundations are being rocked at the Ellsworth house", I believed every word and found deep satisfaction - like completing a difficult chore and reporting back to the taskmaster - that I had <u>stood</u> when I needed to stand.

The thing that mattered most, by far, on the day of Ben's funeral was remembering and honoring that fantastic boy. But a little subplot played out as I fulfilled an unspoken request to stand. The poem below, which has become the final song and anthem of the musical, captures some of that emotion. At the end of a sometimes dark, sad musical, this message of hope and determination is what I hope people take with them as they exit the theater.

"Still Standing"

Standing still a moment, carving out this time.
Reflecting on the landscape of this life of mine.
Peaks too high to conquer, streams too wide to cross,
Troughs too deep to walk through without incurring loss.

Yet here am I still standing tall, despite the rough terrain.
Yes, one like me survived the storms and walked through wind and rain.

My wings are torn and tattered but I know I still can fly.
I may not soar unfettered, I may not rise too high.
Record it in the book of life and bind it with a seal
That I, unbowed, unbroken - I am standing still!

Only God knows where the path of life will yet lead me.
I do not even ask to know, and do not need to see.
It is enough to know that I'm loved and not alone.
And with those truths I thankfully march into the unknown.

Still standing, I will fight the good fight!
Still searching for glimmers of light!
Feet still on the ground, I can still be found
Standing still!

Ben's Death

Oh, how does one do justice to a life and a death? Let me at least try.

Ben was a beautiful chubby, soft-skinned baby boy, our second son. He grew up skinny but athletic. He was a reader and an excellent student. He was a kind boy who was mindful of others. As we moved every few years during his childhood and adolescence he made lasting friendships wherever we lived. Ben was loving, happy and very lovable.

In his teenage years he was little problem. Any behavioral issues related to getting along patiently with his siblings and over indulging in video games. He surprised us at age 17 with his desire to be a U.S. Marine. He wanted, and we wanted for him, to be an LDS missionary as well. The Marines were the only branch of the Service that would allow Ben to go through Basic, Combat, and Specialty Training for six months, then exit the Marine Corps, serve a mission and then return with a five year commitment to the Marine Reserves. Those six months of paid duty would also allow him to earn most of his money for his mission. Amy and I were still surprised. Although my father served in Navy in WWII, I was not a veteran and we seldom spoke of the military in the house. We knew that the Marines were infamous for a brutal 13 week Basic Training.

We asked Ben to do a few things before he decided. We asked him to talk to at least a few people who loved their Marine Corps experience and a few who hated it. Then we asked him to pray and fast for an answer. He did all of that and was convinced that it was the right thing. So we got on board and encouraged him in every way possible. Ben's Basic Training was perhaps the most formative three months of his life. Physically he put on about 20 pounds of muscle. We have learned since that he was assigned to a company in San Diego that was later dismissed or punished for crossing the line of harassment and brutality. Although hard for us non-military people to fully grasp, the drill sergeants, in that insular environment, are able to create an atmosphere of total fear and control. We learned later that Ben was absolutely convinced at least once that he would be killed in the next few hours by his drill instructor. He and the others were shoved, pushed into objects, and verbally threatened over and over. As a result, he sought solace. Ben deepened his religious convictions, had more effective prayers, and learned to appreciate family and the other good things in life more.

It was a different Ben that we picked up at the graduating ceremony in San Diego. He was stronger physically, mentally and spiritually. [Note: Lest anyone think that I am justifying the ends by the means, I do not support or condone the approach used by the USMC. I believe there are other ways to create the soldiers that our country needs.] He was even more ready to be a great missionary.

Ben's Marine Corps Boot Camp graduation, 2004

Ben was called to the Argentina Rosario Mission and was asked to the report to the Missionary Training Center (MTC) on his 19th birthday, June 22nd, 2005. Amy and I took him there and handed him over to the Lord. That is an emotional rollercoaster. We were so pleased to have him doing something so important and sad to be without him for two years. By all accounts he was an excellent missionary in the MTC and in Argentina once he arrived. He was learning the language quickly and loving the people and his companions. On the morning of December 2nd all seemed very good in his and our worlds.

By noon that day he was gone and we were in shock. Ben and his companion were going about their duties in the southern part of the city of Rosario when Ben got too close to a train and paid for it with his life. His companion was spared the trauma of having to see Ben's remains as he darted for help as soon as he saw Ben fall under the train.

The infrastructure of the LDS church kicked into gear. Ben's mission president was notified and he rushed to the scene, comforted Ben's companion, started to make arrangements for Ben's remains to be cared for, and notified the Missionary Department of the church. Only a few hours later, our local Stake President (lay local ecclesiastical leader of around 3,000 members) and his first counselor sat in our living room. President Turk said, "There has been a terrible accident in Argentina and your son, Benjamin, has been taken." These words are etched in my mind. That seemed surreal and impossible to Amy and me. Missionaries don't die. Ben doesn't die. Not our Ben. It is impossible to adequately describe the emotion. It was shocking, wrenching, painful beyond anything we could imagine. Our brains and hearts were dealing with the loss but then other thoughts crowded in. We knew we would need to get Ben's brothers and sisters home quickly and let them know and comfort them. We wanted Ben's body back. We knew loving friends and family would be coming soon to smother us with love and help. My boss needed to know as I would be abdicating any duties for a while.

We found our children and brought them home. I got the girls from high school. Although I wanted to tell the girls at home, I am not a good actor. They sensed that something was horribly wrong, pressed me, I told them and we held each other and cried in the parking lot. I picked Ethan up from his college class and we had a few sacred moments alone. At home we were all blanketed with love and food by our family and ward.

The hours and days that followed are a blur. We planned the funeral and wrote an obituary but mostly we comforted and were comforted. Ben died on a Friday. We buried him on the following Friday.

On the Wednesday we went with our stake president and bishop to receive Ben's remains and to then deliver them to the funeral home. We drove to the Cargo Terminal. I didn't even know it existed. I've still only been there once. Our good boy did not arrive at Terminal 3 on a Delta flight, like most returning missionaries do but rather as a piece of Delta cargo. Amy badly wanted to touch Ben's body but the mission president and the stake president urged us not even to consider it. So we didn't.

On the Thursday evening our girls participated in an annual Christmas dinner and singing event that the high school's music department puts on. Amy and I attended, even though it was the night before Ben's funeral. I remember feeling that it was good and appropriate that we continued to parent and support our girls.

Friday was sacred and hard. About 1,300 people attended the funeral. LDS missionaries belong to the church, it seems, so people came. Afterwards many people commented that it was the most powerful, meaningful funeral they had ever attended. I was grateful that we honored that good boy.

In retrospect, Ben lived a short but great life. He was everything a father could hope for from a son.

The following are the comments made by me and our daughter, Emily, at Ben's funeral.

My Comments:

I am very grateful for our children and that they have the strength and fortitude to stand before you and express their feelings in word and in song. I stand before you representing Amy and our family. I shall attempt to describe how we feel about this fine boy and about his passing.

First I would like to say that we are extremely humbled by the prayers, love, flowers, support, favors, emails, phone calls, letters, gifts, and food, food and more food, that have been given from the heart by so many people. You have loved us and carried us and have given us a tutorial on how to be Christ-like. We will never, ever forget that love and support and we know that you will be blessed for your goodness. We thank our Heavenly Father for you multiple times every day.

We are telling people that Ben has been transferred to the 'Paradise North' mission. We are not being flippant. We believe that with all of our hearts. And that simple statement tells you a few things about our core beliefs - we believe in a loving Father in

Heaven and in His Son Jesus Christ. We believe that that Son lived upon this earth and died for our sins so that we may live together again with Him and our families forever. We believe there is a plan of happiness and salvation given to us whereby we might be saved. We believe that man is that he might have joy, and we believe many other things that pertain to the kingdom of God that President Turk and Elder Lees will describe to you through scriptural evidence in a few minutes. Let me add my witness to their testimonies in advance of their remarks. What they will tell you is true and, if understood and embraced, will bring you lasting happiness in this life and in the world to come.

If an angel appeared to Amy and me and said "I've got good and bad news. The bad news is that we're going to take your boy at a young age. The good news is that you get to completely define the circumstances under which we take him." If Amy and I had been given that task, I want you to know that we would have put him EXACTLY where he was on the day he was taken from this earth. He was serving the Lord and inviting people to come to Christ, he was endowed and temple worthy and clean, he was happy, and he was blessing the lives of all those around him. Of course we didn't want Ben to go now.

Sweet memories of Ben come flooding over me. I remember Ben buying, learning to play, and then performing for me Pachelbel's Canon simply because I said I loved the music. I remember him offering to carry my pack out of Havasupai and the Grand Canyon, I remember him taking on near guardian status of the little boys when he learned they have the same life-shortening disease that Ethan has. I remember the cuddliest, most tender, soft skinned little boy.

But I would like to tell you a little more about Ben in his last months. Ben's mission president, President Hutchison, has passed us letters especially for us from himself and from missionaries who worked with him in the MTC and in Rosario. These are priceless and nearly holy to us as they describe a little of Ben and in them we take great comfort and strength. In summary, they describe a Ben who was happy, loving, driven to know the scriptures and the language, a shoulder to lean on, and very proud of his family at home. We almost thought they were describing someone else's boy ☺. Just a few examples:

Ben's dear companion when he passed, Elder Millett, wrote "Elder Ellsworth was an amazing friend. He was a wonderful, wonderful example for me. I learned many things from him in our short time together, and I appreciate the companionship and more importantly the friendship we had. He loved his family, he loved the work, and he had a rock solid testimony of this work and of the Savior. He spoke like a champ and taught like one too, although he was the last to admit it. He had no problem stopping the hardest looking contact and giving a pure, strong testimony of the restoration of the true gospel of Christ. I have absolute confidence that he is already settled into his next pench (apartment), with his new, better-looking companion, teaching like mad to his ancestors this same gospel of good news. I know that his body, while lost now, will one day reunite, whole, perfect, without blemish or spot through Christ's infinite atonement. He passed away in the Lord's vineyard, and as such he was taken into the Lord's house to do an equally important work. I pray for his parents, that they can know that he is well. That I know. He is well." By the way, if you have been praying for Ben and for us, please throw in Elder Millett as well.

An Argentinian Elder said, "He pulled smiles out of people with just looking at them. He transmitted happiness like energy coming from all of his body."

Another Elder described how proud Ben was of his family. Ben particularly liked to tell people about the twin boys and called them 'my boys'. Then, when people misunderstood, he would have to say, "well, they aren't MY boys."

An MTC Elder said, "In the MTC he was known as the Marine... He didn't want to 'blow his cover' down here in Argentina (he actually just didn't want people to have preconceptions about him being tough and crusty). So.. he would always joke with us that he would break our hand in one steady movement if we told anyone else he was a Marine." That sounds kinda tough and crusty.

His MTC companion said, "he had a way of making you feel like you were the greatest person... down here it was always so nice to see him, you always felt so much better after talking to him, you felt like you could go back to your area and convert the world."

Another MTC district member said, "...(In Elder Ellsworth)... I met a man who had it all. He had that little twinkle in his eye that made him a friend to everyone. He had a voice of authority that would pierce you to the very soul. He was a man that was willing to sacrifice his life for his family, his freedom and ultimately his God. A man of faith, a man of virtue, a man of honor. "

Now that is pretty heavy. It's probably not how Amy and I would have described Ben. We would have said he was a very good boy who was trying hard to be a good missionary. We would have said that the regrets he took with him to the mission field were playing too many video games and quarreling with his siblings. We are so pleased to see how far he had come and that he just kept getting better and better. We love our Ben.

Elder John Groberg said, "There is a connection between heaven and earth. Finding that connection makes everything meaningful, including death. Missing it makes everything meaningless, including life." Understanding and believing the gospel of Jesus Christ - making that connection between heaven and earth - is a wonderful thing. We will miss Ben a great deal but we also know that nothing is really wrong here. No foundations are being rocked at the Ellsworth house. Far from it. God is in his heaven. We are all in His hands. While the reasons for an untimely death may escape us, we also know from an apostle that true disciples are portable. Ben was portable. We are happy to leave it at that for now, knowing that this separation is temporary, that we'll see him again, that he is happy and busy, and that he is pure and clean. What great comfort the gospel gives. I want you to know that this is not idle hoping or wishing but is based on sacred spiritual experiences that we have had and that all men can have that confirm the truth of these things through unmistakable and undeniable whisperings of the Holy Spirit. So we will go forward with some sadness but also great joy and hope, glad that we had him so long and that he brightened our lives.

Let me finish with a sacred experience, which I believe is OK to share in this setting. When our two girls were very young I was given - for some reason - a vision, for lack of a better word, of what my girls would look like and be like when they were in their teens. While the vision was fuzzy and lacked clear detail, I knew it was a gift from God to guide Amy and me in our parenting. In the vision the girls were beautiful and strong, and it was clear to me somehow that they were pure and clean and that they were happy. That vision provided me strength through the years and I knew that one day, if we raised them right, I would happen upon the girls at some instant and, like déjà vu, I would know that the earlier vision had been fulfilled and that it would bring me inexpressible joy. That glorious moment, for which I will sing praises forever, came in August. I walked into my bedroom and saw my family there, Ethan in his chair, the boys and Amy on the floor, and the girls sitting on the bed… and everyone beaming. As the sight sunk in, I knew what I was seeing and I focused on the girls. They were (and are) sweet and clean… but why were their smiles so big? Because they were talking to Ben on the phone from Atlanta as he was en route to his mission in Argentina. Isn't heaven sweet? Isn't our Heavenly Father kind? This vision of the girls was a whole family vision all along with Ben right at the heart of it.

Brothers and sisters, and you are all truly my brothers and sisters since we have the same Father, I sincerely pray that, starting now or sometime very soon, Ben's death, or his temporary parting, can be a smiley face for you and not a frowny face. I pray that when you see his Jeep or his house or his family or even his headstone, it can remind you that his was a good, happy, meaningful life, and that our Father in Heaven took him home and into His loving arms. That he went as well prepared as a man can be. And finally let it be a challenge to you to strengthen your own connection between heaven and earth so that we all may someday find ourselves in the happy place our dear Ben finds himself in now. That is what we will do.

Amy and I share this with you in the name of Jesus Christ. Amen.

Emily's Talk:

My name is Emily. Ben is my big brother.

Benjamin Robert Ellsworth was born on June 22, 1986, the second child born to Cory and Amy Ellsworth. Ben was born in Dayton, Ohio and was preceded in the family by older brother, Ethan, and was followed by sisters Atley and Emily and later by twin boys, Cade and Colby.

This is the last minute we got to see our Ben in this life. He was boarding a bus to drive the few blocks to the MTC.

Ben was a cuddly, chubby, easy-going baby and toddler. But he was a biter, which terrorized his siblings. He quickly turned into a wiry, active, happy, busy little boy. He was a good sibling, loving the girls as they came into the family. Ben loved sports and made friends easily.

Ben and his family moved around a lot and Ben got to see the world. When he was four, the family moved to Toronto for 2.5 years. Ben went to kindergarten and first grade in Canada. Then the family moved to Hong Kong for 2.5 years where Ben excelled in sports, academics and the hand bell choir. His folks hesitated to let him play soccer the first year since school officials had needed to shoo a few cobras off the field the previous month. And, once, after a handbell choir practice in the third grade and at the wise old age of eight, when his parents had forgotten to pick him up, he casually and calmly hailed a cab, instructed the cab driver in Cantonese how to get home, enjoyed the ride, and showed up at the apartment door to ask his Mom if she had 30 Hong Kong Dollars to pay the driver.

When the family moved to London for three years in 1996, Ben was 10 and growing up fast. Ben was a great and serious Scouter in London, earning badges and honors quickly. With the Scouts, he stood on the shores of Normandy, camped in the rain in Germany, hiked the trails of rural England and cooked award-winning cobbler. In school, Ben was a fine student and played sports including rugby, which suited his taste for mud and physical contact. Ben enjoyed several trips to continental Europe, including a ski trip to the Alps with Dad. Ben made dear friends in those formative years. Even then Ben was known for a big heart and a love of laughter. At the same time he had a very serious side, thought deeply, and often held his feelings to himself.

When the family moved to northern Virginia in 1999, Ben was 13. He made friends quickly, loved his Ward, played sports, and was a good boy at home and everywhere else. He flew alone a time or two when flying to an EFY and felt no hesitation at all - he was proud of his ability to find his connecting flight in the Chicago O'Hare airport. Ben had no trouble committing to early morning Seminary and loved the cold climate. In Virginia, Ben was supportive of his family and cheered the birth of the twin boys.

When the family moved to the ancestral home of Mesa in 2001, Ben was the only child who had difficulty making the move. He missed Virginia and his friends and the cold weather. To him, Mountain View was too big and he saw too many LDS kids taking the church for granted. His uneasiness only slowly decreased but was aided by the lasting friendships he made with boys in his own ward. Those friendships became more precious to him as time went by so that, before his passing, he was constantly asking in letters how they were. Early in the stay in Mesa, he learned that both of the twins had the same awful, life-shortening disease that his older brother had. Ben took the news hard and, thereafter, seemed to feel a guardianship over the twins and over Ethan. His position as the only healthy boy was not lost on him and he felt a desire to succeed, at least partially for them.

With graduation came a new desire for adventure, a chance to grow and learn and to serve his country in the Marine Corps. After evaluating his options and after careful prayer and fasting, he entered Marine Basic Training in the Fall of 2004, knowing that after all of the training, he would be released to serve his two-year missionary service for the church. Marine Basic Training is 13 weeks of terribly hard work under almost constant emotional duress. This was by far the hardest thing Ben ever did. When he graduated he said he was proud of the accomplishment but would not wish the experience on anyone. With deep feeling, he also said "Having lived through that, I now know I can do anything!". With such an experience comes a chance to appreciate one's blessings. Ben's love and appreciation for his family grew immeasurably during his 6 months of training in the Marines.

At this point Ben was now a mature, strong, confident, loving, outgoing young man and was ready to serve a mission. He had earned the money required, had rounded his character and had managed to remain true to the standards of the Church even in very difficult surroundings. And while he prepared and waited he only wanted to spend time with parents and siblings and friends. He took Ethan to movies, took his sisters to lunch and provided advice to them, and played with the twins, who viewed Ben as their own private jungle gym. Everyone around him thrilled as Ben received a calling from a prophet to report to the Missionary Training Center on June 22nd, 2005, to serve in the Argentina Rosario mission for two years and to preach the gospel of Jesus Christ to the people of that area. As his parents dropped him off at the MTC in Provo, Utah, Ben was confident, happy, faithful, determined, bright and shiny. As Ben himself might have said, "he was all that… and a bag of chips".

His two-month MTC stay was great for him and he was eager to jump into the work in Argentina. As he arrived in Rosario in August, he jumped into the work. He was learning the language quickly, loved his companions, and was learning to love the people deeply. Just before he lost his life in a terrible tragedy on December 2nd, according to his Mission President, Ben "had bright light in his eyes. He was happy and had an infectious smile. His companion and fellow missionaries loved him deeply. He made people feel good."

Early on his mission, Ben was affected by and loved the poem, "Footprints", which is printed in the program and tells the story of Christ carrying us when we are unable to do it ourselves. Ben died knowing that the Savior of the world loved him and had sacrificed His own life so that we all might live again. And Ben was sharing that message with all who would listen.

When a person leaves this life, whether they want to or not, they leave a legacy. Here is Ben's legacy:

- he loved his family
- he loved his God and was serving Him
- he believed in the saving power of Jesus Christ
- he built people up and made them feel good
- he gave hugs
- he could do really hard things
- he protected his loved ones
- he had a plan and was right on track
- and he just kept getting better and better

And that's about as good as it gets.

We will miss you, Ben. In the name of Jesus Christ, Amen.

In Loving Memory

Benjamin Robert Ellsworth

The Death of LDS Missionaries

At the end of 2013, there are about 80,000 LDS missionaries serving around the world. That is a steep increase from previous years and is attributable to an age change that allows young men to serve at age 18 instead of age 19 and young women to serve at age 19 instead of age 21. As a result of the increased numbers, missionary deaths have also increased. At least 12 missionaries have died in 2013. Historically we have lost only 3-6 per year it seems. I use the word 'we' because LDS missionaries belong to the entire church. Most members pray for all of them, interact with some of them locally, and have family members serving. The loss of a missionary is always very sad.

As the result of losing Ben we pay much more attention than before to any reports of missionary deaths. From a distance we grieve with and pray for the affected families. In some cases, where appropriate, we have reached out. I have done some homework on missionary deaths and find the results telling and faith-building.

According to various sources, the worldwide death rate for 80,000 people in the ages of most of our missionaries would yield anywhere between 70 and 209 deaths annually. We have 12 in 2013. That is not only low but remarkably so. And I would argue that a logical discussion of the risk factors would imply that LDS missionaries are in more situations more often that would put them at risk for injury and death. Missionaries are often on bikes in traffic. They are also often in the toughest neighborhoods. They eat anything they are served. In some places there are still natural prejudices against Mormons (and the young men stand out with their suits, ties and name tags). On my mission I was chased with an ax and was brushed at least twice by vehicles traveling 30 mph or faster while riding my bike. Most missionaries can tell similar stories.

On the other side, missionaries are not likely to be in war-torn areas and are extremely unlikely to have issues with alcohol or drugs. On balance, I think that believers can put the daily protection of LDS missionaries into the miracle category. Non-believers would have difficulty explaining it away. I believe that God and his angels protect our missionaries. The death - or taking - of a missionary in those relatively small numbers tells me that, if they are taken, they are needed or that it is simply their time. Thank God and thank goodness that we are not mourning the loss of 209 or even 70 of our precious young missionaries every year.

Ethan's Death

As I wrote earlier, Ethan's death was the death of a thousand cuts for him and us. He broke our heart from the day we knew he had this terrible disease. He broke it every time there was something he wished he could do that all the other boys did. He broke it when he included 'a new set of muscles' on his Christmas list and asked God for new muscles in his prayers. When he had his first muscle biopsy, at age 7, the hospital staff prepared him for the simple surgery (a tiny slice of muscle from his thigh). We got a chance to say good luck as they wheeled him by on the gurney. Clutching a new stuffed animal, he looked cute and pathetic. We had obviously not prepared him well enough as he whispered to Amy and me, "When they're done with my muscles, will they put them back in?" We reassured him but had to turn our heads to hide our tears from him. We cried buckets of tears for our good Ethan through the years.

That's not to say, however, that Ethan's life was sad. He had plenty of fun, laughter, and accomplishment along the way. Ethan was cute and handsome from day 1. His red hair and infectious smile made him a favorite wherever we went. He was smart enough and made friends easily.

He went with us through all of our moves. He moved to South Carolina when he was 2, Germany then Ohio, at 3, Toronto at 7, Hong Kong at 10, London at 13, Virginia at 16, and Arizona at 18 (as a high school senior). He never complained. He loved the adventure even though getting around with a wheelchair was very trying in some of those places.

The comments that Amy and I gave at Ethan's funeral provide more insight into his life and personality.

Cory's Comments:

Ethan has two loving, talented sisters. Atley has married Camden and Emily will soon marry Brigham and they are extraordinary young men. Ethan has little brothers in Cade and Colby who are good boys. And he has a younger brother in Ben whom he loves very much and who must have been his welcoming committee when he passed. Ethan is with Ben. They are well and happy and I'm happy for Ethan.

The reason that I am happy for Ethan is rooted in the faith and set of beliefs that Ethan, his family and so many of you hold dear. We believe in a loving Father in Heaven and in His Son Jesus Christ. We believe that Jesus lived upon this earth and died for our sins so that we may live together again with Him and our families forever if we live worthily. Indeed we believe that life goes on and that, in the spirit world where Ethan now resides with Ben and other loved ones, there is joy and fellowship. To paraphrase what I also said at Ben's funeral, Elder John Groberg said, "There is a connection between heaven and earth. Finding that connection makes everything meaningful, including death. Missing it makes everything meaningless, including life." Making that connection between heaven and earth is a powerful thing. We will miss Ethan very much but we also know that nothing is really wrong here. God is in his heaven. We are all in His hands. While all of the reasons for physical impairment and a shortened life may escape us now, we are happy to leave it in God's all-powerful hands. Knowing that this separation is temporary, that we'll see our Ethan again, and that he is happy brings great comfort. My testimony to you is that this is not idle hoping or wishing but is based on unmistakable and undeniable sacred spiritual confirmation from the Holy Spirit that we have had and that all men can have. So we go forward with sadness but also great joy and hope, glad that we had him so long and that he enriched our lives.

I echo Amy's heartfelt thanks for the many prayers, cards, emails, flowers, and food that have come our way from loving family and friends. We are surrounded by wonderful people.

There was always plenty of tickling, laughter and wrestling at our house. We played Tickle Time and Doctor Derang-o. Doctor Derang-o was a horrible child-tickling-and-eating creature that would sometimes overtake my body. Since I was bigger and stronger than the boys I usually got the better of it. Because of that, Ethan always claimed that he and Ben will be hiding behind some bush or hedge in the next life and that I am in for a huge surprise attack. I look forward to that.

Ethan could be hardheaded figuratively and literally. When he was a very little boy he and I would bump foreheads like billy goats. I was always surprised that his head was so hard and that he wouldn't give up even when I knew both of us were dizzy. It was our little game. Ethan's grandparents came to visit us in Ohio and Grandpa Bowden had Ethan on his lap. Grandpa looked away for a moment, Ethan decided to play the head game, and Grandpa turned right into it. I saw and heard the collision of heads and heard Grandpa mutter a mild oath as he passed out for a few seconds.

Ethan has a well-developed sense of humor, which was still active to the end of his life. As I put him to bed about a month ago he was so tired that he couldn't keep his eyes open. He had spent time with our Stake President, Terry Turk, that day and they had discussed Ethan's funeral so it was on his mind. I made small talk and told him, jokingly, that I planned to perform an interpretive dance at his funeral. Thinking he wasn't even paying attention, he surprised me by saying, "in the buff, Dad". And then a few seconds later he said "Oh, that's a disgusting thought". In the hours after Ethan died, I thought of a few of Ethan's friends who needed to know that he had passed and I wanted to jot the names down before I forgot. I grabbed the first pen I saw, which promptly jolted me with a big shock. It was a gag pen that Ethan had bought at Christmas. I am sure he got a big laugh out of that one.

Ethan was adventurous. I remember waterskiing when Ethan was 10. I had him stand as best he could on my skis while I held him with one arm and held the ski rope with the other. Ethan's 70 pounds and my being limited to one arm made it hard to get out of the water. But I remember clearly realizing at the time that this would be the first and last time that this child would ever water ski. So we made it up and skied for a short while and fell together and laughed hard. He never skied again. And other things he missed completely in this life. He never shot baskets with his dad and brother. He never drove a car, never wrestled with his little brothers, and never experienced romance or marriage.

But he did so many other things. He played 'Oliver' in a wheelchair in a middle school play, he made good friends everywhere he went, he made hard decisions, he had a job, he was a genius on a PC, he loved and supported "1856" The Musical as webmaster and chief cheerleader. Once, when we were living in London, he and I went for a three-day trip to Paris. He did much of the planning and I made the mistake of telling him we should go in style. So we piled his manual wheelchair into a chauffeur-driven Jaguar limo to the train station. Then, first class under the English Channel in the Eurostar train, into a nice hotel in downtown Paris, and then on to the sights. He laughed as we strolled in the rain, as we ate and ate, as we jangled his body and nerves on the cobblestone streets, and as one of his wheels fell off. He was an adventurer.

He was brave. He was a human pincushion, he had so many shots and IV's and had so much blood taken through the years. To keep his back straight he was full of wires and screws and rods. His X-rays looked like the miscellaneous drawer at the hardware store. He dealt with hard things when he found out that his twin brothers have the same disease that he has and when his good brother Ben died.

He was loving. Anytime I returned from being away, the first thing he always said was, "I missed you", in a distinctive, loving way. He loves his brothers and sisters and he cherishes his good mother.

He was good and noble. In the days since his passing, Amy and I have come to understand that in a much deeper way through sweet feelings and promptings. We believe there are few souls who could go through the constant refiner's fire that he was put through and yet come out the other end of the furnace with a smile on his face and with his faith bright, intact, and strong.

I wrote a poem a year ago, which has become a song. It represents Ethan on his deathbed singing his last words to Amy and me. I didn't consult Ethan on it but rather the song reflected how I hoped and prayed he would feel as he left this life. A month ago or so Amy and I sat with him and we played the song for him and let him read the lyrics. He cried all the way through. I quietly asked if it was how he felt. Through tears he said, "Dad, that's exactly how I feel".

The lyrics that he loved and blessed and therefore adopted are:
'I had….. a thousand dreams and maybe two, And some might that think that none of them have yet come true, It isn't so. It seems to me that life is more than bucket lists, I've come to see. I walked alone, I even ran (well, kind of), I stood and fell and stood again, just like a man, So thankful for the peace I've known and for the precious loving ones I call my own. I saw this life through my own lens. It wasn't bad and not so sad and now it ends, With few regrets and fewer fears, I'll miss you both. I'll see you soon. Now dry your tears".

Ethan knew we would need plenty of information off his iMac and kept it well organized. There are many of our important files, pictures and bits of information among his three or four terabytes of storage. The day after his death, we tried to access his files but found some important ones were password protected. We tried all of the previous and obvious password options and none worked. I was beginning to worry. But after searching, Mary Thomas finally found a document that gave us his password - "I miss Ben". He does not need that password anymore.

Last night I found a letter that Amy and I wrote to Ethan when he was 11. In it we said, "A few months ago in our night time prayers, Atley (who was five at the time) prayed, 'Please bless Ethan to feel better when he's finished with Muscular Dystrophy'. The way she worded that, I believe, is important. She made it sound like you had uses for MD and that when you have learned what you need to learn from MD you can move on. I have thought a lot about her prayer. I believe you are courageous and special and that having MD will teach you many valuable things that many people never learn - such as great patience, sympathy for people with all kinds of sufferings or handicaps, learning how to graciously accept the gifts and time of others, learning how to rely on the help and love of your Heavenly Father". He learned all those things and more.

In closing, Ethan left a voice message for the twins. It is sweet and precious. At the end he bears his own final witness and I believe it is worth sharing. He told them in part, "I know the gospel is true, and I know that Jesus died for us, …and I **absolutely** know without a doubt that once I die I'll get to see Ben and Grandpa Joe and all the people that love me that I don't even know exist yet". And he finished, as I do, with "in the name of Jesus Christ. Amen"

Amy's Comments:

Our family would like to thank you for your love and support. We are so thankful for you.

Ethan wanted me to give his life history and I'm honored to do so. Ethan Joseph Ellsworth was born on March 15, 1983 in Provo Utah. Cory was attending BYU and working part time. I had finished beauty school a few months before. Ethan's was a hard labor and delivery that lasted 24 hours. Ethan was a beautiful baby and child. His red hair and sweet smile always got him noticed. He was also very strong willed (aka stubborn) That's from the Ellsworth side. He did not like to sleep!

When Ethan was a year and a half old we moved to South Carolina for Cory to start an international MBA program. Part of the program was an internship and we went to Germany for six months. Wherever we went it seemed that all the little old grandmas would just have to touch his hair and tell us how darling he was.

Cory graduated and off we went to Ohio for our first real job and just in time for the birth of a new brother! Ethan loved Benjamin and they became best buddies. Ohio was where Ethan learned to ride a bike and climb tall trees and often get stuck so his dad had to come to the rescue. He also played t-ball. Two sweet little sisters were born and he loved them too.

When he was seven we had concerns about his physical strength. Watching him run as if in slow motion worried us. After visiting different doctors he was diagnosed with Duchenne Muscular Dystrophy on August 8, 1990. We were heartbroken that our beautiful boy would not have the life every parent hopes for their child. Instead we would have wheelchairs and splints and hospital beds. Ethan was a happy boy despite it all and we decided to make his life as full and exciting as possible. In January of 1991 we moved to Toronto, Canada. He made friends and had lots of fun with his family.

After Toronto we moved back to Ohio only to find out, after a few months, that we were going to Hong Kong. Ethan enjoyed the many moves and the new things to see and discover. Things always seemed to work out for him and us - sometimes miraculously. For example, when we moved to HK, Ethan was already in a wheelchair most of the time and was ready to start middle school. We were still a little inexperienced about handicap accessibility and went to HK not fully understanding the lack of any accessibility. HK is built on the sides of mountains! But we felt that it would work out. The school that Ethan was to attend had three different campuses - grade school, middle school and high school. The grade school and high school were not accessible at all. But they were just finishing the new middle school that was fully accessible with ramps and elevators and was just down the road. The school was ready to admit him but said that their emergency plan required someone strong enough and willing to carry him to safety in case of a fire or loss of power. Then a young Chinese art teacher, who was a body builder on the side, gladly volunteered. He was also an LDS bishop and turned out to be a great friend to Ethan.

These coincidences were in fact miracles and tender mercies. I could tell similar stories about each place we lived. Heaven intervened to allow Ethan to enjoy his adventures. Ethan made some very good friends in HK and kept in touch with them.

After two and a half years Cory had two opportunities for a job with his company- one back to Dayton, Ohio or in London, England. With much thought and prayerful consideration in what would be the best for Ethan we chose England and never regretted it for a minute. We were told that Ethan would not be allowed to go to the American school where the younger children would go because they weren't equipped to deal with handicaps but that there was a good school with provisions for handicapped kids, where Ethan should be happy. Well if the older people here can remember a movie called "To Sir With Love", that place was just like it and Ethan had his eyes opened to many new things. He went a year to that school and I went to the American School and told them what he was dealing with and would they please reconsider. They had an elevator so he could get around and they said yes. I know our prayers were heard. His last two years at school there were wonderful. As always the best kids became his friends. The last e-mail Ethan sent was to one of those good friends from American Community School.

Ethan and I went to Stratford-upon-Avon with his 8th grade class to study Shakespeare and had a blast! He loved driving into London with the family and going to shows and museums, castles and so many wonderful places. He has such fond memories of England and the branch we were in, where he went to early morning seminary with Cory as the teacher.

By 1999 his back was curving and that was bad for breathing. The doctors recommended spinal fusion surgery where they put steel rods along the spine and wire them to the vertebrae. It is a very serious surgery that needed much thought and consideration. We all decided that we would rather have it done in the U.S. So Cory started to ask the company he worked for about coming home. There was nothing for him in Ohio and we started looking at other companies. Ethan had heard of a great high tech company called Cisco Systems and Ethan was all over Cory telling him to try them and it worked! They moved us to northern Virginia that summer.

In September, Ethan had the surgery and a painful long recovery began. But he had already made some good friends in the young men's organization at church and they came while he was in the hospital and painted his pink room a more manly color. That January the twins were born. That started a new way of life for our family. Ethan loved those babies very much and would be sad that he couldn't hold and play with them like he wanted to. But he found joy in watching them and interacting with them as much as he could. We have video of Ethan and year old twins in his bed bopping to "You Can't Touch This." It's great!

We moved home to the motherland of Mesa, Arizona in July of 2001. Ethan had his senior year at Mountain View and graduated in 2002. He started at Mesa Community College in the fall and decided he wanted to serve a mission. He was called to the Regional Family History Center in Mesa and met many wonderful senior missionaries. They loved him and he loved them. It was a great experience and he was proud of that accomplishment.

It hurt Ethan deeply when he learned that Cade and Colby were affected with the same disease that he had. He often told Cory and I to take them to fun places. We went to Disneyworld when they were three and he just loved watching them.

Ethan loved his family and had a special closeness with Ben and kind of lived through him as Ben got a driver's license, his Eagle Scout award, joined the Marines and went on his mission. Those were things he wanted to do.
 Ethan loved it when he and Ben would take our big green van and go to a movie and then get fast food. They had some fun times in that van, and it was almost too much for him to bear when Ben died on his mission. He could not understand why he had to live with this horrible disease, know what his little brothers would have to go through and lose his healthy, strong brother. He really had to dig deep inside and figure out if all he had been taught was true, and if this life was worth all the pain.

Ethan is a hero to me, and one of God's noble and great ones. I think of his life and how much he suffered, often silently and alone and how bravely he moved forward and endured the frustration of being a prisoner in a body that couldn't move and gave him pain.

Ethan has some wonderful friends that have done so much to bring him some fun and happiness. A few examples in the last few weeks - Seth bringing him a really nice ASU sweatshirt that he wore everyday and Dave staying with him and bringing PF Chang's - his all time favorite. We are so thankful for all of his sweet friends and the love they showed him.

I hope someday to be worthy to be with the amazing men that are my sons. Ethan's last few days were hard for Cory and me to watch. He wanted so much for Ben to come and get him. Ethan was not afraid to die, just afraid of suffocating and struggling. He prayed that he would die in his sleep and the Lord gave him that tender mercy.

Someday I hope to be able to watch when Ben came to get Ethan and say, "Come on, big brother. It's finally time to go. You have finished your work." And then watch the smack down as they wrestled together. While we miss and grieve our loss of Ethan, I am so happy for him and the freedom from his body and pain.

I know my boys are together again and that I will see them one day and that they are beautiful, faithful and strong in their testimony that God lives. Jesus Christ is His son and our Savior, and because of Him, Ethan and Ben and all of us will have perfect bodies. I love you Ethan! Give Ben a big hug for us.

In Loving Memory

Ethan Joseph Ellsworth

Twin-isms

Our twins have always had the ability to make us laugh. As a toddler in a diaper, Colby learned to walk around and occasionally pat someone on the bum and ask, "Are you poopy too?"

I overheard them talking when they were about four years old. They were discussing what they would do to any intruder in our home. They had long been fascinated by the baseball bat that I keep by my bed. They knew it was my preferred form of self-defense. They were one-upping each other tales of what they would do to a robber. Colby said he would use a cheese grater to take the robber's skin all off. Cade countered that he would whack their knees off with a baseball bat. Colby, grabbing a pale blue baster, that for him reminded him of some of the enemas he had received, said, "I'd give him an enema... even if he didn't have a problem!"

Cade, wielding a flashlight, told Colby he was going to shine it up Colby's bum. Colby pondered a few seconds and said, "To do that you'd need to pull down my pants...but don't". Colby's unintended comedic timing has always been excellent.

On the day that Ben died, we were smothered with love and concern by many of our friends. One sweet family brought Krispy Kreme donuts and even some donut-maker hats. The little boys, five years old, put on the hats and walked through the house asking everyone, "DO (intonation on the 'do') you want a donut? It was a ray of sweetness on that very bad day. The twins have made us laugh from their first days.

Ethan's Last Message

Ethan recorded a voice message directed to the twins in late December, 2008 or early January, 2009. Ethan passed away on January 17th, 2009. Here is the text:

This is Ethan, your big brother. Hey, I just want to leave you some recordings. This audio one I'm gonna leave you and hopefully I'll get to a video one. I just want to leave you guys with a little something cuz you guys know that I'm not feeling very good lately these days and soon I'll get to go see Ben. So I want to leave you guys some of these messages so that, after I'm gone, you can listen to my voice, so you don't forget my voice.
I just want to tell you guys how much I love you and will miss you once I'm gone but I want you to know that once I'm gone I'll ALWAYS, ALWAYS be there for you and I hope that you'll be able to feel me near you after I'm gone.
I want you guys to be tough cuz, from my perspective, only us three know exactly how hard being in wheelchairs is so we gotta stick together.
I want you guys to know that the ONLY way I've been able to get through this life is to rely on Mom and Dad and our family and the gospel. The gospel is so enormously helpful because we know that, once we die, that's not the end. So many people believe that but we don't. We believe that, when I'm dead, I'm gonna be able to see Ben and that's gonna be so cool. I'm gonna be able to walk and jump and do all those fun things. And when you join us, you'll be able to run and jump and walk and everything that you couldn't do and that'll be a cool day to be with you boys.

Sorry, I'm trying to get through this without being emotional. It is hard.

As you guys get older it's gonna get harder cuz you're gonna be in power chairs and those are fun at times but sometimes you'll be discouraged and I want you to know that all you have to do is pray and you'll feel better. I promise you that cuz it has helped me.

I want you guys to have fun. Make sure you always put a little time aside to have fun cuz, pretty much, that makes life bearable, I've found. And I know Mom and Dad - you guys will want to play video games - and Mom and Dad will complain and say you play those too much, which I usually did. But you won't be able to do a lot of stuff outside so video games are fun. But don't play them as much as I did because so there are so many other things to do. You can be reading. There are so many great things out there that you can do besides playing video games.

I want you boys to know that you have - let's see if I can get through this - THE best parents. So if you ever need any help, or if you're ever not feeling good or feeling depressed, just go to them and they'll help you. Plus you have Atley and Emily and Camden and Brigham pretty soon. That'll be so cool. You'll have brothers-in-law and sisters to help you. That will be very cool.

And hopefully once I'm gone you guys can go do a couple of fun trips. I want Mom and Dad to take you to places like where we used to live and you can see where we used to live and what we used to do because I think that's important for you guys to see.

Just, in closing, I just want you to know how much I love you and how much Mom and Dad love you and the rest of our family and especially how much Heavenly Father loves you.

So stay strong. Remember, this life's just short. It may seem long and hard and a pain in the butt but if I can get through it you guys can.

I'll leave that with you and bear my testimony that I know the gospel is true and I know Jesus died for us and I know Joseph Smith was a prophet. And I absolutely know that, without a doubt, that once I die, I'll get to see Ben and Grandpa Joe and all the people that love me that I don't even know exist yet, that I'll get to meet pretty soon.

So I'll say that in the name of Jesus Christ. Amen.

I Won't Let Anything Bad Happen to You

Growing up on a dairy, I was exposed to more than my fair share of danger, particularly around the large bulls and cows. My father would often give me a task or a challenge that seemed dangerous. His many years of experience, and perhaps occasional dumb luck, allowed him to have a good feel for what was dangerous and what wasn't. When I looked at him with that "you've got to be kidding me!" look, he used a line that I took to heart. "I wouldn't let anything bad happen to you", he would say. Usually that was enough for me and I would jump in with both feet, whether it was herding ornery cattle or doing a half gainer off the swimming pool diving board. It almost always worked. I never had an experience that led me to think my Dad had lost his mind and that his expressed insurance policy was ever invalid.

That sense of protection continued through my twenties. While there were mild disappointments, I was kept far from any truly earth-rocking experience. No parents or siblings died or divorced. I made all of the sports teams. Every girl that I was deeply interested in fell for me. My mission in Germany was a great success and building block for life. I found Amy - the love of my life - shortly thereafter. We furthered our education. Precious children came along. Life was indeed charmed and I suppose I felt impervious to any serious painful events. I took on my father's belief that I could somehow protect my family and my world.

That all came crashing down in August of 1990 with the diagnosis of seven-year-old Ethan's Muscular Dystrophy. I was completely unable to provide a cure or even much relief for my beloved firstborn. I was so lost. I wondered why I didn't have the same magical touch that my father had. I felt so inadequate and helpless as I cared for my little, now strangely vulnerable family. Starting in that horrible summer of 1990 and for many years thereafter, I sat in the figurative classroom of heaven, learning one of the most important truths that heaven or life has to offer. It is this: One of our most important tasks in this life is, not to keep bad or hard events from our loved ones, but rather to set an example for them of how to behave and move forward with faith when such dark-cloud events envelop us.

I was motivated to learn the lesson. I have seen, from time to time, the horrifying looks of fear, panic, or depression on the faces of those whom I love the most and who look to me. Those horrified eyes were searching mine for answers, for comfort, for direction, for peace. I knew I had to provide at least a modicum of those sweet, comforting emotions if I wanted to pass the test of parenthood. I am not certain if I have passed. But I have tried. Tried when my oldest wondered when and why he would die early. Tried when he lost the ability to walk. Tried when Amy and I had to tell our four oldest children that their beloved younger twin brothers had the same life-shortening disease from which their older brother suffered. Tried when each member of our family struggled with the traumatic loss of our only healthy son on his mission. Tried as we buried him. Tried as watched our eldest pass to the next life and join his brother.

If I have passed the tests, I give full credit to a loving Father in Heaven, who slowly but surely imparted the lesson. I learned that the protectionist doctrine, which I believed as I heard it from my dear father, is a well intended but a false doctrine. I learned that growth and wisdom do not come from avoiding pain but rather confronting it with a humble and submissive and brave heart. I learned firsthand that, as a wise man once said, "The gospel of Jesus Christ is not insurance against pain. It is resource in the event of pain". I learned that the love of heaven continues with us through any trials and that the preponderance of painful events in our lives is not an indicator of anger or dislike from heaven.

My experience can be analogous to our Heavenly Father's interaction with us in this wondrous plan of salvation. I imagine to myself how He might yearn to say to each of us, "I won't let anything bad happen to you". But His plan is to allow pain, to allow suffering but to be there with sympathy, empathy, and love in his eyes and in his fingertips. His plan allows us to 'fight the good fight' and 'finish the course'. When we reach the finish line we will not be coddled and naive but rather tattered and torn but tested and proven. It hurts and heals. It is risky. Not everyone will come through it with their faith intact. But it is a necessary process. And we are never left alone. I am thankful for that.

The Fundamental Tone Of My Existence

Parents who lose children gain membership in an unfortunate club. Finding people who can empathize based on shared experience is important. Members of that club often reach out to each other, sharing love, remembering the day of passing of friends' children, sharing books or quotes or articles that might be helpful. A dear friend, Randy Bradford, who, along with his sweet wife, Melissa, lost their precious 18-year-old son Parker several years ago, shared a book with me. It is entitled, "Lament For a Son" by Nicholas Wolterstorff, who lost a son in a mountain climbing accident. I found it profound. Here are a few excerpts that resonated deeply with me:

"When we gather now there's always someone missing, his absence as present as our silence, his silence as loud as our speech. Still five children, but one always gone. When we're all together, we're not all together."

"Is the death of a child any easier when vitality has wound down? If some disease had wasted him away, sapped his energy, made him, weak, would death then have seemed a proper closure? But then all the pain would have been in seeing the winding down."

"All around us are his things: his clothes, his books, his camera, the things he made - pots, drawings, slides, photos, notes, prayers. They speak with forked tongue, words of joyful pride and words of sorrow. Do we put them all behind doors to muffle the sorrow or leave them out to hear them tell of the hands that shaped them? We shall leave them out.

We will not store the pots, nor turn the photos. We will put them where they confront us. This as a remembrance, as a memorial."

"I've become an alien in the world, shyly touching it as if it's not mine. I don't belong any more. When someone loved leaves home, home becomes mere house."

"Sometimes I think that happiness is over for me. I look at photos of the past and immediately comes the thought: that's when we were happy. But I can still laugh, so I guess that isn't quite it. Perhaps what's over is happiness as the fundamental tone of my existence. Sorrow is no longer the islands but the sea."

This last quote hit me more than any other part of this wonderful book. It helped explain the melancholy mood that I found to be my most common emotion.

As time moved on, though, my attitude towards this quote has changed. With all respect to Nicholas Wolterstorrf, I believe I cannot accept a change in the fundamental tone of my existence, especially given the theology in which I so deeply believe. God is in his heaven. He loves us. He has a plan for each of us. My deceased sons are not exceptions to the plan - they are part of the plan. Our souls continue on. My sons are in another place, another world. They are happy and busy there. Amy and I will see them again once we die. Our parting was very, very sad but is temporary. Therefore, as odd as it may sound, everything is as it should be. There is nothing wrong here. Painful and hard, yes. Wrong, no. So I will fight the melancholy and try my very best to make sorrow the islands and happiness the sea.

The Next Fifty or Ten or Twenty or Whatever

There are still some things I want to do in this life. Some are activities while some are habits or longer-term opportunities. Here they are, roughly in order of importance.

- Raise our boys with love until they join their brothers
- Love and support Amy until one of us dies
- Be there for my daughters, their husbands and their children. Be a great grandpa
- Be there for my friends and family
- Laugh and smile - a lot
- Serve at least one LDS mission - preferably more
- Attend the LDS temples on a regular basis
- Provide financially for my family
- Give often of my time, talent and money - look for opportunities
- Stage "1856" and "Crosses" every few years
- Continue to write poetry and music
- Learn to play an instrument well
- Learn at least one more language - Mandarin or Spanish or Russian
- Travel - some of the places that I would still like to see are: Antarctica, Israel, Russia, the Silk Route, and the outback of Australia
- Have a thankful heart and find maximum joy in the journey

I may be forgetting a few things but that's pretty much it. I think I'll get started. I can hear one of the twins calling.

www.ingramcontent.com/pod-product-compliance
Lightning Source LLC
Chambersburg PA
CBHW020347170426
43200CB00005B/80